W9-ATP-430

# Seven Masterpieces
## *of* 1940s Cinema

DAVID GLENN HUNT
MEMORIAL LIBRARY
GALVESTON COLLEGE

# Seven Masterpieces
## *of* 1940s Cinema

Inga Karetnikova

DAVID GLENN HUNT
MEMORIAL LIBRARY
GALVESTON COLLEGE

HEINEMANN ■ Portsmouth, NH

*To Dimitri and Leon*

**Heinemann**
A division of Reed Elsevier Inc.
361 Hanover Street
Portsmouth, NH 03801–3912
www.heinemanndrama.com

*Offices and agents throughout the world*

© 2006 by Inga Karetnikova

All rights reserved. No part of this book may be reproduced in any form or by any electronic or mechanical means, including information storage and retrieval systems, without permission in writing from the publisher, except by a reviewer, who may quote brief passages in a review.

The author and publisher wish to thank those who have generously given permission to reprint borrowed material:

Excerpt from *Hitchcock on Hitchcock: Selected Writings and Interviews* by Sidney Gottlieb. Copyright © 1992. Published by University of California Press. Reprinted by permission.


**Library of Congress Cataloging-in-Publication Data**
Karetnikova, Inga.
    Seven masterpieces of 1940s cinema / Inga Karetnikova.
        p. cm.
    ISBN-13: 978-0-325-00962-9
    ISBN-10: 0-325-00962-7
    1. Motion pictures.  I. Title.

PN1994.K294 2006
791.43'75—dc22                                    2006019541

Editor: Lisa A. Barnett
Production service: Melissa L. Inglis
Production coordinator: Vicki Kasabian
Illustrations: Dimitri Karetnikov
Cover design: Catherine Hawkes, Cat & Mouse
Typesetter: Tom Allen/Pear Graphic Design
Manufacturing: Louise Richardson

Printed in the United States of America on acid-free paper
10  09  08  07  06    VP    1  2  3  4  5

# Contents

# Acknowledgments

I am deeply grateful to Leslie Johnson, Leita Luchetti, Jon Kiefer, Robert Gerst, Don Mullare, Peggy Troupin, Veronica Zolina, Cindy Rowe, and Diane Carmody Wynne for their time and attention given so generously to my work. Very special thanks go to my husband, Leon Steinmetz, and my son, Dimitri Karetnikov, for their unfailing help. My deepest gratitude to my insightful and loyal editor, the late Lisa Barnett.

# ✒️Introduction

This book is called *Seven Masterpieces of 1940s Cinema.* I chose seven films because seven is a magic number, and the 1940s because it was the most remarkable, tragic, and heroic decade of the twentieth century: the time of unprecedented suffering and unprecedented heroism; of the horrors of war and the exhilaration and yet complexities of peace.

It was not easy to select films for this book. There were other strong potential candidates: *Casablanca, Citizen Kane, The Best Years of Our Lives, My Darling Clementine*, and *Brief Encounter* among them. Yet the films chosen here, American (*The Great Dictator, Notorious*, and *It's a Wonderful Life*), Russian (*Ivan the Terrible*), French (*Children of Paradise*), Italian (*The Bicycle Thief*), and Japanese (*Rashomon*), complement each other and together re-create, to an extent, the cultural and political atmosphere of the 1940s.

Except for *The Great Dictator*, the films in this book are not about historical events of the 1940s—documentary films depicted the events as they were occurring; feature films usually needed distance to reflect upon them. But the films I discuss are saturated with the atmosphere of that time. One always feels it and is aware of its allegories. When, for instance, the priest in *Rashomon* laments the horrible time that came upon his country (the action takes place in eleventh-century Japan), one can't help thinking about the Japan of the 1940s—Pearl Harbor, the atomic bomb, the defeat and shame of the nation. (In his memoirs, Kurosawa described how, after the defeat, his countrymen were sitting in their doorways, their swords drawn, waiting for the emperor's order to die, which luckily never came.)

Each chapter, dedicated to a specific film, tells about the historical and political atmosphere in which the film was made, discusses the film's narrative, and analyzes the cinematic devices that are used. And it certainly talks about the film's director. Everyone knows that there are many contributors to a film's creation. That is especially clear now, when we see at a film's conclusion the endless stream of their names, really, an army of people. Yet it is the director who is the supreme commander. This is why we say "a Capra film" or "a De Sica film," the same way we would say, for instance, that it was Wellington's victory at Waterloo, even though there were thousands of officers and men who fought there and without whom that victory over Napoleon could not have been possible.

The films discussed in this book came to us with their sensibility and their worldview, but they are not just something from and about the past; they are still relevant to us emotionally, intellectually, and aesthetically. They continued experiences of their predecessors in film and other arts. So they are not one artist "thick," but many artists "thick."[1] They have a very strong human element; they are compassionate and they generate compassion, and they are masterfully made—in short, they are *masterpieces*. Of course, film history cannot focus only on works of great masters. All works of a period, celebrated and not celebrated, the matters of their production and distribution, studio requirements, stars, and mutual influences on each other are aspects of film history. But this book is not intended to be a film history of the 1940s. My task is more modest—to write about several films of that period.

They come from different countries, belong to different cultural traditions, and were made in different political and social climates by different masters and in very different styles. Thus, *Bicycle Thieves* is very close to reality. De Sica was among the first directors to turn a film into a *slice of life*. Hitchcock, to the contrary, wanted his film to be, as he said, *a slice of cake*, because, in his words, if someone wants a slice of life there is no need to go into a movie theatre—there is plenty of it on the street outside. Carné's *Children of Paradise*, based on European theatrical and artistic traditions, is quite removed from both De Sica's and Hitchcock's work, while Eisenstein's epic *Ivan the Terrible* is alien to all of them and certainly to Capra's parable-like *It's a Wonderful Life* and Kurosawa's enigmatic *Rashomon*.

Never before have these particular films been grouped together, put next to each other, revealing, in spite of their differences, that they have certain things in common, as people of the same generation might have: they all have clear continuity of action, and they do not sacrifice the narrative for anything. They do not like jump cuts or freeze frames. The camera never exists in its own right. Even in *Notorious*, although Hitchcock's fascination with the camera's behavior is well known, the camera was used only to make the narrative more intriguing. It was just another character *within* the story rather than a self-indulging artistic device outside of it.

There is also in these works a similarity in the basic trust in the medium of film—nothing yet of the convulsive competition with television, which would happen soon, but at that time television had not yet turned into a dangerous and victorious rival.

One last remark: the book starts with *The Great Dictator* (1940) and ends with *Rashomon* (1950). The latter completes the 1940s on a high artistic level, and makes a transition to new decades when *film* would become *cinema*.

*Seven Masterpieces of 1940s Cinema* is for people of various walks of life who are interested in films—those who remember and love old films and those who want to learn about them either independently or in a school or college environment.

In the book readers will discover how the films were made, how the plot (conflict, climax, crisis) and characters were developed, which cinematic devices were used and why. They will go from the pages of text to the viewing of films on tapes and DVDs, and will recognize the choice of mise-en-scènes and mise-en-shots, gaining the skill of *seeing,* noticing details, grasping visual hints—in short, they will be developing what is called *an educated eye*.

I deliberately wanted this book to be free of scholarly jargon and esoteric theories, which so often create a wall between readers of film books and films; I strived rather to write a book that would be like an inviting bridge, connecting the readers and the films. I also tried, whenever possible, to introduce the voices of people who created or participated in creating these film masterpieces.

## Note

1. This idea was expressed in Kenneth Clark, *What Is a Masterpiece?* New York: Thames and Hudson, 1981, p. 11.

# THE GREAT DICTATOR

## Charles Chaplin

|  |  |
|--:|:--|
| director: | Charles Chaplin |
| producer: | Charles Chaplin |
| script: | Charles Chaplin |
| cameramen: | Karl Struss, Rollie Totheroh |
| editing: | Williard Nico |
| assistant directors: | Dan James, Wheeler Dryden, Bob Meltzer |
| music: | Charles Chaplin, Meredith Willson with paraphrases of Wagner and Brahms |
| art director: | Russell Spencer |

*cast*

*People of the Palace:*

|  |  |
|--:|:--|
| adenoid hynkel, dictator of tomainia: | Charles Chaplin |
| benzino napaloni, dictator of bacteria: | Jack Oakie |
| schultz: | Reginald Gardiner |
| herring: | Billy Gilbert |
| garbitsch: | Henry Daniell |

*People of the Ghetto:*

|  |  |
|--:|:--|
| jewish barber: | Charles Chaplin |
| hannah: | Paulette Goddard |
| mr. jaeckel: | Maurice Moskovich |
| mrs. jaeckel: | Emma Dunn |

Black and white
*running time:* 126 minutes
*first release:* October 15, 1940, Capitol and Astor Theatres, New York
*awards:* Nominated for the Academy Awards for best picture, best
actor, and best screenwriter for Chaplin, 1940. Jack Oakie (supporting
actor) and Meredith Willson (music) were nominated as well.

✳

Charles Spencer Chaplin was born in London in 1889 into a family
of music hall entertainers. His father, Charles Sr., was an incurable alco-
holic, and his mother, Hannah, an incurable adulteress. Chaplin was
not even sure who his real father was.

In 1890 Charles Chaplin Sr. departed for America, leaving his wife,
the baby Charles, and the baby's half brother, four-year-old Sydney,
without any financial support. Sydney later became one of the most
important people in Chaplin's life, entirely devoted to him.

Hannah was mentally unstable, but she was a loving mother and
a wonderful performer.[1] Chaplin's first appearance on the stage was at
the age of five. His mother lost her voice in the middle of a song, and
to appease the audience, the stage manager made Charlie go on in her
place. He did everything to entertain the crowd—sang, danced, and
performed imitations, including one of his mother. The audience was
ecstatic and threw money on the stage.

Being in and out of special institutions became routine for Hannah,
and her two sons were condemned to workhouses, streets, and schools
for orphans and destitute children.

In his childhood and early adolescence, Chaplin "passed through
virtually every strong experience which was to illuminate his art."[2] It
was at that early time that he developed his worldview, his social
sympathies and humanity, his sentimentality and his irony.

At eleven, when he was performing with a clog-dancing troupe,
he upstaged the star—there was already an air of excellence about him.
In a couple of years he thought of organizing a comedy group and calling it the Millionaire Tramps. Later in life, as Chaplin himself admitted, he became a millionaire by creating and playing the tramp.

At the age of seventeen, he was hired by Casey Court Circus as "a
boy comedian" who "sang, danced, and did imitations." He obsessively
polished his techniques; he was a perfectionist and a "solitary man without camaraderie."[3]

In 1908 Chaplin joined the troupe of Fred Karno, a remarkable producer and master of clowning and pantomime.[4] People who knew Chaplin at that time recalled that he wasn't very likeable. He lived like a monk, never allowing himself anything except his work (all his professional life he would work hard to attain perfection), never drinking or spending money on luxuries, and putting every penny in the bank. His ambition was the theatre, and he wanted to play dramatic roles, not vaudeville or the music hall. In fact, he never lost his attraction to drama.

In 1909, with Karno's company, he was playing at the Folies Bergeres in Paris. In 1910 they left London for an extended tour in the United States and Canada. Stan Laurel,[5] who also was a performer for Karno, recalled that when their ship neared the American shore, Chaplin shouted: "America, I am coming to conquer you!"

In New York he caught the attention of the legendary Mack Sennett, the creator of the *silent film slapstick comedy*. This genre, with its uproariously funny visual humor, and the combination of the arts of mime, clown, vaudeville, and gags, was a purely American phenomenon, like jazz and skyscrapers.

It was after the second United States tour, in 1913, when Chaplin was hired by Sennett's company in Hollywood for $150 a week. (In less than two years the Mutual Film Company would pay him $10,000 a week—an unheard of sum for a movie actor.)

It was a hard decision to go from his growing success at Karno's to a totally unknown field, which in England, more than in any other country, was looked down upon. But he was attracted to the novelty and the free spirit of the screen. Certainly, he could not have realized at that point how crucial his decision was: in music hall, with his talents, skills, and virtuosity, he could become superb, even the best performer; cinema made him a genius.

First of all, he created his film persona—a tramp in a pair of oversized baggy pants and oversized shoes, which he put on the wrong feet, an undersized coat and a derby hat, a bowtie and a bamboo cane. The last touch was a black toothbrush moustache. He knew that Sennett expected him to be much older. The moustache would add age without hiding his expressions. So, the character was ready— the funny little man, the tramp.[6]

But from the very beginning he also was "a gentleman, a poet, a dreamer, a lonely fellow, always hopeful of romance and adventure . . . but he was not above picking up cigarette butts or robbing a baby of its candy."[7]

In the first year of his new career, he learned everything about the camera, about being in front of it and dealing with the space that differed so significantly from the stage, and he made 35 two and three reelers.

His first film was released in 1914, and in less than two years he became an international star. No one before Chaplin had achieved world fame so quickly in any art. Charlie, Charlot, Carlino, Carlos, Carlitos—the tramp, the clown—he had no age, no race, no home, no country.

Chaplin brought to film, the most modern art of his time, the experience of the ancient arts of pantomime, the commedia dell'arte, and the circus. Blending opposites—old and new, funny and sad, common and elitist—was the expression of Chaplin's artistic personality. He proved that the opposite of the funny is not the serious, but the *not* funny. He was the first to gradually introduce drama to comedy and made the screen truly intimate.

The public adored him. His films were shown even at the fronts of World War I. Military convoys would carry Chaplin films along with weapons and provisions. He was the soldiers' favorite.

When Chaplin visited England in 1921, a veteran wanted to give him all of his medals because, he said, of what that fellow had done for the men at war: we would forget everything and laugh.

People laughed, but their laughter was not indifferent, as laughter is over a custard pie. The public cared about that naïve and unselfish fellow.

Among numerous one to three reelers, made between 1914 and 1921, the most significant were *The Tramp* (1915), *The Pawnshop* (1916), *The Immigrant* (1917), *A Dog's Life* (1918), and *Shoulder Arms* (1918).

In *The Tramp* he accepts rejection from a girl he loves, and leaves. "For the first time, he makes his classic exit: he waddles sadly away from the camera up a country road, his shoulders drooped, the picture of defeat. Suddenly he shakes himself, and perks into a jaunty step as the screen irises up upon him."[8]

In the spring of 1918, Chaplin, with Douglas Fairbanks[9] and Mary Pickford,[10] was on a two-month tour for the Third Liberty Loan bond campaign to support, as he said, "the great army and navy of Uncle Sam." People in Virginia, North Carolina, Kentucky, Tennessee, Mississippi, and Texas—everywhere he went—were buying bonds, and millions were raised for the war needs.[11]

*The Kid* (1921) was Chaplin's first feature-length film, "a picture with a smile and perhaps a tear," as the opening title says.[12] The film became incredibly successful and was distributed in some fifty countries, and even Chaplin's costar, five-year-old Jackie Coogan, became so popular that the pope granted the boy a special audience.

He only directed the next film, *A Woman of Paris* (1923), a drama with no trace of comedy. It was made, to a large extent, to let his former costar Edna Purviance[13] start her own career independent of him.

*The Gold Rush* (1925) was the picture Chaplin wanted to be remembered by. It was about the tramp who came to the Klondike to search for gold. The film was again a blend of humor and specifically Chaplinesque pathos. The film was called the greatest and most elaborate comedy ever made.

For *The Circus* (1928), Chaplin was presented with an honorary Oscar "for versatility and genius in writing, acting, directing, and producing." The *New York Daily News* wrote that *The Circus* was "a screaming delight from fade in to fade out." Chaplin wrote that the film had a poetic and touching ending, "with the circus slowly packing up and moving off leaving me quite alone on the ground."[14]

Chaplin worked on his next film, *City Lights* (1931), for three years. The invention of sound recording[15] did not change anything in his work. He could afford to ignore sound. His *silence was still golden,* the public and critics had to admit. Only he could turn the plot and clichés of Victorian melodrama in *City Lights*—a blind flower girl, her poor grandmother, and a ragged benefactor whom she takes for a millionaire—into an expression of intimate feelings of love and humanity.[16]

*Modern Times* (1936), as *The Gold Rush*, *The Circus*, and *City Lights* before it, blended comedy, romance, and pathos, "but what makes [it] decidedly different [are] the political references, which keep intruding into Charlie's world."[17] It was his last silent film. Chaplin himself noted in his memoirs that he started feeling that the art of pantomime was gradually becoming obsolete.[18]

At the end of the film, the tramp walks, as he has done in several other films, down the road to the horizon, but now he is not alone— he has a companion, a lovely waif. The actress who played her was Chaplin's wife, Paulette Goddard, and certainly, at that time, the image of happily going together had a personal meaning for him also.[19]

The year after the premiere of *Modern Times,* in 1937, "Alexander Korda had suggested I should do a Hitler story based on mistaken identity. Hitler had a moustache like the Tramp's so I could play both parts. . . . The story took two years to develop and another year to prepare," Chaplin explained.[20]

So *The Great Dictator* (1940) was Chaplin's first talkie.

The film script about a Jewish barber, a soldier of Tomainia, and about Hynkel, the dictator of the country, was finished in the late summer of 1939. In September the shooting began and continued till March 1940. As usual, there were numerous takes, sometimes as many as forty.[21]

The film premiered on October 15, 1940, in New York. "The review of *The Great Dictator* was mixed. The New York *Daily News* said that I pointed a finger of Communism at the audience and most of the critics objected to the long final speech. But the public loved the film," Chaplin remembered.[22] The film was called a frank attack on Nazism. But there were negative responses, too.[23]

In London *The Great Dictator* opened in December 1940. The British were delighted. The Barber's last speech was quoted and reprinted, and was compared to Lincoln's Gettysburg Address and to Winston Churchill's famous speech given a few months earlier, in May 1940, in the British Parliament. "I have nothing to offer but blood, toil, tears and sweat," said Churchill. "You ask what is our policy? I can say: it is to wage war, by sea, land and air, with all the might and with all the strength that God can give us; to wage war against a monstrous tyranny in a dark lamentable catalogue of human crime. . . . What is our aim? . . . Victory, victory at any cost . . . for without victory, there is no survival."

Churchill's vision was bold and realistic, unlike Chaplin's utopian and idealistic vision. Anti-Nazism became Chaplin's passionate political commitment. He was happy when at the end of the war General Eisenhower personally requested a dubbed French version of the film for the newly liberated France.

In 1941 Chaplin was in a Hollywood delegation to the inauguration of President Roosevelt, whom he had met before and regarded very highly. "Roosevelt's reception was cool, however, and his only comment about *The Great Dictator* was to complain about the difficulties [the film] had caused with pro-Axis countries in Latin America."[24]

Chaplin was deeply involved in the campaign for the opening of the second front in Europe and was really upset to realize how much pro-Nazi feeling there was in the United States.

*Monsieur Verdoux* (1947) completely abandoned the tramp image, which had been Chaplin's identity for more than thirty years (the

Jewish Barber in *The Great Dictator* was, after all, also the tramp, only slightly transformed). Chaplin called *Monsieur Verdoux* a "comedy of murders," but the public of the 1940s was not ready to comprehend the film's metaphor for the cynicism of contemporary society. The film was rejected by the public and critics. The day after the premiere in New York there was a press conference, but it looked more like an interrogation of Chaplin. The director was accused of being unpatriotic to America and was reminded about his remark that he was "a patriot to humanity as a whole." His accusers said that he thought about himself as a "citizen of the world" but never applied for American citizenship; that he was "taking our money" but had some conflicts about taxes; that he had suspicious political views and was a Soviet sympathizer and a Communist. Chaplin stated that he had never belonged to any party, that he had always wanted to make films, not revolutions, that he was a peace monger, and that during the war, he sympathized very much with Russia because he believed that it was "holding the front" and for that he owed Russia thanks.[25]

The bizarre situation in his private life was also widely discussed. True, his romantic adventures had been notorious.[26] His marriage to Oona, the daughter of the celebrated American dramatist Eugene O'Neill, in 1943 was a real scandal. She was eighteen, Chaplin was fifty-four. She was recommended for a part in his film *Shadow and Substance*. He never made that film but he married her. After some years, Oona stated that she keeps him young and he makes her mature. It was the happiest of his marriages, and it lasted thirty-four years, until Chaplin's death. They had eight children.

His last film in the United States was *Limelight* (1952), in which an aging clown, Calvero, saves a young ballerina from her attempt at suicide; they live together; after some time she leaves, becomes a celebrity, and comes back; he gives his last performance and dies on the stage.

This sentimental drama was in a way very personal to Chaplin. After all, he was an aging clown. Most of the actors in the film were members of his family: his sons from his first marriage, Sydney and Charles Jr.; his half brother Wheeler Dryden; and three of his small children with Oona—Geraldine, Michael, and Josephine. Although Oona didn't play the ballerina, the actress Claire Bloom was very much her type, and a couple of times, in some shots, Oona substituted for her. The greatest American comic, Buster Keaton,[27] also appeared in the film.

In September 1952 the Chaplin family departed for England on the *Queen Elizabeth*, and soon Chaplin learned that a reentry permit would not be granted to him by America, and that many theatres in the United States had canceled showings of *Limelight*.

But he was happy to be in London. The premiere of *Limelight* was a triumph there. In Paris, Oona and Chaplin were invited to lunch with the president; Chaplin was made an officer of the Legion d'Honneur. The premiere was attended by the French Cabinet and the diplomatic corps, but the American ambassador did not come.

In the beginning of 1953 the Chaplins made their home in Switzerland, in the town of Vevey. In 1954 Oona renounced her U.S. citizenship.

In 1962 Chaplin received an honorary doctorate from Oxford, especially pleasing to him since he had never even finished high school and loved to learn words by reading dictionaries.

Two films made in Europe, *A King in New York* (1957) and *A Countess from Hong Kong* (1967), could not be qualified as total failures, but they were not successes either. But everybody would agree that Chaplin had earned the opportunity to just toy with his medium in his golden years.

In 1971 the twenty-fifth Cannes Film Festival made a special award for his total oeuvre. Finally, the Academy of Motion Picture Arts and Sciences decided to award him an Honorary Oscar and invited him to the United States. The prohibition against his return had been dropped and forgotten long before.

He arrived in New York in the spring of 1972. This was his first and last return to the United States after twenty years in Europe.

In Philharmonic Hall in New York, some fifteen hundred people gave him a standing ovation. Next was Hollywood, which Chaplin remembered as an unknown suburb when he first came there in 1914. At the Academy Awards ceremony, the music composed by him for his films was playing and clips from his films were screened. The last clip was from *The Circus*: the tramp is alone in the field after the circus has left. Those who watched the ceremony on TV recall how from this shot, the camera moved to a tight close-up "of the white-haired Chaplin coming out onstage to the shouting crowd. He was dignified and he was crying. It was the real ending of *The Circus*, [and] it was the real ending of his life."[28] A special award of the Golden Lion in Venice in 1972 and knighthood from the queen of England in 1975 were only some biographical additions.

Chaplin died of heart failure five years later, in 1977, on Christmas morning at his home in Vevey, Switzerland. He was eighty-eight.

But there was one more unintended Chaplinesque twist. Shortly after his funeral, the coffin with his body was dug up by two Eastern European immigrants, who hid it in a cornfield and demanded a ransom. They did not succeed, however. After several weeks the police recovered the unopened coffin and it was brought back to the Vevey cemetery.

The work on *The Great Dictator* started in October 1938. By that time Hitler's political opponents in Germany had already "disappeared"; the alliance with Mussolini—the Rome-Berlin Axis—was formed (October 1936) and then joined by Japan (1940); the German army occupied the Rhineland (1936), annexed Hitler's motherland, Austria (1938), and in the same year occupied Czechoslovakia. Anti-Semitism was the official government policy and the Kristall Nacht, when Jewish businesses and property were attacked by the government and mobs, had already happened. And yet Hitler was taken rather as a frightening but passing fad. Even Thomas Mann,[29] Germany's great mind, did not take him seriously. The extent of Hitler's power and evil was suspected by only a few.

We should keep in mind that the work on *The Great Dictator* started *before* Hitler's army invaded Poland (September 1, 1939) and England and France declared war on Germany; *before* the bomber raids over England; *before* the extermination camps and the "final solution" in 1941; *before* the invasion of the Soviet Union, the so-called Operation Barbarossa in 1941; and *before* Pearl Harbor and the United States' entrance into World War II in December 1941. Until that time the Americans did not want to be involved in what they thought of as a European crisis, and the interventionist-isolationist division between Americans was very strong. (Even the national hero Charles Lindbergh talked about backing "strength and peace" instead of "weakness and war"—he was a supporter of Hitler anyway.) Soon, however, American public opinion started shifting from an isolationist to an interventionist position.

When in October 1940 *The Great Dictator* reached the screen, Hitler, the war, and the storm troopers were not the best topics for laughter. Chaplin himself admitted: "Had I known of the actual horrors of the

German concentration camps, I could not have made *The Great Dictator*; I could not have made fun of the homicidal insanity of the Nazis. I wanted to ridicule their mystic bilge about a pure-blood race."[30] But still *The Great Dictator* was a brave anti-Nazi action made in the United States, where at that time there were a lot of Nazi sympathizers and the film was the only direct assault on Hitler.

Obviously we have a different perception of the film than viewers did in 1940. In our minds we see a broad montage of events, and we know how it all ended—Hitler in his bunker at the chancellery as the Soviet army neared the place, giving poison to his one-day wife, Eva Braun,[31] before shooting himself. He did not die with his soldiers, who were still fighting in the streets of Berlin. He was no Wagnerian hero, as he loved to imagine himself.

It was before the release of *The Great Dictator* that the comparison of Chaplin and Hitler had started, certainly as a humorous paradox. It was triggered by the look-alike moustaches, Hitler's real and Chaplin's fake, just a detail of his artistic persona. "He stole my moustache," Chaplin repeated to the press. The joke obviously outraged Hitler, and it was not a surprise that in the infamous Nazi book *The Jews Are Looking at You*, Chaplin was called "a disgusting Jewish acrobat."[32]

There were some other similarities besides the moustache. The two were born just four days apart in the same year: Chaplin on April 16, 1889, and Hitler on April 20. They both never finished school, adored their mothers, had blue eyes and dark hair, were short, had strong wills, and were fanatical about what they were doing. Here the similarities ended and differences began:

Chaplin was a highly professional man; Hitler never had a profession.

As a very young man, before World War I, Chaplin gained recognition, praise, and applause and was the best at what he was doing. Hitler, on the contrary, at that time was a frustrated artist, bitter and jealous, twice rejected by the Academy of Art in Vienna, who dreamed about power and revenge while working as an assistant to a house painter.

In 1914, Chaplin, the British vaudeville performer, started his career in Hollywood and in two years became a superstar. Hitler's first and only success at that time was the Iron Cross, which he received from the German army.

Chaplin could express everything without words; even his back could convey loneliness or a feeling of joy. Hitler, for many years an agitator and propagandist of the German Socialist Worker Party, believed in the appeal of rhetoric more than in any other force, as he wrote in *Mein Kampf*.

Chaplin was a cosmopolitan, a passionate internationalist; Hitler was a fanatical militant xenophobe who struggled for "one blood, one state, one führer."

Chaplin loved romance and women, was four times married, and had ten children; Hitler was indifferent to romance, probably impotent.[33]

In the 1930s Chaplin and Hitler were among a few of the best-known people in the world. They were connected by the extremities: Hitler made people cry more than anyone else; Chaplin made people laugh more than anyone else.

*The Great Dictator* was Chaplin's first film with words, his first talkie. People would joke that he started talking at fifty. The switch to sound did not change Chaplin's style—the same masterly pantomime and intimate openness of his face, the same absence of a personal name for the main character. He is just the Jewish Barber, but the rest of the characters have names, including the barber's "double," Hynkel.

Already the credits of *The Great Dictator* establish Chaplin's intentions, both political and comedic. He divides the cast list into two groups: "People of the Palace" and "People of the Ghetto."

The first group contains Adenoid Hynkel, identified as a chancellor and dictator of Tomainia (a telling pun on *ptomaine*, a poison produced by bacterial decay, and *mania*—the madness.) There is also an answer to Italy's Mussolini, one Benzino Napaloni, the dictator of Bacteria, and Hynkel's top aides, Garbitsch and Herring—parodies, respectively, of Goebbels, Hitler's closest ally and propaganda chief, and Goering, the field marshal, air force commander, and organizer of the Gestapo.

The credits then give a hint of mischief: "Note: Any resemblance between Hynkel the dictator and the Jewish Barber is purely coincidental."

Then the great story begins.

*1. A final title sets the scene at the end of World War I, 1918, and a battlefield fades in. The camera sweeps across the front lines.*

This is the first Chaplin film in which, from the very beginning, the relationship of the action with the specific historical events is established.

We hear a voiceover: *"In the last year of the world war, the Tomainian nation began to weaken."*

*A group of soldiers loads shells into the cannon with an enormous plunger. Holding the firing cord is a private, the Jewish Barber with trademark moustache and comic bearing.*

The Barber is almost the same as the tramp in *Shoulder Arms*, the film made by Chaplin some twenty-two years before, during World War I. The Tramp appeared there in a military uniform, tormented by danger, fear, explosions, hunger, and homesickness, but still clownish and funny. The drama and the laughter in *The Great Dictator* also blend harmoniously. The beginning of the film looks like a sequel to *Shoulder Arms*.

*The blast startles the Barber off his feet. The shot falls notably short of the target. Another shell pops out of the barrel and lands softly below. The Barber is stuck with the duty of examining the dud. Though dutiful and alert, the Barber also has trouble with an antiaircraft gun, a grenade, a machine gun, and even with recognizing the enemy; he gets lost in the battle smoke and finds himself behind enemy lines.*

*2. The Barber hears the cries of an exhausted pilot on the ground nearby, "Can you fly a plane?" the pilot asks. "I can try!" the Barber replies, and they take off.*

Here the beginning of a relationship between the Barber and the pilot of the enemy army, Schultz, is established. We see a series of gags in the teetering plane, which eventually runs out of fuel and crashes into a swamp.

Schultz survives, but Tomainia has lost the war. The crash leaves the Barber with amnesia—we get a glimpse of him sleeping in a hospital bed.

The twelve minutes of the introductory sequence—the *exposition*—have more than fifty shots. *Long shots* (a few extremely long) establish the image of the world the Barber finds himself in, and various *medium shots* show how he exists in and reacts to this world.

*3. A montage of quick, overlapping images suggests the passage of time: crowds in the streets, a spinning printing press, a series of newspaper head-lines: "Armistice!" and "Peace!" and concluding with "Depression," "Riots in Tomainia," and "Hynkel Party Takes Power."*

*4. We see the Barber strolling on the hospital grounds, doffing his hat at a nurse, sniffing a flower. The voiceover tells: "Meanwhile, the Jewish Barber suffered a loss of memory and remained an inmate of the soldiers' hospital for many years. He was ignorant of the profound change that had come over Tomainia."*

*5. Dissolve to the dictator Hynkel shown from the back. He is making a tense speech to the masses. The narrator explains that "under the new emblem of the double cross, liberty was banished."*

The "double cross," as an emblem, is Chaplin's answer to the swastika, and as a phrase it is a pun: Hitler's apparent revival of the German economy and national spirit turned out to be a double cross of the greatest order.

A cut to the frontal view of the dictator reveals his resemblance not only to Hitler but to the Jewish Barber as well. Chaplin's love for contrast in *The Great Dictator* comes to the highest point: nothing can be more opposite than the Barber and Hynkel.

*Hynkel continues his charged speech, full of nonsense words and German gibberish: "Democratien stoonk!" "Libertad stoonk!" "Wiener Schnitzel."*

It was known that Hitler practiced oratorical skills in front of a mirror and studied the photographs and documentaries of himself addressing the crowds. He was very attentive to the sound of his own voice, its modulations from restricted dramatic tension to paroxysms of ecstasy.

*Hynkel enjoys the rousing applause he has inspired; he is very excited. He takes a glass of water and pours some down his pants. He even pours water in his ear and spits it out of his mouth* [Chaplin's nostalgic recollection of an old clownish stunt].

*The crowd robotically salutes. He waves sharply to silence them and continues his indulgent, barking oratory.*[34]

Chaplin analyzed and closely studied the führer's speaking at the Nuremberg Nazi Party rally of 1934, which was portrayed exhaustively in Leni Riefenstahl's film *Triumph of the Will*.[35] He repeated and exaggerated Hitler's movements and gestures, turning everything into grotesque.

*Hynkel makes a comment about the need for Tomainians to tighten their belts and his minister of war, the oafish, fat, and very emotional Field Marshall Herring, makes a gesture of loyalty by literally tightening his belt. The moment he sits, however, his belt pops open.*[36]

*Führer continues his speech. His eyes are wide and full of hate, his inflection growling and inflamed. But the commentator remarks, gently: "His Excellency has just referred to the Jewish people."*

In the ten-minute scene of twenty-five shots, the speech takes more than half of the time and is presented in seven medium shots with an almost steady camera in order not to break the continuity of Chaplin's performance—the incredible virtuosity of grotesque movements and sounds.

*The event concludes with more formalities: Hynkel poses with a baby for a photo, sneering, then wipes his hands and gets in his limousine for a cruise along Hynkelstrasse, the avenue of culture. Tomainia's "masterpieces," versions of familiar statues, raise an arm to hail the dictator.*

A failed artist, Hitler had a very personal and painful attitude toward art. He collected paintings of old painters, hated modern art, and patronized only those artists who glorified him and his totalitarian regime.[37]

*6. In the car, Hynkel asks Garbitsch his opinion of the speech. "I thought your reference to the Jews might have been a little more violent," Garbitsch replies. "At this time violence against the Jews might take the public's mind off its stomach."*

*7. Dissolve to the ghetto. It is a modest and shabby but lived-in neighborhood, except that storm troopers patrol the streets. We see the ghetto's inhabitants, Mr. Jaeckel, an elderly dignified man, and the pretty laundress, Hannah.*

The name Hannah had a special significance for Chaplin. This was his mother's name. In Chaplin films prior to *The Great Dictator* characters usually did not have names but were indicated as the Flower Girl, Millionaire, Artist, and so forth.

*8. Hannah emerges with a basket of laundry. She stops short to see some storm troopers smashing windows and grabbing vegetables from a street ven-*

dor. When Hannah stands up to them, the storm troopers pelt her with the stolen vegetables and humiliate her.

9. A clinical office at the hospital, where two administrators discuss the amnesiac barber. They discover that he's left but decide that he's harmless.

10. Dissolve to the Barber returning after many years to his shop. He takes the boards off the windows and opens the door, dons his barber's coat, and notices the dust and cobwebs everywhere.

The three following scenes could be treated as one scene because there is no time interruption in the action. Yet the setting is slightly various and the themes are shifting.

Outside, the storm troopers deface the Barber's shop, writing "Jew" on his windows, as they have marked other buildings in the neighborhood. The Barber starts to scrub it off. Here we see a silent slapstick of splashing the officers with their own paint. Hannah helps by leaning out her window and whacking everyone including the Barber (by accident) with a frying pan. She brings the Barber inside the courtyard and explains that the police won't help. She also admires his courage. "That's what we should all do: fight back," she says.

How to respond to Nazism was a burning question for America at that time. Hannah could use only her frying pan, Chaplin, his film.

11. More troops arrive, and the Barber puts up a fight, but soon the street is mobbed with soldiers. They ooze around corners and quickly outnumber him. In no time, the situation has escalated beyond the comfortable confines of comedy: the storm troopers make a noose and prepare to lynch the Barber.

For the viewers of the 1940s, storm troopers were not an object of laughter, and soon after the film was released, Chaplin himself realized this.

12. Schultz, who has been promoted through the ranks, arrives in a limousine. Luckily, he recognizes the Barber as the man who saved his life. "Strange. And I always thought of you as an Aryan," he says.

"I'm a vegetarian," the Barber replies innocently.

The only thing that the Barber had in common with the real dictator was that Hitler also was a vegetarian.[38]

Schultz promises that the barber and the people in his neighborhood won't *be bothered again. "Oh, it's no harm," the Barber says, the noose still around his neck.*

The camera here is more active, although often the movement is expressed in front of the camera—in the mise-en-scène rather than *by* the camera.

*13. The scenery changes to the dictator's palace—elegant, spacious, with high ceilings, statues and frescoes, chandeliers and grand staircases. Hynkel, enormously busy and full of a sense of self-importance, is now satisfied, now enraged. He has people licking envelopes for him, painting his portraits, and sculpting his busts; inventors show to him ludicrously foolhardy new weapons. He plays the piano, takes advantage of his secretary, and has more meetings, one more ridiculous than another.*

No matter how grotesque Hynkel's actions are, Chaplin based them on real aspects of the führer's personality and his habits, certainly exaggerating them: Hitler's restlessness, his doing simultaneously many things without finishing them, and the swings from hysterical fits of rage to melancholic dreaminess while listening to music. The latter was described by Winnifried Wagner, the composer's daughter-in-law, who was platonically in love with Hitler and saw him as a Wagnerian hero.

*14. Hynkel decides to invade the nearby country of Osterlich. To do it, however, he will need to borrow money from a Jewish banker. He discusses this with Garbitsch. Until the loan is secured, he orders that persecution of the ghetto's Jews should temporarily stop.*

Osterlich is obviously Austria, Hitler's homeland. In 1938, the son of Austrian soil, as he sometimes was called, but now the führer of Germany's Third Reich, occupied the country.

*15. Mr. Jaeckel getting a haircut. He fills the Barber in on recent Tomainian history. The Barber's business is slow, Jaeckel explains, because so many of the local men have been taken to concentration camps. Well aware of the growing affection between Hannah and the Barber, Jaeckel suggests the Barber expand his business to include women—beginning right away with Hannah. Jaeckel leaves them alone together, and Hannah sits in the Barber's chair.*

Although the next scene is the direct continuation of previous action, it is so different in theme, tone, and mood that it could or even should be treated as a new scene.

*16. The Barber absent-mindedly lathers Hannah's face for a shave. It prompts a shared laugh. The Barber starts over.*

With an element of old-fashioned movie-screen magic, the film dissolves directly from the image of Hannah before her makeover to a more prettified image thereafter. The camera moves closer and closer to Hannah and stops at her face—the first close-up in the film and one of few.

*17. Hannah goes outside to get some potatoes, and when she trips on the curb, the nearby storm troopers are attentive and polite. She doesn't quite know what to make of it and says directly to the camera, "Wouldn't it be wonderful if they'd let us live and be happy again?"*

The shot fades out.

*18. Back in his palace, Hynkel, prone to irrational rages, hearing of a factory strike, orders: "Have them all shot. I don't want any of my workers dissatisfied." Garbitsch strokes Hynkel's ego, compares him to Caesar, and leaves him alone with his delusions of grandeur. In an ecstasy, with a wicked laugh, the dictator dances with a balloon—an inflated globe.*

It is hard to believe that the performance, which looks so spontaneous, was scripted by Chaplin: how Hynkel moves hypnotically toward the globe, one hand on hip, one outstretched; how he finds he can do what he likes with the globe; how he laughs ecstatically; or how he bounces the globe from toe to head to rear.

The megalomaniacal nature of Hynkel (Hitler), his craziness, sentimentality, and fantasy of world domination, is expressed in the dance, accompanied by Richard Wagner's *Lohengrin*. It is the reminder of Hitler's beloved composer and of the German knight in shining armor, Lohengrin, the prince of the Holy Grail—the mythological root of Germanness.

*The balloon world is fragile, and eventually it pops in the dictator's face, leaving him distraught.*

It was said by many critics that in the dance with the balloon globe, Chaplin surpassed even himself, reaching the highest point of virtuosity as a performer and as a director.

*19. A dissolve to the barber shop, where the Barber gets a kind of dance number of his own. Playing through his radio is a Brahms Hungarian Dance, to which the Barber precisely choreographs an intense and amusing shave of his client.*

The nonverbal balloon and shaving scenes are quintessentially Chaplinesque: an unreachable height of poetry, humor, sarcasm, and plasticity.

*20. Mr. Jaeckel and his friend play chess. They are suspicious of the recent peace in the ghetto. Meanwhile Mrs. Jaeckel helps Hannah prepare for her date with the Barber.*

*21. Dissolve to the palace. Learning that his loan has been refused, Hynkel fumes. He wants to take his rage out on the ghetto, but Schultz tries to dissuade him. This protest gets him arrested. "Remember my words," Schultz says. "Your cause is doomed to failure because it's built on the stupid ruthless persecution of innocent people."*

How prophetic the phrase is! Is it just Schultz saying this, or rather Chaplin himself articulating his own prediction?

*Schultz is hauled away, leaving the dictator to another violent and silly tantrum.*

*22. The Barber is getting ready for his date. He is clearly unaccustomed to formality and overdoes it, wearing both a pocket watch and a wristwatch.*

In *The Great Dictator* romance is less important than in other Chaplin films; we can even say that it is not important at all. Hannah could have been just his sister, not his date, and nothing would have changed in the film.

*23. All the neighbors wait to see the Barber and Hannah off on their date. Sharing a cheerful mood, they stroll down the street and decide that things aren't so bad after all. Maybe to give Hynkel another chance, they start to buy buttons supporting him. But just then the dictator's voice comes roaring over a loudspeaker, full of nasty fury. Hynkel's angry face is inserted for an instant, and then the camera goes back to the ghetto street.*

This second close-up in the film works as a strong visual emphasis on the dark and inhuman nature of Hynkel—a contrast to the previous close-up on Hannah, with her innate goodness.

*Hannah and the Barber give back the buttons. Hynkel shouts to attack the ghetto and everyone panics. All of the people out in the streets suddenly flee, leaving the Barber and Hannah standing alone together, dumbfounded, and then they hurry to safety. The Barber loses his hat and goes to pick it* up but is repeatedly startled by the blare of the dictator's voice, which sounds like a roaring animal. Again, Hynkel's face is inserted.

The moment crystallizes the tone of the whole film: it is frightening and funny at the same time.

24. *The Barber manages to slip out of a storm trooper's hands. The locals congregate in the courtyard, and Mr. Jaeckel tells the men to take a stand against the encroaching troops. The Barber orders a Nazi trooper "out!"*

25. *Hannah and the Barber watch his shop go up in flames. She says they can start over, but she can't keep from crying.*

26. *The scene dissolves to Hynkel happily toying with one of his pianos.*

27. *Fade in on the roof at night. Hannah and the Barber are watching the stars, which, she observes, will always remain out of Hynkel's reach. Mr. Jaeckel comes up to inform them of a secret meeting with Schultz to take place downstairs.*

28. *Schultz calls on the men of the neighborhood to commit their resistance to Hynkel. One of them must become a martyr, he explains, to rid them all of the tyrant. It is decided that they will all be given puddings, one of which contains a coin, and whoever gets the coin is thereby elected. Hannah has put coins in all of the slices; several of the men try to get rid of their coin. Finally, Mr. Jaeckel, who has always seemed an honorable man, declares that the duty is his.*

29. *The next day the storm troopers close in again. Schultz and the Barber scamper and hide, allowing for a bit of slapstick humor, but eventually the soldiers capture them.*

30. *Headlines tell us that Schultz gets sent to a prison camp and, after a dissolve to him and the Barber in the camp among the prisoners, the screen fades out.*

31. *Hannah, Mr. Jaeckel, and the others have finally fled to the vineyards of Osterlich with their rolling hills, fertile vines, and plenty of sunshine. Hannah writes an optimistic letter to the Barber, and the screen dissolves to him in his cell reading it.*

32. *Fade in on the dictator and his closest subordinates—they are ready to march on Osterlich. Hynkel pins a medal on the overly emotional Herring,*

*but with the information that Napaloni, the dictator of Bacteria, has mobilized his men on the Osterlich front, he becomes furious with Herring and yanks off all his medals, and even some of the buttons on his jacket. Hynkel gives an impulsive order to declare war on Napaloni but becomes suddenly sheepish when Napaloni himself calls to discuss the situation.*

*33. Hynkel's troops, in formal regalia, are waiting to greet Benzino Napaloni at the train station. The train can't quite find the appropriate resting place. The rotund and boisterous Napaloni refuses to step off the train until a red carpet is presented before him. When the Bacterian dictator finally approaches the Tomainian dictator, they can't decide whether to salute each other or shake hands. They make their way to the car, and the crowd greets Napaloni enthusiastically. Hynkel is unnerved by the warm reception for his rival.*

Hitler and Mussolini formed an alliance, the Rome-Berlin Axis, in 1936, joined by Japan in 1940.

*34. Hynkel is pacing his office. "At all costs, Napaloni will not invade Osterlich," he shouts. Garbitsch suggests to humiliate Napaloni. But he suddenly appears and surprises Hynkel with a big slap on his back. "Hinkie, my dictator frien [sic]!" he says in Italian immigrant English. The intimidated Hynkel gets tongue-tied.*

Chaplin delights in making these leaders into burlesque characters. The whole scene has the comic directness and simplicity of old European street theatre and of American slapstick comedy.

*35. At the buffet of a formal ball, discussions about Osterlich get heated, and a food fight between the dictators ensues, and when an inquisitive reporter peeks through the door, he gets a pie in the face—a classical slapstick stunt.*

*Garbitsch convinces Hynkel to sign a treaty with Napaloni and then violate it. Hynkel agrees, and he and Napaloni finally embrace.*

*36. Fade in to the prison; we learn that two prisoners have escaped in officers' uniforms. The alarm sounds, and the troops scramble.*

*37. Dissolve to the escapees, none other than Schultz and the Barber, heading for the border along a deserted road.*

*38. Meanwhile Hynkel, alone in his rowboat, is contemplating his plans for a secret invasion. He zealously shoots at some ducks and falls into the water. Two storm troopers discover him and take him for the escaped barber.*

It's the last we'll see of Adenoid Hynkel.

*39. The Barber and Schultz pass some soldiers on the road and worry that they'll be spotted. But the soldiers, of course, mistake the Barber for Hynkel, and he and Schultz are therefore welcomed with fanfare into the village of Pretzelburg. They're led to a limousine. The Barber almost faints, but Schultz props him up.*

*40. A quick montage of dissolving headlines: "Ghettos Raided"; "Jewish Property Confiscated." Shots of storm troopers coming down hard on the ghetto.*

*41. The Osterlich countryside, where the peace is ruptured by Hannah's scream. Storm troopers charge the house, round up the other residents, slap Hannah and Mr. Jaeckel down, and idly eat their grapes. Finally a last headline: "Osterlich Crowds Await Conqueror."*

*42. We see the sons and daughters of the Double Cross crowds, and the gathered troops, as the limousine arrives. The Barber and Schultz advance toward the podium. Herring and Garbitsch notice that Hynkel is somehow different and that Schultz has returned, but they dare not speak aloud and stand stiffly with their arms raised in salute.*

*Garbitsch makes some welcoming remarks. "Today, democracy, liberty, and equality are words to fool the people," he says. "We frankly abolish them." The Barber is astonished by what he hears. "You must speak," Schultz tells him. "I can't." "You must. It's our only hope." "Hope," the Barber repeats, softly.*

Even at this tense dramatic point we cannot help but realize the double meaning of the words "you must speak." For more than ten years Chaplin had heard them said by his critics, who demanded sound, not silent films, from him.

The Barber appeals to the Tomainian Nazi soldiers with the plea not to fight for the dictator but to take power from him and enjoy peaceful life. What a naïve and idealistic attempt. The last words of hope are addressed to Hannah. The speech is six minutes long and consists of three shots on the Barber and two on Hannah listening to him. (One of the Barber's shots is eighty seconds long while the average Hollywood shot at that time was seven seconds long.)

*43. Hannah lifts her head as if she hears him: "Wherever you are, look up! Look up, Hannah! The clouds are lifting! The sun is breaking through! We are coming out of the darkness into the light!" She looks up at the immense sky.*

This is the last shot of the film.

We can see in the chart in Figure 1–1 how the line of narration is broken by the switches from the world of the Barber to the world of the dictator Hynkel. The breaks are accentuated by fade-outs: the screen goes to black, creating a short pause before the new action resumes. The forty-three scenes of the film vary in duration from a few seconds to ten minutes. They are filmed primarily in medium and long shots by a camera that rarely tracks or pans, as if it doesn't want to disturb Chaplin's performance. There are only two close-ups in the whole film (an unusually small number). They are used for strong emphasis: in scene 16 to show how open and attractive Hannah's face is, the image of the humane, and two close-ups in scene 23 on Hynkel's abhorrent and ugly face, the image of the wicked.

As we know, the film is based on the contrast between the vicious and insane dictator and a kind little man, the Barber. They are identical in appearance. We know that the action culminates as the dictator, while duck hunting, is arrested by the storm troopers, and the Barber, in a stolen military uniform, is mistaken for the dictator and treated accordingly. This double mistaken identity is pleasantly symmetrical and gives a certain balance to the film. As the scene diagram in Figure 1–1 shows, the same balancing effect results from the two long speeches, one by the dictator (scene 5), the other by the Barber (scene 42), and the two "dances": the dictator performs with the globe (scene 18), and the Barber does his "hand dance" when shaving a client (scene 19). Also contributing to the balance is the film's running time: it is equally divided between the two characters. Forty-six minutes are given to the Barber and forty-seven minutes to the dictator.

In *The Great Dictator* Chaplin wears two masks, constantly exchanging them—from the Barber to Hynkel and back to the Barber again. Only at the very end of the film do the masks come off: through the Barber and Hynkel, Charles Chaplin himself appears with his passionate call against the war and aggression. The little barber would be incapable of delivering such a speech, and it certainly could not be expected of Hynkel.

The film was strongly criticized for having uninventive camera work and for being slow to change angles and distances. But these

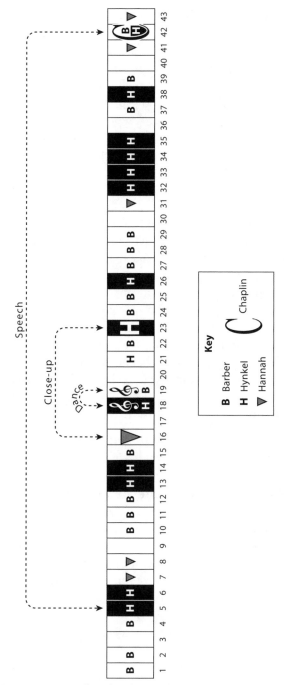

*Figure 1–1. Scene Diagram for* The Great Dictator

critics failed to notice that the dynamic inventiveness and fluidity all were in Chaplain's performance. The camera's function here was to capture it and deliver it unaltered to the world audience.

The film was also criticized for its structure—too loose, with fragmented narration and its ending left unresolved. It was criticized for its long speeches and especially for its concern with hot political issues, something that was unacceptable by Hollywood standards. But political issues were precisely what Chaplin was aiming at.

In the film we recognize the actual historical personalities (although grotesquely transformed) and events—hints at Nazi rallies and Hitler's annexation of Austria (called Osterlich in the film) and headings with references to world events.

*The Great Dictator* is a political satire, and Chaplin unfolds the frightening realities of his time in a burlesque spectacle full of gags and puppetlike characters: the doll-like brave girl, the wicked dictator, and the lovable simpleton (his loss of memory makes him even more of a mindless puppet). "I'm the clown, and what can I do that is more effective than to laugh?" was Chaplin's position. All his skits and stunts came from old theatrical and circus traditions, from the most common and accessible entertainment—the street performance—and he made the screen the largest street ever. Chaplin could not care less whether *The Great Dictator* would conform to Hollywood standards. His political goal was to strip Adolf Hitler of his powerful eminence, to make fun of him, to ridicule his greatness as if asking, "Is *this* the great dictator?"

## Appendix

### From Richard Meryman's Interview with Chaplin[39]

I don't think one can do humor without having great pity and a sense of sympathy for one's fellow man . . . humor does save one's sanity. We can go overboard with too much tragedy. Tragedy is, of course, a part of life, but we're also given an equipment to offset anything, a defense against it. I think tragedy is very essential in life. And we are given humor as a defense against it. Humor is a universal thing, which I think is derived from more or less pity. . . . There is a lot of sorrow to life, there's plenty of trouble in the world, and I think to make a picture showing the possibility that there is another aspect to life is very charming. It's not the question of what life is, it's a question of what the possibilities are.

Cruelty is a basic element in comedy. What appears to be sane is really insane, and if you can make that poignant enough they love it. The audience recognizes it as a farce on life, and they laugh at it in order not to die from it, in order not to weep. It's a question of that mysterious thing called candor coming in. An old man slips on a banana and falls slowly and stumbles and we don't laugh. But if it's done with a pompous well-to-do gentleman who has exaggerated pride, then we laugh. All embarrassing situations are funny, especially if they're treated with humor.

## Notes

1. "If it had not been for my mother," Chaplin wrote, "I doubt if I could have made a success of pantomime. . . . It was through watching and listening to her that I learned not only how to express my emotions with my hands and face, but also how to observe and study people." David Robinson, *Chaplin, His Life and Art*, New York: McGraw Hill, 1985, p. 18.

In 1921 Hannah was granted permission to immigrate to the United States. She lived in California in comfort and wealth, with all the attention of her famous son. Now and then she was unwell and forgetful. Once, when present at the shooting of *The Gold Rush*, she suddenly looked very embarrassed and whispered to Chaplin: "Charlie, I have to get you a new suit." She died in 1928.

2. Roger Mannvell, *Chaplin*, Boston: Little, Brown, 1974, p. 51.

3. Randolph Churchill, "At 50 Chaplin Begins to Talk," *The New York Times Magazine*, 1939 (30 July), pp. 10–12.

4. Pantomime is an old traditional European genre; it was stimulated by the laws of eighteenth-century France, which forbade dialogue in all performances, except on the stages of the Theatres Royal. The Chinese and Japanese theatre had its pantomime traditions with more ritualistic rules.

5. Stan Laurel (1890–1965), an English-born mime and comedian, from his twenties lived and performed in the United States. He and Oliver Hardy (1892–1957) were the most successful film comedy duo of the time.

6. Chaplin was not much over five feet tall. He said that if he were a couple of inches taller, the image of his tramp would not have been possible.

7. Alan Dale, *Comedy Is a Man in Trouble*, Minneapolis: University of Minneapolis Press, 2000, p. 36.

8. Robinson, p. 143.

9. Silent-film star Douglas Fairbanks (1883–1939), with Mary Pickford, Chaplin, and Griffith, formed United Artists Film Company to distribute their film productions. He was Chaplin's closest friend.

10. Mary Pickford (1893–1979) started at Griffith films at age sixteen. She became an adored actress known as the Girl with the Golden Hair and America's Sweetheart.

11. A lady donated twenty thousand dollars to sit next to Chaplin at a dinner.

12. The theme of a child left by his parents was very sensitive in the post-war time, when many children were orphans.

13. From 1915 until 1923, Edna Purviance was the leading lady of Chaplin's thirty-five films. Contrary to the widely held opinion that Chaplin was indifferent and unfair to women who were close to him, he supported Edna for some thirty years until she died in 1958.

14. Charles Chaplin, *My Life in Pictures*, London, Sydney, Toronto: Bodley Head, 1974, p. 232.

15. The attempts to introduce sound to motion pictures go back to the very end of the nineteenth century. But the so-called talkie revolution happened in 1927 in Hollywood with the first talkie, *The Jazz Singer*.

16. Chaplin recalled that he worried about *City Lights*: Would the public accept a silent film at that time? He went to the premiere in Los Angeles with Albert Einstein and saw how he was wiping his eyes. Then he realized that his worries were unnecessary.

17. Charles Maland, *Chaplin and American Culture,* Princeton, NJ: Princeton University, 1989, p. 150.

18. Although this is a silent film, a step toward words was made in a song Chaplin composed and sang in the film with nonsensical, nonexistent gibberish lyrics: "Se bella piu satore, je notre so catore."

19. Paulette Goddard and Chaplin met in 1932, were officially married in 1936, and separated amicably in the very beginning of the 1940s. She was his third wife. The first was Mildred Harris (1918–1920); the second was Lita Grey (1924–1928), the mother of two of his sons, Charles Jr. and Sydney, whom he loved and cared about. The boys had a very good relationship with Goddard and continued seeing her after the divorce.

20. Alexander Korda (1893–1956), internationally known director and producer.

21. Chaplin's shooting ratio—the amount of footage shot as opposed to the amount of footage in the final print—was legendary, unheard of, sometimes as high as one hundred to one.

22. Chaplin, *My Life in Pictures,* p. 28.

23. Rudolph Arnheim, famous art historian and a recent refugee from Hitler's Germany, wrote: "Charles Chaplin is the only artist who holds the secret weapon of mortal laughter . . . but instead of unmasking Nazism he unmasked a single man, the great dictator. . . . This good film should have been better." Quoted in Robinson, p. 508.

24. Robinson, p. 510.

25. Screenwriter Ben Hecht recalled how the press called Chaplin wicked or traitorous, and how untrue and unjust it was.

26. In 1943 there were court hearings about a young actress' accusations that Chaplin had fathered her newly born daughter. Despite a blood test proving that he was not the father, and even though the first jury acquitted him on all counts, the second jury melted at the touching sight of the mother and child and ordered him to pay child support until the girl was twenty-one.

27. Buster Keaton (1895–1966), legendarily famous from the late teens to the thirties; his appearance in the film gave a boost to his dying career.

28. Stanley Kauffmann, *Before My Eyes,* New York: Harper and Row, 1974, p. 418.

29. Thomas Mann (1875–1955), one of the most influential writers of the twentieth century, received the Nobel Prize for literature in 1929.

30. Chaplin, *My Life in Pictures,* p. 268.

31. Hitler married Eva Braun the day before.

32. Chaplin's ethnic background was not clear. For some reason he was evasive about it. Probably, he felt that any specific notion of his ethnicity would automatically deprive the tramp of his universality.

33. Hitler was emotionally attached, in his pathological way, only to his niece, Geli, who committed suicide or maybe was killed by him or at his request in 1931. Eva Braun was just his submissive follower, not a lover.

34. Before shooting started, Chaplin watched all the newsreels of Hitler. He returned often to a particular sequence showing the führer at the signing of the French surrender, and as he left the railway carriage, he seemed to do something like dance steps. Chaplin would watch it with fascination, exclaiming, "Oh, you bastard, you son-of-a-bitch, you swine. I know what's in your mind." Dale, p. 49.

> Adolph Hitler was disturbed when he heard Chaplin was at work on *The Great Dictator,* and there is some evidence that Hitler actually saw the film. According to an agent who fled Germany after

working in the film division of the Nazi Ministry of Culture, Nazi authorities procured a print and Hitler screened the film one evening in solitude. The following evening he again watched the film by himself. That is all the agent could tell Chaplin. In relaying the anecdote, Chaplin said, "I'd give anything to know what he thought of it." Jeffrey Vance, *Chaplin, Genius of the Cinema*, New York: Harry N. Abrams, 2003, p. 250.

35. Leni Riefenstahl (1902–2003), director and actress; her documentary on the Nuremberg National Socialist Party Convention in 1934, *Triumph of the Will*, has been called the most powerful propaganda film ever made.

36. The man is the easily recognizable Hermann Goering—the Luftwaffe commissioner who controlled the police and security forces and organized the Gestapo. He was grossly overweight and shed his pounds only during the Nuremberg trial of the Nazi war criminals. Sentenced to hang, he managed to commit suicide a few hours before execution, but still his corpse was hanged.

37. Hitler collected paintings from the seventeenth through the nineteenth centuries, which mainly came from the Gestapo-confiscated private collections of people who emigrated or were arrested or executed. He hated modern artists, especially the German Expressionists, calling them degenerates. In the 1930s, works of the German modernists were sold abroad, destroyed, or simply burned.

38. Hitler could not eat meat because, he explained, it meant the death of a living creature; he drank only water and herbal teas, did not smoke, and could not tolerate smoking in his presence.

39. Published in Jeffrey Vance, *Chaplin: Genius of the Cinema*, pp. 363, 364.

# CHILDREN OF PARADISE

## (LES ENFANTS DU PARADIS)

### Marcel Carné

| | |
|---|---|
| director: | Marcel Carné |
| producer: | Raymond Borderie |
| screenplay: | Jacques Prévert |
| cinematography: | Roger Hubert |
| production design: | Alexandre Trauner |
| costumes: | Antoine Mayo |
| music: | Joseph Kosma, Maurice Thiriet |
| editing: | Henri Rust, Madeleine Bonin |

*cast*

| | |
|---|---|
| garance: | Arletty |
| baptiste deburau, the mime: | Jean-Louis Barrault |
| frédérick lemaître: | Pierre Brasseur |
| pierre-françois lacenaire: | Marcel Herrand |
| jéricho, the old clothes man: | Pierre Renoir |
| nathalie: | Maria Casarès |
| count edouard de montray: | Louis Salou |

Black and white
*running time:* 195 minutes
*released:* March 1945, The Palais de Chaillot, Paris
*awards:* Nominated for the Academy Award for best original
screenplay, 1947

Marcel Carné was born in Paris on August 18, 1906. He was an only
child in a working-class family; his father was a cabinetmaker. His
mother died when he was only five. This clearly affected Carné: in

almost all of his films, love is inseparable from suffering and loss.[1] He later observed that although he was too young to fully comprehend his mother's death at the time, losing her left him with a painful sensitivity. That, too, is evident in his films.

His grandmother raised him, supporting his earliest creative interests. She bought him the "magic lantern," a projector with which he put on slide shows for his neighborhood friends (some of whom would later act in his films). From early on, his appetite for cinema and theatre became voracious.

At sixteen he started working with his father, but soon left him and took a series of odd jobs, meanwhile studying filmmaking and photography at the Ecole des Arts et Métiers. When he thought of working on films, he recalled, he couldn't even dream of being a director, only maybe a set manager.

At the age of twenty-two, Carné met Jacques Feyder (1885–1948), one of the most authoritative French directors, who hired Carné as his assistant on the comedy *Les Nouveaux Messieurs* (*The New Gentlemen*, 1928). This was the best possible schooling in technical and artistic perfection, in the secrets of putting a poetic touch to melodramas, in an attention to minute details, sets, and costumes, in theatrical elegance of performing, and in picturesque shots.

After the film was finished, Feyder left for Hollywood. Carné, meanwhile, was recruited by the military and served for a year in the Rhineland. Upon his return to Paris, he worked as an assistant cameraman, made some short advertising films, and soon switched to writing about films. He won a writing contest and got a job at *Cinémagazine*, a weekly film journal in which he published articles and essays until 1933. His firsthand experience with making films gave him an authority and insight that readers respected. But he returned to filmmaking and in 1929 made *Nogent, Eldorado du Dimanche*, a short documentary about the Sunday adventures of Paris' working class. The film was noticed and even inspired René Clair (1898–1981) to hire Carné as one of his assistants. He was working on *Sous Les Toits de Paris* (*Under the Roofs of Paris*, 1930), soon to become a French classic.

In 1933 Jacques Feyder returned to France and Carné returned to his side as his assistant. The maestro taught Carné to look more at old masters rather than follow new fads, to not be afraid of being traditional, "to mistrust theories of the cinema and to work directly from his heart and mind."[2] Carné was sensitive to Feyder's aesthetic and political conservatism, but his own sympathy was with left-leaning ideas, and by 1934 he joined the Association of Revolutionary Writers and Artists, mainly Communist intellectuals connected to the famous newspaper L'Humanité. It was a time, Carné recalled, of intense political turmoil in France, and he was on the side of the proletariat, but his involvement in political life was rather of a romantic nature. During an antigovernment demonstration, Carné was injured, but not seriously. More significantly, though, Carné's budding political affinities had caused some friction with Feyder.

"Politics is a distorting mirror," Carné would later say, realizing the dangers of political oversimplification and renouncing his callow commitments. All his ambitions and involvement now and forever were only with films.

French filmmakers have always been proud that their country was the geographical and cultural birthplace of the film art form. The brothers Louis (1864–1948) and Auguste (1862–1954) Lumière projected their very first film on March 22, 1895, in Paris, at the Boulevard des Capucines, where the Impressionists used to exhibit their paintings. It was a documentary of less than one minute. A couple of years later, Georges Méliès (1861–1938), using a camera more imaginatively, created the first short fiction films. It is remarkable that Carné's *Children of Paradise,* in a way, combines these two lines, using some real characters in a fictional story.

One of the first film production companies, Charles Pathé's (he was called the Napoleon of the cinema), was French, and eventually the company became a movie empire, the world's largest, before World War I and before Hollywood's ascendance to the very top.

Unlike the American film industry, with several principal companies controlling the market, with the studio system and clearly defined film genres, in France, since the beginning of the 1920s, there were numerous independent producers. French cinema didn't have genre division, and often directors, not producers, had the final say at all stages of filmmaking, from the script to the final cut.

In France, the general attitude toward cinema was also different: film was considered a work of art, not just an entertainment, and the director was regarded as the artist.

In the 1920s, some French filmmakers were a part of the Parisian avant-garde: they rejected narrative and any connection to theatre or literature and treated film as a synthesis of painting, music, and architecture. Diverse avant-garde groups had one thing in common— passion for new discoveries in cinematic language and technique.

They brought to the French film a spirit of independence, artistic freedom, and strong interest in experiment. This culminated in the Surrealist films of dreams, aggression, and erotic imagery and of the violent collision of the conscious and subconscious.[3]

In the 1930s, when Marcel Carné's rise to stardom began, the mainstream of the French cinema became a mixture of lyricism and realism, called *poetic realism*. A film would look like reality but would be thoughtfully and elegantly structured and have a strong intention to go "beyond the face of things," to their symbolic and metaphysical meaning. Carné became the master of poetic realism.

In 1936, he got an offer to adapt to film a pulp gangster novel. It became his feature debut, *Jenny* (1936). His choice for a scriptwriter was the Surrealist poet Jacques Prévert.

*Jenny*, the first of their eight collaborations, a poetic realism melodrama, "ignored class struggle without ignoring the class differences."[4] The director's view of the world appeared pessimistic, with neither belief in nor promise of any positive values. But Carné's artistic sensitivity gave the film an aesthetic quality, as if the director wanted to compensate for the imperfection of life with the refined, accomplished images of his art.

Released in the same year, *Le Crime de Monsieur Lange* (*The Crime of Monsieur Lange*, 1936), by Jean Renoir (1894–1979), was much more politically and socially oriented. At that time, Renoir's artistic reputation had been already established, though he had not yet reached the professional excellence of his classics, *La Grand Illusion* (*Grand Illusion*, 1937) and *La Regle Du Jeu* (*The Rules of the Game*, 1939). From the 1940s, Carné's status would be defined by some as superior, by others as inferior to Renoir's.

*Jenny* had mixed reviews, but with this film, Carné found his professional identity and demonstrated his creative power. As it was noticed, already Carné, the master, could be seen emerging from Marcel, the novice. Already by the end of the 1930s, no one doubted Marcel Carné's place among the so-called big five of the French cinema, along with Jacques Feyder, Jean Renoir, René Clair, and Julien Duvivier.[5]

Carné and Prévert worked in constant dialogue. Generally, the director would choose the performers to populate each film, and the writer would write or rewrite with them in mind. Their films *Drôle de Drames* (*Bizarre*, 1937) and *Le Jour Se Lève* (*Daybreak*, 1939) showed the oppressed, ominously gloomy atmosphere of France on the threshold of the war. Especially expressive was their *Le Quai des Brumes* (*Port of Shadows*, 1938). After the war it was said that the film's depressive, fatalistic pessimism and low spirit contributed to France's defeat. Carné answered that a film can be a barometer of its time but the makers of barometers are not responsible for the storms they forecast.

Carné's direction was careful, disciplined, formal, enriched by Prévert's elevated vision and witty wordplay. Carné did not tolerate improvisation. The master of intelligence and taste, he knew precisely what he wanted with each scene, each shot, and he directed accordingly.

In September 1939, Carné was drafted into the army: Hitler invaded Poland, and its ally, France, declared war on Germany. Years later he recalled that at the time he felt both resigned and fatalistic.

In May 1940, the German army crossed the French border and in six weeks entered Paris. The eighty-five-year-old marshal Philippe Pétain, a national military hero, signed the armistice—a total and humiliating surrender. France's new so-called Free State was formed in the south, in Vichy (a well-known health spa), with Pétain as its president. The northern, eastern, and western parts of France, including Paris, were occupied by the Nazis. The choices left to the French were joining Charles De Gaulle's Free Forces Army, emigration, the underground resistance, or collaboration with the Germans.

It happened that Carné's case came closest to the latter: he did not emigrate as Renoir, Clair, Feyder, Duvivier, and some other filmmakers and actors did. But Camus, Cocteau, and Sartre[6] did not emigrate either.

Strangely enough, the occupation was one of the great periods of French cinema. There were two main reasons: with the fuel restrictions, cinemas (and theatres, which also flourished in these years) were places people could go to keep warm, and there were no American films, which meant that there was no invincible competition. "The French public flocked to the darkened theatres to see a world they had lost or one that existed only in their dreams, they went to the movies because it was the only outlet they had, and they went in greater numbers than ever before in history."[7]

The Nazis did not dismantle the French film industry, but they made every effort to control it. Early in the occupation, Goebbels established the French Propaganda Department with the Film Control Board, overseeing and dominating all aspects of film and media production.

Carné inevitably had to work with the German authorities, first when making his highly accomplished film *Les Visiteurs du Soir* (*The Devil's*

*Envoys*, 1942), a medieval *period piece*, and certainly, when making *Children of Paradise* (1945). This film, the highest peak of his cinematic glory, was made while his country was experiencing its lowest fall.

There was nothing about war in *Children of Paradise*, and it did not discuss Nazism. Still, the film contained a clear anti-Nazi message. It was made by *ignoring* political reality, and it stated indirectly that Germany was not *über alles* (above everything), that art was *über* Germany, *über* the war, *über* the Nazis—in essence, *über* everything. Carné's poetic resistance was the only one he could mount under the reality of occupation. "Amidst the despair of military defeat, the French cinema needed to prove to itself and to the world that France was not dead." The film was the epitome of Frenchness, and it demonstrated that the national spirit had survived.[8]

*Children of Paradise* premiered in Paris in early March 1945, after the city had been liberated but before the war had ended. The film's initial Paris run lasted more than a year. But the chances are that even if you went to Paris right now, the film would be playing somewhere.

In the next half century, Carné made fourteen more films, but he couldn't seem to get out from under *Children of Paradise*. He was often compared to Orson Welles, who was always measured against his early masterpiece, *Citizen Kane* (1941).

In the 1950s, Carné's love for the exuberance of theatrical spectacle, the elegance of his style and his pessimism, seemed dated to the young generation of New Wave[9] filmmakers, first of all François Truffaut (1932–1984) and Jean-Luc Godard (born in 1930). Their interest in contemporary characters and themes, location shooting, handheld cameras, improvised dialogue, the intimacy of their films, and most of all, philosophy of moral indifference were incompatible with Carné's world.

Yet his film *Les Tricheurs* (*The Cheaters*, 1958) was considered by Le Figaro to be "the best French film of the year," and even Truffaut had to admit that the New Wave directors were influenced by it. Still, Carné was their favorite target. He stated that the *New Wave* assassinated him, but by doing this it assassinated the cinema as well.[10] Truffaut's critique of Carné was purposely insulting.[11] Yet, years later, he publicly declared, "I've made twenty-three films, and I'd give them all up to have done *Children of Paradise*."[12]

In the 1950s and 1960s, almost as a rule, when Carné's films were shown, the theatres were full, but the press was usually skeptical and unfriendly. In the 1970s, a writer wrote in an open letter to Carné that of all the directors of his generation or that which preceded it, he knew of not one who, after having been adored (in the 1930s and early 1940s), had been so knocked about, ridiculed, reviled, and rejected as he.

Carné's film *Les Assassins de L'Ordre* (*Assassins of the Law*, 1971) was strongly criticized in France, was praised outside the country, and earned Carné the Life Achievement Award at the Venice Biennale, along with John Ford and Ingmar Bergman. Very soon it was mentioned in the press that Marcel Carné lived in total poverty, and only financial help from his friends prevented him from asking for public assistance. "Let's not exaggerate. I'm not a billionaire, but I am not a tramp," he answered. "When I have very little money, I manage. When I have a lot, I spend it."[13]

His next film, *La Merveilleuse Visite* (*The Wonderful Visit*, 1974) was almost laughed at for its idealism, "lack of authentic instinct," and a "reactionary aesthetic." "How . . . could I not have understood that [today's] viewer wants 'blood and ass'? And nothing else. . . . Are there today, in this nation, people still capable of dreaming?"[14] Carné responded. His last film, *La Bible*, was made in 1977, a documentary devoted to the Byzantine mosaics of a Sicilian basilica.

Carné's work spanned six decades, and he made twenty-two films. But when in 1980 he became a member of the French Academy, no one doubted that this happened because of *Children of Paradise*.

Marcel Carné died on October 31, 1996.

Jacques Prévert, a poet and writer, was born in 1900 in Neuilly-sur-Seine, a suburb of Paris, to a working-class family. He attended a Catholic school and left it at age fourteen, thoroughly soured on religion. He had an imitation talent, loved the theatre, especially burlesque and comedy, but did not want to be a performer; he preferred writing, and with his brother, Pierre, he wrote verses, screenplays, and song lyrics.[15] Prévert's gregarious personality, combined with his liberal politics, brought him into close contact with various political and artistic groups of Paris. During the late 1920s and early 1930s he associated with the Surrealists, and he wrote regularly for an actors collective called the Groupe Octobre, dramatizing social issues of importance to France's working class.

Prévert's politics sometimes got him in trouble with censors, but his writing held a broad popular appeal. He distributed his poems not only by publishing them but by simply passing them out among his friends. Simple, clever, lovelorn, and irreverent, they were eventually published together in 1946 and the collection became a bestseller immediately and is still a popular book of French poetry.

Prévert was an immensely creative screenwriter. He considered film an art and believed cinema and poetry were almost the same thing. It was said that Prévert was the "first poet able to shout, sob, and laugh by means of the camera."[16]

Prévert and Carné met during a screening of Renoir's *Crime of Monsieur Lange* (1936), which Prévert wrote. They became fast friends. "Both born of the working class, both educated at the school of life, we shared the same window of the world, we liked the same authors and artists and ignored the others," Carné said in his speech to the French Academy in 1980. *Jenny* (1936) was the first of their collaborations, through which their partnership was formed. They completed one another in a harmonious counterpoint—Prévert, the joyfully irreverent poet, a rebel against conventional forms, and Carné, conversely, a pessimist as a man and a traditionalist as a filmmaker.

*Children of Paradise* was their seventh film. The partnership ended very soon after their next film, *Les Portes de la Nuit* (*The Doors of the Night,* 1946).

Prévert did continue writing, in various forms, for the rest of his life. He remains an admired poet and writer in France. He died in 1977.

Jean-Louis Barrault (1910–1994) should be credited with partial authorship of *Children of Paradise*. He was a celebrated dramatic actor and mime who could "speak with his legs, reply with his hands, with a look, with a shrug,"[17] as was said about mimes in the film. One of sources of his mime inspiration "was the Russian revolutionary theatre of Vsevolod Meyerhold in the first decades of the twentieth century." Barrault was also a connoisseur of theatre history and had collected biographical information on the greatest French mime, Jean-Gaspard Deburau (1796–1846), and on the remarkable French actor Frédérick Lemaître (1800–1876). He wished to intertwine their lives in a play or a film and explore the relationship between pantomime and spoken performance. In his memoirs Barrault called it "continuity between a gesture and a word."[18] It was *The Great Dictator* that first gave Barrault the idea. "At the heart of it all was Charlie Chaplin," he later said. "When I first learned that Chaplin was going to speak in his film, I remember rushing to the theatre simply to hear the sound of his voice. This was an exceptional theatrical event for me."[19]

In 1942, Barrault, then the reigning star of the Comédie Francaise, met Carné and Prévert. "We were in a café in Nice," Prévert recalled, "and Barrault said, 'Why not make a film about the Funambules . . .

the pantomime . . . the Boulevard of Crime . . . Deburau.'"[20] It was the beginning of *Children of Paradise*.

Prévert rented space in a remote farmhouse near Nice. It proved to be a fertile workspace for all principal members of the creative team. Alexander Trauner, the art designer who from the first day worked together with Carné and Prévert, was relatively out of danger there (as a Jew, he was prohibited to work in France by the French law of 1940).

The farmhouse became the center of preproduction. For six months, Carné, Prévert, and Trauner wrote, planned, sketched, and talked through their work in progress.

Barrault had told the team everything about the Boulevard of Crime itself, with its performances, abundance of genres and forms, both high and low, about mime. In the twentieth century it was a fully ingrained and beloved national tradition, thanks largely to the artistic genius of Jean-Gaspard Deburau in the nineteenth. But Deburau was also famous for his unusual and high-profile murder trial. When one day subjected to a surprise barrage of insults from a man on the street, Deburau struck and killed the man with his walking stick. Parisians flocked to the trial, not so much from concern about his crime and possible punishment but simply because they were curious *to hear the mime speak*.

*Children of Paradise* doesn't include Deburau's crime. The movie's mime, Baptiste, does perform a version of it only in a pantomime. The mime in the film is uncorrupted and innocent, an honest naïf, a genius of movement and imitation, an unhappy man who twice loses the love of his life—Garance. The casting choice for her was Arletty, the French Garbo, as she was often called.

A former factory worker, then a secretary, Arletty (Leoni Bathiat, 1898–1992) had performed in music halls during the twenties, had been a model for artists, among them Braque and Matisse (the film's Garance, we will learn, posed for Monsieur Ingres), and was a singer, a comedienne, and a movie actress. Her luminous film and theatre work made her a Parisian favorite and an international movie star. Her wry and daring humor had a streetwise appeal, yet her elegance, refined poise, and model beauty made her seem especially lofty and unattainable. As it was written about her, "Arletty lends her admirable face and her deep set eyes in which, from time to time, some unconfessed dream can be seen."[21]

By the time of *Children of Paradise*, Arletty had become a very visible and complex cultural icon. She simultaneously represented the sophisticated allure and free spirit of French culture and, in light of her affair during the film's production with a Luftwaffe colonel, an associate of Herman Goering, that culture's shameless collaboration with the German occupiers. But she did not see her affair as a betrayal of her country. As Andre Bazin said, "[This woman] knows how to live with impurity."[22] Her resulting arrest for "collaboration with the enemy" prevented her from attending the *Children of Paradise* premiere but did not detract from her widespread mystique; in fact, it probably intensified it. "My heart is French," she later quipped, "but my ass is international."

Another dramatic focus of *Children of Paradise* was Pierre-François Lacenaire, a notorious nineteenth-century criminal, the so-called Dandy of Crime. This historical Parisian character preserves his identity in the film.[23]

*Children of Paradise* was France's most expensive motion picture to date (58 million francs, about $1.25 million). Postwar journalists teased Carné with the catchphrase "Je dépense, donc je suis" ("I spend, therefore I am"). At the Victorine studios in Nice, a one-hundred-meter outdoor set was built for the Boulevard of Crime, with almost fifty building fronts. More than fifteen hundred extras were hired. Clearly, Carné had a resolute vision for his project.

Film shooting started in August 1943. Though it hardly seems obvious from the film's appearance, the production during the occupation did take a toll. Transportation was unreliable, film stock and other basic resources were intermittently unavailable, funding was cut, and sudden blackouts were common. Curfews made some important exterior night shots impossible, so they had to be re-created later, at great expense, in a studio.

When discovered to be of Jewish decent, the film's original producer, André Paulvé, was fired, and Carné worried constantly about several other Jewish members of his crew. The Germans pressured Carné to use collaborationists—French citizens who fully endorsed and cooperated with the Nazi regime—for extras, but he evaded the mandate as best he could. In the studio, an extra was arrested, suspected of having a connection to the underground resistance, and was never seen or heard of again. Another actor was later discovered to be too closely connected to the Nazis. And of course the film's lead actress, meanwhile, was having a passionate affair with a German officer.

But under Carné's relentless command, the crew persevered, and *Children of Paradise* premiered in two parts in Paris in early March 1945.

Set in early nineteenth-century Paris, *Children of Paradise* tells about four very different men connected by their common love for a notorious and enigmatic woman, Garance. They are Baptiste Deburau, the mime; Frédérick Lemaître, the aspiring actor; Pierre-François Lacenaire, the poet and celebrated criminal; and the naughty Count Edouard de Montray. They all love Garance, but none, ultimately, can have her, even the mime Baptiste, whom she adores. Garance and Baptiste have to separate and resign themselves to unwanted relationships.

The main axis of the film's locations is the Boulevard du Temple. This bustling and seamy sector of mid-nineteenth-century Paris was known for street theatres and commedia troupes such as the Théâtre des Funambules.[24] When this film's action takes place, according to Prévert's original treatment, the boulevard "has become the temple of melodramas, of bloody denouement—in a word, the Boulevard of Crime."[25]

## Part I

### *The Boulevard of Crime*

The film begins as if it were a play, with a stage curtain across a proscenium arch. After the knocking sound customary in old French theatre for signaling a show's beginning, the lights dim, the camera closes in on the curtain, the opening credits scroll by, and the curtain rises. It reveals not a conventional stage set, but, rather shockingly, a lifelike city street: the Boulevard du Temple. Carné brackets the entire film with a reiteration of the panoramic view from the same high angle he presents at the beginning. The setting, crowds, and performances here are presented with almost a documentary authenticity.

*1. A panoramic visual overture: a tightrope walker, the dancers, clowns, acrobats, a monkey on stilts, a Hercules lifting weights, "a whole crowd of people—good, simple people wholeheartedly enjoying themselves."*[26]

This is a visual shorthand of the themes of *Children of Paradise*—theatrical performance, daring adventure, romance, fate, vanity, displays of power.

*On a platform a barker is shouting and inviting the public inside the tent behind him: "Come in and see the Truth herself!" Here Garance is behind a tent curtain, sitting naked in a rotating tub and looking at her own reflection in a hand mirror.*

Already subject to the gazes of men who have paid to look at her, Garance is introduced as a mysterious, even mythic, object of unrequited desire—like Helen of Troy or rather like the biblical Bathsheba, whose beauty first riveted King David when he saw her taking a bath. But, she is a contemporary, her name *Garance*, which obviously rhymes with *La France*.

*2. The freewheeling actor Frédérick Lemaître is inquiring about work with the Funambules. He spots Garance outside on the boulevard and pursues her. The camera moves with them, and they're shown in intimate reversing two-shots, from just enough distance to see them among the boulevard's streaming crowds. A natural performer, Frédérick flirts, brazenly but charmingly, and Garance gently rebukes him.*

*3. The screen dissolves to the public scribe sign, then to Pierre-François Lacenaire, the scribe. He is writing a letter for his client: "My love and my life . . ." The man listens to the words anxiously.*

Lacenaire, we will learn, is contradiction itself: a poet-playwright and also a murderer and an impeccably dressed dandy.

*Lacenaire's henchman, Avril, comes in. Lacenaire spots Garance outside—she is nearing his office.*

For all his theatricality, amply provided in this film, Carné makes subtle but effective use of cinematic language. First, by moving the camera to steer our attention, and second, for the same purpose, by cutting: Lacenaire looks at Garance off screen, and the film cuts to a shot of what he sees, and then back to him, revealing his reaction.

*Garance enters, and clearly she and Lacenaire know each other well. He even calls her his "guardian angel."*

The Garance-Lacenaire connection is notably not sexual. Prévert's storyboard notes even describe Lacenaire as impotent; Carné said on several occasions that Lacenaire was gay, and that the film's ambiguity on this subject was designed to elude censorship.

*"You are the only woman I have ever approached with neither hatred nor*

contempt," Lacenaire says. "I don't love you either," she replies. Lacenaire speaks eloquently about his alienation, his unique and yet unrealized greatness, and his "declared war on humanity" and at the same time proudly calls himself a "petty thief from necessity . . . murderer by vocation."

Lacenaire is framed in a medium close-up against the window with confining bars on it—certainly it works as a premonition.

Lacenaire is interrupted by the arrival of the Old Clothes Man, Jéricho, a frightening vagabond wanderer, informer, and spy, hated by everybody, who wants to trade in Lacenaire's stolen goods. The presentation of Jéricho, as unambiguously filthy and repulsive, reveals the authors' attitudes about informers in their own time. How ironic it is that the actor first cast in the role turned out to be a Nazi sympathizer and an informer.

4. A direct cut to a moving shot, a street view of the Théâtre des Funambules. Here is our first sight of the mime Baptiste, the main character of the film. "Sitting on an upturned barrel is a young man with a whitened face and colored wig; stiff as a waxwork, silent, fearful, ridiculous and vulnerable . . . gazing blankly at nothing."

The camera settles just above the heads of the assembled crowd, for a direct, straight-on view of the outdoor stage, but soon the image cuts to closer, lower-angle shots, from the crowd's perspective. The camera controls our attention, preserving the sensation of a live theatrical performance. Carné establishes a direct equation between audiences in the film and audiences of the film.

Baptiste's eyes are fixed on something out of the shot. In a reverse angle we see Garance in the crowd watching the performance. Meanwhile Lacenaire steals a gold watch from a bourgeois who is making boorish passes at Garance. But now she is accused of stealing his watch. Baptiste comes to her rescue. A constable asks if anyone witnessed the incident. "Me. I'm a witness. [I saw] everything," shouts Baptiste, and all faces turn in astonishment toward the speaking mime. What follows is a masterful pantomime of what really happened—a performance full of virtuosity and persuasion—convincing even the policeman that she is not guilty.

This is one of many episodes of the film when we see how life and performance interpenetrate and influence each other.

To express her gratitude, and perhaps other feelings as well, Garance throws a rose she has been wearing in her hair to Baptiste. She blows him a kiss and disappears into the crowd, leaving him transfixed.

5. *Backstage of the Funambules theatre. A chaos "made up of bizarre props and fantastic sets, among which acrobats, dancers, dwarfs, men with bird heads, devils . . . go about their business." The Old Clothes Man, Jéricho, is also here. He predicts to Nathalie, a young actress, the daughter of the stage manager, that the man she loves will marry her.*

Soon we'll learn that she loves Baptiste.

*Frédérick, full of hopes, appears at the backstage, talks to Nathalie, and then explains to the stage manager that he wants to become an actor. They talk amidst noises and screams onstage, backstage, and in the audience. "And what an audience!" says the manager. "They may be poor, my audience, but they are worth their weight in gold. Look, there they are; up there, in the Gods!" He points out the top galleries, the so-called Paradise.*

*The enthusiastic crowd is notably lower class, rowdy and unrefined, with ragged clothes; many dangle their legs over the edge of the balcony.*

*After a scandal and chaos onstage, the curtain is brought down and the audience demands that the play continue. It's a happy moment for Frédérick; he'll replace Harlequin, Baptiste will replace Pierrot, and Nathalie will continue her role as Colombina.*

This is a classical trio of the commedia dell'arte.[27] The camera leaves the stage before they start playing.

6. *Baptiste, in the makeup and the costume of Pierrot, is in the dressing room with Nathalie. We follow her startled gaze—the flower given to Baptiste by Garance has caught her eye.*

*Nathalie kneels before Baptiste: "I want you to love me," she says. Though he doesn't even know who Garance is, Baptiste confesses to loving the woman.*

*The stage manager asks them to be ready for the next scene. "You know the plot," he says. "You love her, she laughs in your face, so you weep like a baby." Before they go on, the screen fades to black.*

7. *After the show Frédérick and Baptiste share a drink and a conversation on the nature of their art. Frédérick confesses his ambition to one day become a great actor. "You don't need [words]," he tells Baptiste. "You speak with your legs, you reply with your hands, one look, a shrug of the shoulders, two steps forward, one step backward and there you are! . . . They've understood everything, up in the Gods!"*

*Baptiste, talking in his dreamy way, replies that those up in the Gods* understand everything. "They're poor people, and I'm like them . . . their lives are small, but they have big dreams. . . . I want to move them, to frighten them, to make them cry."

8. Baptiste offers to help Frédérick get a room at a boardinghouse, the Grand Relais, and introduces the aspiring actor to its owner, Madame Hermine. Baptiste then decides to take a late-night stroll outside.

Madame Hermine, plump, no longer young, but coquettish, is delighted by Frédérick's attention. She shows him to his room and more. The scene evokes a burlesque romance. "Good night. The key's in the door," she says.

"I always leave my door open," he answers. . . . "A pretty lady might stroll into my room."

"A pretty lady. . . . Really, young people today make difficult demands," she says, pouting.

9. A dissolve brings the action to the alley, where Baptiste meets a blind beggar.

This scene is lit rather dramatically, with splashes of moonlight and gas lamps—a direct tribute to the chiaroscuro of Friedrich Murnau,[28] one of Carné's favorite filmmakers. Baptiste and the beggar adjourn to the Rouge Gorge—the Red Breast—a seamy dance hall so named because its last owner was killed by having his throat cut. From Baptiste and the beggar, the camera moves to the wider view of all of the action inside the dance hall. A key light focuses our attention on Baptiste's eyes, and the editing is again motivated by what he sees.

10. In the Rouge Gorge, with a comedic trick, the beggar reveals not only that he is not blind but that he is hardly as downtrodden as had been implied. "Can't believe your eyes, funambulist?" he asks an astonished Baptiste. Apparently toying with the blurred distinction between performance and reality, the beggar explains that while inside the Red Breast his sight is restored.

Once again Jéricho appears and forewarns of Lacenaire's impending arrival. Lacenaire and Garance do arrive, with Avril and some others in tow. Garance plays coy and eventually tires of Lacenaire, who says he wants her. "You have a head too hot for me, Pierre-François, and a heart too cold," she answers.

Garance gladly accepts Baptiste's invitation to dance. "Be careful," she tells him, warning that Lacenaire and his companions "can be very nasty." "It doesn't matter. I'm so happy," Baptiste replies. On Lacenaire's order,

*Avril throws Baptiste through a window, but the mime returns right away with great dignity and humor, dusting himself off, replacing the flower Garance gave him, and gracefully fighting back. He leaves with her. Lacenaire dismisses them and concentrates instead on making his criminal plans.*

11. *Baptiste and Garance stroll through the moonlit alley. She admits her surprise at his response to Avril. Baptiste tells her that he had a rough childhood and at that time learned to defend himself. When he was unhappy he dreamed, hoped, and waited. "Perhaps it was for you that I was waiting." Baptiste is overwhelmed by her beauty, but Garance explains that she is "simply alive." It begins raining; they go to Madame Hermine's boardinghouse.*

12. *A room in the boardinghouse. Finally Baptiste and Garance are alone together and he becomes embarrassed when Garance starts to remove her rain-soaked dress. "Please Baptiste, don't be so serious," she says in a tone of both innocence and experience, "I'm not what you dreamed of me. I'm simple—very simple." She invites him to spend the night with her, but Baptiste loses his nerve and runs out, leaving Garance.*

13. *In a nearby room, Frédérick tries to get a grasp of playing Othello. He hears Garance singing and finds her. They both smile.*
     The scene fades out.

14. *Fades in to the exterior of the Théâtre des Funambules. People are invited to come and see the performance—a "grand, fantastic, exotic, pyrotechnic pantomime."*

15. *On the stage is the statue of Arthemise (Phoebe), the goddess of the hunt and moon. This is Garance. The camera moves across the audience to find Edouard, the count. He is smitten with Garance, who is onstage. "Have you ever seen a more splendid creature?" he asks his two dandified companions. Poised, refined, and immaculately dressed, the three of them are the utter opposite of "the Gods" in the balconies.*
     The camera's sweeping gesture, seeking the count out, summons our attention as if to suggest that he will be an important character in the story.

*The performance is Baptiste's. He is Pierrot, hopelessly in love with a statue of Phoebe, played by Garance. He loses her to a more successful suitor, Harlequin, played by Frédérick. As soon as Baptiste appears onstage, in a*

comically graceful routine of chasing a butterfly, the crowd roars its approv-
ing welcome. Baptiste's display of love for Phoebe moves the Gods to rapt
silence. While Pierrot dozes off, Harlequin appears and charms Pheobe away.

Pierrot readies himself for suicide, but he is inadvertently rescued from
the attempt by a young woman played by Nathalie.

Baptiste's art seems to imitate his life.

Baptiste observes that the rapport between Garance and Frédérick has
continued offstage; he becomes downtrodden, forgets himself onstage, and
falls out of character completely.

16. Garance comes backstage and she and Frédérick retire to the dressing
room together. "Not happy, not unhappy," Garance says. "We're somewhere in between. We're not in love." Frédérick says that Garance called out
Baptiste's name in her sleep—and that "Othello killed Desdemona for much
less." The count enters, preceded by an enormous floral bouquet, and offers
his card—in case, he explains, Garance should ever need help or protection.
As the count leaves, Baptiste arrives, jealous and increasingly upset. In a fit
of self-hatred, he runs to a mirror and actually crosses out his own reflection.
Garance tries to soothe him, but then Nathalie enters, also jealous and upset.
"I know that all the love that there is in the world for Baptiste is mine. . . .
Go ahead and smile," says Nathalie to Garance, who replies, "I always do."

17. Under a false name, Lacenaire occupies an apartment at the Grand
Relais, where he and Avril try unsuccessfully to rob and assassinate a debt
collector. They flee the scene of the half-committed crime. Back at the boardinghouse, the incident is reported. A gossipy crowd gathers. Jealous Madame
Hermine (she still cannot forget Frédérick's charm) falsely accuses Garance
of being Lacenaire's accomplice. Garance is interrogated.

Here the tension is heightened by an increase in the number of
shots and acceleration of the editing between them: back and forth
between Garance and the inspector interrogating her.

The situation presents Garance with a need for both help and protection: she
shows the card given to her by the count and explains that he should be
informed of this judicial error. The status of the count saves Garance now,
as did Baptiste's performance in the beginning of the film.

After a series of close-ups to reveal the surprised expressions of
those around her, and Garance's peculiar smile, Carné ends on a
slightly removed and painterly tableau: Garance, the brightest element

in the composition of the shot, is at the very center of everybody's attention, including ours.

*The curtain falls, signifying the end of Part 1.*

## Part 2

### The Man in White

*"Several years passed" is written on the screen.*

*18. The curtain rises again, and again we view the boulevard in a wide shot. The camera pans to follow a carriage speeding by with Frédérick, now a famous actor, and a lady on each arm. But his success is not without its perils.*

Such a change—in the beginning of Part 1, Frederick didn't have a job and nobody knew him.

*19. After some flirting in his luxurious if disheveled dressing room, the actor is besieged by angry creditors and jealous husbands. They attack him and beat him up.*

*20. Frédérick does show up for rehearsal, his costume torn and tattered from the backstage battle, and the play's three authors quarrel with his "modifications" to their text.*

Carné and Prévert seem to delight in depicting the authors as a trio of buffoons—personages of a skit.

*21. One of the authors shouts, "Stop! That's not written in the play." Frédérick snaps back that the play was empty and needed "little padding."*

The film cuts frequently between the action onstage, the excited audience, the flabbergasted prompter and conductor, and of course the enraged authors. As a matter of historical fact, the play's real authors gladly accepted Lemaître's "modifications," which helped the actor make his famous performance as Robert Macaire.[29]

*Frédérick pulls the authors onstage for a confused curtain call. Once safely backstage, they accuse him of having "insulted the dramatic arts" and challenge him to a duel.*

*22. To his surprise, Frédérick finds Lacenaire in his dressing room. The dandy criminal sits calmly, toying with the bejeweled brooch given to Frédérick by Garance years ago. Frédérick snatches it away.*

The brooch reminds us of what these characters already have in common. The scene is an intense contest between two men who both feel compelled to control any situation that befalls them—Frédérick, confident that he can improvise through anything, and Lacenaire, confident that the law is beneath him.

*Lacenaire plans to rob Frédérick, but the actor doesn't hesitate to hand over some of his money. "Perhaps fate sent you," he says. "I won the lottery last week."*

*Such generosity, Lacenaire explains, in fact has saved Frédérick's life; had he refused, the consequences would have been dire. "I can assure you," Lacenaire says, revealing the dagger in his belt, "the blade doesn't retract into the handle."*

At the height of the tension, the exchange of medium close-ups is rapid and urgent. But the tone and pace change with Frédérick's demonstration of generosity.

*Avril comes in and Lacenaire explains that he is a great fan of Frédérick's; the delighted actor invites the two crooks to dine with him.*

*23. The following morning. This is the first and only time that the action of Children of Paradise leaves the city. An evocative scene is set, with a fog-shrouded forest, photographed in a very painterly style to look earnest and brooding.*

*Frédérick, Lacenaire, and Avril arrive, drunk and stumbling, for the duel. Frédérick says he is ready to "exchange bullets." Lacenaire and Avril will be his seconds. The theatre director, who hates the thought of losing his greatest box-office draw, tries to talk Frédérick out of it, but to no avail.*

Life and theatre seem entirely entwined here. Frédérick and his seconds play the scene with openly theatrical flourish and comic exaggeration. And in the same way that a theatre curtain opening to reveal a teeming boulevard is bold and surprising, this playlike exchange within the carefully composed yet organic textures of a very real forest provides a striking effect. The camera exits this scene early, before the duel even begins.

*24. Frédérick is wearing a sling on one arm—he has only been injured. He attends Baptiste's performance—the mime, too, has become a star. The tickets are sold out, but Frédérick manages a special seat next to the mysterious woman who, he was told, lately has attended every one of Baptiste's shows. To Frédérick's surprise, the woman is Garance. They speak briefly of their past. "It was with that man . . . with his arms laden with flowers, that you disappeared, wasn't it?" Frédérick asks. "And where did you go? To India, perhaps?" "It's true, I did go to India," she says, "[but] I lived most of the time in England . . . in Scotland . . . [but] Paris is the only place I love."*

*Baptiste's appearance onstage interrupts their conversation. The stage is shown in a long shot, as seen from Garance's box.*

*Baptiste's Pierrot has stowed away on the carriage that brought the object of his affection, played by Nathalie, to an aristocratic house party. He tries to follow her inside but clearly doesn't meet the dress code, and the house's guard tosses him back into the street.*

*Garance raises her eyes to Paradise when the audience shouts with laughter and she smiles nostalgically. "I used to laugh like that once . . . to burst out laughing, for no reason . . . just laughing . . ." Onstage, the Old Clothes Man appears, and the penniless Pierrot begs to borrow a suitable outfit for the party. When the old man refuses, Pierrot snatches his sword and kills him, takes the clothes he needs, blows a kiss to his love inside the house, and tiptoes offstage as the curtain falls.*

*Frédérick praises the mime's skill. "Baptiste is not acting; he's inventing dreams!" says Garance. "Since the first day I left, not a single day has passed when I didn't think of him." Watching her, Frédérick becomes jealous, but probably he realizes that he might use that feeling to understand Othello. He thanks Garance, offers to tell Baptiste that she is there, nods, and goes out.*

*25. At the backstage, Frédérick greets Baptiste. The two actors exchange compliments, and we learn that Nathalie and Baptiste are together and they have a son, also named Baptiste. "I'm not beautiful, Frédérick, just happy," Nathalie says. But a moment later, Jéricho arrives to tell Nathalie that Garance has returned.*

Here the *reality* and the play come very close again in showing two ragmen—the *real* one, namely Jéricho, and the pantomime version, played by Baptiste's father. Jéricho accuses the elder Deburau of stealing his identity for the play.

*26. On his mother's orders, the five-year-old Baptiste visits Garance's box to tell her his family is happy—and that she is beautiful. Frédérick, meanwhile, informs Baptiste of Garance's presence in the theatre. Even the mask of his makeup cannot conceal Baptiste's uncontrollable feelings. He makes*

his stage entrance but can't concentrate on his performance. Nathalie recognizes something wrong immediately. Some quick, wordless cutting reveals
her response, the conductor's, and Baptiste's. He stops his performance, in
front of a demanding audience, and leaves the scene to find Garance. But
it's too late: she has already left.

It is not the first time the order of a staged scene is upset by the
chaos of "real life" in *Children of Paradise*.

27. *A long shot of Garance ascending the staircase in the count's enormous
home eventually reveals another surprise appearance from Lacenaire, who
intercepts her. In wide, flowing, sumptuous shots, the camera implies a
strong contrast between this "real" mansion and the artificial one of the
Funambules' recent pantomime.*

*In their methodically paced exchange, Garance observes that as a crim-
inal Lacenaire has become a celebrity. He agrees but adds that he would prefer literary success. "It hurts me so to find you unchanged. I'd prefer to find
you ravaged, submissive," Lacenaire says. He asks her about Baptiste, "your
friend, the acrobat. . . . I had the absurd idea of killing him, the acrobat! . . .
You might just as well shoot a draught, a ray of moonlight."*

*As Lacenaire leaves, he encounters the count on the stairs, and they have
a tense confrontation, a power struggle emphasized, by an old theatrical tradition, just by their placement in different planes on the staircase—Lacenaire
stands several steps below the count. After Lacenaire leaves, the count con-
fronts Garance, whose love he knows he still hasn't won.*

We see the distance between the two; they literally are placed far
apart, and for most of the scene they don't even look at each other.
Finally Garance promises the count that she'll tell all of Paris that she's
madly in love with him, if that is what he wants, but she confesses that
there has always been another man whom she truly loves. But now she
wants to leave Paris. The camera stays on her, in a medium close-up,
and fades to black.

28. *The Funambules' windows are dark, and there is a sign announcing the
cancellation of Baptiste's performance. We see him alone in his old boardinghouse room, sulking. Madame Hermine tries to help, but Baptiste
doesn't want anything. She leaves, runs into Nathalie and tells her where to
find Baptiste. Nathalie hasn't lost faith that he'll soon be all right.*

29. *Frédérick's premiere as Othello. The moving camera directs us to
Baptiste as a spectator on one of the balconies and then to Lacenaire. He*

*watches with keen interest this play about jealousy and revenge; so does the count in the mezzanine, sitting next to Garance. All of them see that Frédérick sends his lines and his intense gaze directly to her. An enormous bouquet arrives at Garance's box, very much like the one with which the count first courted her. The count reads the note: "Othello is no longer jealous. He is cured. Thank you."*

The bouquet *motif* contributes to the film's symmetry and balance.

*30. The public is leaving the theatre. In the crowd Baptiste and Garance notice each other. They go outside to a terrace. We see them in expressive pools of shadow and light. "I never forgot you. . . . It's you who prevented me from becoming old and stupid, and spoiled," she says. "I thought you didn't want to see me again. . . . And I thought I had lost you forever!" says Baptiste.*

*Lacenaire is watching them. Having hatched a devious plot, he joins Frédérick and the count in the foyer, interrupting their verbal sparring match. With a grand theatrical gesture Lacenaire pulls back the glass door curtain. Now the embracing Baptiste and Garance are exposed. Frédérick points out, "Jealousy belongs to all, if a woman belongs to none." Frédérick once again gets called to a duel, this time with the count. Lacenaire is delighted.*

*31. Baptiste and Garance retire to the same secluded room at the Grand Relais. Everything is the same as it was during their first evening together years ago, including the velvety shadows and radiant moonlight. "You were right, Garance," Baptiste says, "love is so simple." "Yes, when you love each other," she answers. They are pressed closely together and sway gently sideways to sit down on the bed, as the camera pans toward the open widow.*

*32. Lacenaire and Avril surprise the count at the Turkish baths—one final exotic and highly stylized location. Lacenaire kills the count, with calm, wordless precision. The camera is kept on Avril, who is shaken. "My poor Avril," Lacenaire says, "the play is finished. You can go now." "And you?" asks Avril. "Oh, me . . . I'll stay here." Lacenaire defiantly awaits his own capture.*

*Baptiste and Garance remain in the same room. "It was a wonderful night," she tells him, but she must leave to stop the duel and, as promised, to profess her love for the count. "He doesn't care if it's not true." She is ready to leave Paris again, if it will save Frédérick's life. Anyway, she has to go. "But, why?" Baptiste cries. "You have a very sweet little son . . . and your career . . . and Nathalie." "It's you that I love!" he says.*

*Before Garance can leave, Nathalie arrives. She sees Garance and*

*Baptiste with "their arms around each other. Nathalie stands on the threshold, astonished and distressed." Garance is ready to go. "Easy to go away . . . and then to come back," Nathalie says. "Six years I've lived with him." "So have I," says Garance, "anywhere, everywhere, every day . . . and even at night, all the nights I spent with someone else, all those nights I was with him. . . ." "Garance," Baptiste pleads. "What is left for me?" Nathalie asks as Garance discreetly slips out. "What about me?" She holds him back, but he brutally pulls himself free and rushes out, shouting, "Garance, Garance!"*

*33. Outside, the Boulevard of Crime is crowded and noisy. Garance walks rapidly. Baptiste cannot catch up with her and continues shouting her name while "all around him, indifferent to his despair, the crowds laugh and dance." The boulevard is choked with revelers. Here is also Jéricho, the Old Clothes Man, who grabs the mime: "Come on Baptiste, don't make a fuss. You've had your fun, you can go home now." "Leave me alone!" Baptiste shouts.*

*Garance gets into a carriage. "She is sad, and stares at the floor of the carriage with a vague, far away expression, lost and indifferent."*

*The carriage slowly rolls away; the crowd engulfs Baptiste. "He still cries out, but can no longer be heard."*

And the curtain falls.

When performing at the beginning of the film, Baptiste had crowds at his command, but now, with his art subjugated to his life, the crowd controls him. It is especially, and bitterly, ironic that most of the revelers wear the costume of Pierrot, the character Baptiste made famous, while he now wears ordinary clothes.

Carné brackets the entire film with a reiteration of the panoramic view from the same high angle he presented at the beginning.

Baptiste is the protagonist of the film. We know whom he loves, what he dreams about; we hear about his childhood; we see his father, his wife, and his son; we know how he acts in various situations; and we see his magnificent performances. He is the dramatic center of *Children of Paradise*. In a way, the rest of the characters, in contact with him or just by juxtaposition, reveal different aspects of his personality. (See Figure 2–1.)

For Carné and Prévert, film as a medium was closely related to all arts. In *Children of Paradise* we recognize deep connections with French painting—with the disciplined academic style of David,[30] the aloof elegance of Ingres,[31] and with the whole national culture of visual

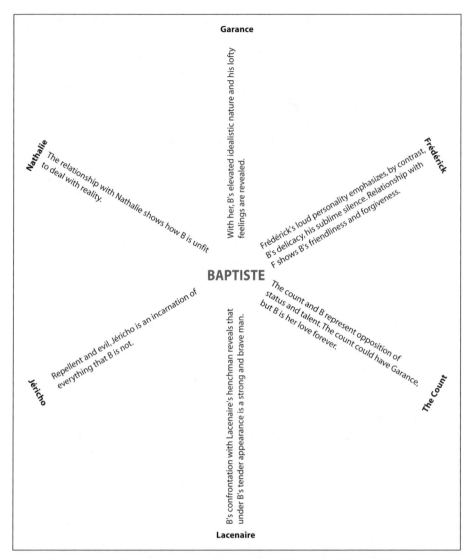

*Figure 2–1. Relationships Between Baptiste and Other* Children of Paradise *Characters*

refinement. We see it in balances of forms, in the film's highly culti-vated compositions and lines, when the edges of the screen could be taken as the frame of a canvas.

The broad scope of characters and the richness of psychological and physical detail of *Children of Paradise* evokes a nineteenth-century

French novel by Hugo[32] or Balzac.[33] But above all influences is theatre. Carné and Prévert even intended the film as a tribute to French drama, to the stage, and especially to actors who so easily and graciously transferred spectators to the imaginary worlds.

In *Children of Paradise*, the spectacle often mirrors reality, but at the same time, it goes much beyond it into the enchanting, mysterious sphere of magic. And what kind of creatures are the performers who in *Children of Paradise* seem both better and worse than we are? In the film, Lacenaire expresses Carné's opinion: "Actors aren't people. They're every man and no man."

There's almost always a performance going on in this film—and reality always tries to intrude on its completion. Frédérick deliberately meddles with his dialogue and stage directions and can't unlock the mystery of Othello until Garance has unearthed his deepest jealousy by telling about her love for Baptiste. Manipulating the others, Lacenaire calls himself the author of a live spectacle in progress. But when the count tries to expel him from the room, Lacenaire snaps, "I'm not a character in a farce!" Even the performances of Baptiste were interrupted by real dramas of life. (The same happened to his prototype, the great Deburau.)

And what do we make of this film's title? What irony, if any, do the authors intend? Literally, as we know, it refers to the cheapest seats in the theatre, "the furthest away from the stage, for the 'people,' that is why it was called Paradise,"[34] said Prévert. And who are the children? "The actors and the audience, too," he stated. Baptiste loves the people; he says, "their lives are small, but they have big dreams," and he is happy to make them laugh or cry. "I was like them," Garance says nostalgically. To Carné, the children stand for actors, "the beloved heroes of the public."

It seems that the title *Children of Paradise* hints at other meanings, too. Maybe that spectatorship altogether is a kind of paradise. Maybe the act of watching a masterful performance, such as the one Carné and Prévert created, restores us to a state of heavenly enjoyment. Or maybe, after all, theatre and art in general are a kind of paradise.

## Appendix

### From Brian Stonehill's Interview with Marcel Carné (1991)[35]
I shot the film during World War II. I was very bold then, and thinking about it now, it was madness to make such a film in a country

lacking necessities. . . . We started working suddenly and furiously . . .
we met with a lot of obstacles. . . . We were very scared. . . .

   *Children of Paradise* is a pretty straightforward story . . . four men
in love with the same woman. . . . And she loves each of them too. The
first man, the mime, is shy. The second one is a lady-killer who can't
love and who does discover true love. Lacenaire is the intelligent one
who wants to impress her. The count wants to appear with that beautiful lady at his side. He begins to love her when he feels her slipping
away. . . . I admire Barrault's sensibility, Brasseur's (Lemaître) ease of
speech, and the breeding of the count. Never has an actor seemed so
noble as Salou. He had so much class. . . . The one I feel most akin to
is Barrault/Deburau. . . . Arletty . . . she was wonderful. She had such
stage presence. Anyway, I had some problems, because she, as we all
know, was the mistress of the Luftwaffe colonel—a well-known one,
actually, whom I met by chance once—handsome, intelligent, well educated. People despised her because of the affair. . . .

   Now about New Wave. They became afraid of appearing old-
fashioned by defending "grandpa's cinema," but they didn't do anything,
nothing important anyway. They never made . . . a *Grand Illusion* or
*Children of Paradise*, forgive my saying so. They made intimate films
with some kind of elevator music. . . . Truffaut said many nasty things
about me. . . . And Mr. Godard. . . . I didn't like many of his movies,
but I found some things interesting, once in a while. . . . When they
say, "At least we can shoot on location, something the old filmmakers
couldn't do." They shot on location, fine. But they owe that to the talents of photochemists and engineers, not to their own. . . .


## Notes

1. See Edward Baron Turk, *Child of Paradise: Marcel Carné and the Golden
Age of French Cinema*, Cambridge: Harvard University Press, 1985, p. 11.

2. Turk, p. 36.

3. *Un Chien Andalou (An Andalusian Dog*, 1929) and *L'Age D'Or (The Golden
Age*, 1930), the collaborations of painter Salvador Dali and filmmaker Luis
Buñuel, were the highest points of shocking Surrealist revelations.

4. Turk, p. 58.

5. Julien Duvivier (1896–1967), devoted proponent of poetic realism. His
most celebrated films belong to the 1930s, including *The Great Waltz* (1938),

made in Hollywood. During the war he moved to the United States, and after the war, he returned to Europe.

6. Jean Paul Sartre, in fact, had no difficulty in getting his work published. He even wrote, probably as one of his existential paradoxes, that "the horror of [the war] was intolerable but it suited us well. . . . We have never been as free as we were under the German occupation." Quoted in Paul Johnson, *Intellectuals*, New York: Harper and Row, 1988, p. 228.

7. Evelyn Ehrlich, *Cinema of Paradox*, New York: Columbia University Press, 1985, p. x.

8. Ehrlich, pp. x–xi.

9. In the late 1950s several French film critics began directing films according to their own theories. They collectively became known as the Nouvelle Vague (New Wave).

10. Marcel Carné, *The Economist*, 1996 (16 November), p. 95.

11. "Marcel Carné, a confused soul, has never known how to evaluate a screenplay, has never known how to select a project," Truffaut wrote. "Carné is a very obstinate cineaste . . . a man who gives a stature to anything he has to film. If what he has to film is intelligent, then he highlights that intelligence; if it's stupid, he highlights the stupidity." *ARTS,* Paris, October 1956 (31 October).

12. *Children of Paradise*, DVD package, Criterion Collection, 1991.

13. Turk, p. 427.

14. Turk, p. 421.

15. Some of Prévert's lyrics, "Autumn Leaves" among them, remain well loved.

16. Turk, p. 44.

17. Jill Forbes, *Les Enfants du Paradis*, London: British Film Institute, 1977, p. 34.

18. Jean-Louis Barrault, *Memories for Tomorrow*, London: Thames and Hudson, 1974, p. 87.

19. Interview with Barrault, December 31, 1999, quoted in Turk, p. 220.

20. Marcel Carné and Jacques Prévert, *Children of Paradise* (film script), London, Boston: Faber and Faber, 1968, p. 10.

21. Jacques Siclier, "The Great Arletty," in *Rediscovering French Film,* New York: Museum of Modern Art, 1983, p. 130.

22. Siclier, p. 130.

23. Pierre-François Lacenaire stood trial for murder at the same time as

Jean-Gaspard Deburau did. History has recorded that the public wanted to hear the voice of the mime Baptiste, but soon defected to the other courtroom where Lacenaire was pompously condemning himself to death.

24. Baron Haussmann's extensive renovation of the city in 1862 razed most of the theatres and completely refaced the area. It is now the Place de la Republique.

25. From Prévert's original *Children of Paradise* treatment, reprinted in the DVD package.

26. All of the script's quotations are taken from Marcel Carné and Jacques Prévert (film script).

27. Commedia dell'arte was a popular Italian improvisational comedy that originated in the sixteenth century. Pierrot was a stock clown character in French pantomime, known for his white-painted face and flowing, oversized white clothing. He is said to have been originated in the mid-seventeenth century but refined and popularized in early nineteenth-century France by the real Jean-Gaspard Deburau. In Deburau's hands, the usually lovesick Pierrot character represented an important transition from the original figures of the Italian commedia dell'arte to the current clowns of modern circuses and films.

28. Friedrich Murnau (1888–1931), celebrated German filmmaker, master of *chiaroscuro* and *subjective camera*.

29. Robert Macaire is a common name in the history of French dramatic literature, sometimes used as a nickname to signify a sly crook or sometimes worse than that. The character originated in the play *L'Auberge des Adrets* (*The Inn of the Adrets*).

30. Louis David (1748–1825), famous French painter and founder of the neoclassical school.

31. Auguste Dominique Ingres (1780–1867), French classicist painter.

32. Victor Hugo (1802–1885), Romantic writer and poet.

33. Honore de Balzac (1799–1850), French classical novelist.

34. Quoted in *Children of Paradise* (film script).

35. *Children of Paradise,* DVD package, the Criterion Collection, 1991.

# IVAN THE TERRIBLE

## (IVAN GROZNY) PARTS I AND II

### Sergei Eisenstein

|  |  |
|--:|:--|
| director: | Sergei Eisenstein |
| screenplay: | Sergei Eisenstein |
| cinematography: | Eduard Tissé, Andrei Moskvin |
| editing: | Sergei Eisenstein |
| art direction: | Josef Spinel |
| costume design: | Lydia Naumova |
| music: | Sergei Prokofiev |

*cast*

|  |  |
|--:|:--|
| ivan the terrible: | Nikolai Cherkasov |
| anastasia: | Ludmila Tselikovskaya |
| efrosinia staritsky: | Serafima Birman |
| vladimir staritsky: | Pavel Kadochnikov |
| prince andrei kurbsky: | Mikhail Nazvanov |
| fyodor kolychev (philip): | Andrei Abrikosov |
| pimen: | Alexander Mgebrov |
| pyotyr volynets: | Vladimir Balachov |
| malyuta skuratov: | Mikhail Zharov |
| fyodor basmanov: | Mikhail Kusnetsov |
| young ivan: | Eric Pyriev |

*part I:* Black and white
*part II:* Black and white; two sequences in color
*running time:* 99 minutes (Part I); 85 minutes (Part II)
*released:* 1945 (Part I), Moscow; 1958 (Part II), Moscow
*production:* Alma-Ata Film Studio (Part I and Part II); Mosfilm Studio, Moscow
*awards:* 1946 Stalin Prize, first grade (Part I), 1946 Locarno Film Festival, Italy, best cinematography

✳

Sergei Eisenstein was born in 1898 in Riga, Latvia (then part of Russia). His father, the city's architect, was a decorated state councilor. His mother, the heiress of a rich St. Petersburg industrialist, was an educated woman with a love of the arts.

The family's only son, Sergei was raised with governesses and tutors. He showed an extraordinary talent for drawing, was exceptionally well read, loved horseback riding, took dance and music lessons, and spoke fluent Russian, German, English, and French. Later in life, he spoke and gave lectures in the language of the country he was in.

His parents divorced when he was ten.[1]

In 1915 Eisenstein enrolled in the Institute of Civil Engineering and Architecture in St. Petersburg.[2] Already at that time, he had developed a lifelong habit for, in his words, mathematical precision and disciplined thinking.

The revolution of 1917 totally altered his life. "If it had not been for the Revolution, I should never have broken with the tradition passed down from father to son . . . only the Revolution gave me the freedom to take my life into my own hands."[3] With his fellow students, he joined the Red Army. He worked on the construction of defense systems, operated telephones, wrote pamphlets, drew caricatures for the army newspapers, and decorated agit-trains. He also organized an amateur theatrical group, in which he directed, starred, and made stage decorations.

In 1920 his military service was over, and by a lucky chance he found a job as a stage designer at the Proletcult (Proletarian Culture) theatre in Moscow. He was thrilled with the work and the first successes of his stylized sets, costumes, and some directing. Above everything else, he enjoyed being among the avant-garde crowd. All of them believed that radical art and radical leftist politics perfectly matched each other. No one could ever have imagined that when revolutionary politicians would obtain total power, the last thing they would need would be avant-garde artists with their freethinking individualism and love for experimentation.

Eisenstein was swept up by the utopian ideas of transforming the world and building a new society. The engineer and architect in him was seduced by the formulas of the Marxist dialectic; the artist in him was attracted to the dramatic conflicts of the revolution. Feelings of guilt over his nonproletarian upper-class background made his devotion to Communism even more passionate, almost fanatical.

In 1921 he entered the school for stage directors organized by Vsevolod Meyerhold (1874–1940),[4] a master of the most original theatrical ambitions and of nonrepresentational stage techniques who believed that what was *said* in movement and gesture was stronger than what was *said* in words. For Meyerhold, Eisenstein designed sets and costumes and invented complex stage constructions.

In 1923 Eisenstein directed his own stage production, *Enough Simplicity in Every Wise Man*,[5] with pantomime, acrobats, clowns, flying trapezes, different types of music and industrial sounds. At one point a short film was inserted into the performance, a spoof that included, among other things, the director himself clowning and bowing in front of the camera.

Eisenstein's generation was striving for everything new and rejecting the past. But no matter how far Eisenstein went with his radical formalistic ventures, he always preserved his deep attachment to the great art of the past, whether it be Leonardo da Vinci's works, drawings by Piranesi, Pushkin's poetry, or the novels of Balzac.

Gradually, the cinema pushed aside the theatre, and Eisenstein entered The State Institute of Cinematography (VGIK) in Moscow, the world's first film school. (Some years later he would be the most celebrated professor there.) It was founded in 1919, when the civil war was still going on and the country was wracked by destruction and starvation. But the Soviet leaders recognized the indispensable importance of cinema for propaganda purposes. "Of all the arts, cinema is the most important for us," stated Lenin in his speeches in the first year of the revolution, and Trotsky openly talked about replacing church services with shows of Soviet propaganda films. Never before and nowhere else had cinema faced such an immense political task.

For three months, Eisenstein attended the institute's motion pictures workshop, conducted by Lev Kuleshov (1899–1970), a remarkable film theoretician and director and an ardent proponent of film editing. According to him (and soon according to Eisenstein, who would go even much further than his teacher), the content of a film depended not only on what was *in* the shot but on what happened *between* the shots, how they influenced each other, and how out of the juxtaposition of the shots a new content was born. For Eisenstein this was the starting point for his many-faceted *montage theory*, which was so elaborate that one wonders whether his films served only to illustrate it.

*Montage*, which was supposed to agitate and ideologically propagandize the audience, became a trademark of the Soviet cinema of the 1920s, just as inwardness, and *chiaroscuro* (the arrangement of light and dark elements in any composition), and the swift-moving camera were the signs of the German cinema of that period.

Although Eisenstein's Russian colleagues had the same political tasks and the same convictions as he, and they all paid great attention to editing, their working methods were different: for Vsevold Pudovkin (1893–1953), for example, editing was an expressive and rather poetic *linkage* of shots, not a *collision* of shots, as it was for Eisenstein. Above everything else, Eisenstein saw montage as a universal method of composition in poetry, literature, and art.

In 1924 he made his first film, *Strike,* abandoning, as he thought, the dramatic narrative of the "bourgeois cinema" with individual heroes and bringing the action of the masses onto the screen. He did not cast actors but just people whose appearance would give an impression of a certain social type, a *typage*—the Menshevik, the priest, the Bourgeois, the Worker. The film had the sharp contrasts of images, scales, sudden dissolves, unusual irises—all to bring the audiences into a chain of emotional shocks that Eisenstein called *montage of attractions.*

*Strike* was the starting point of his work with cameraman Edward Tissé (1897–1961), an inseparable and harmonious collaboration. For more than twenty years Eisenstein and Tissé always worked together, and only in 1943, for *Ivan the Terrible,* for unknown reasons, was Tissé asked to shoot only location scenes, the rest was given to another cameraman.

In 1925, Eisenstein was commissioned by the Soviet government to make a film about the 1905 revolution. He chose just one episode of the event: the sailors' mutiny on the battleship *Potemkin* and the slaughter of the inhabitants of Odessa, who came to greet the sailors (the latter actually never happened).

*Battleship Potemkin* was assembled in a never before seen dynamic of visual images, new speed, and a sharp contrast of shots taken from changing distances and various points of view—the best example of what Eisenstein's montage is. "Eisenstein became an international celebrity and the principal ambassador abroad of Soviet culture . . . . For left-inclined intellectuals *Potemkin* came . . . like a message from an unknown, exotic and hopeful world. . . . [The film] was much more popular in Berlin than in Moscow."[6] *Battleship Potemkin* has become legendary, and it was praised as the most effective propaganda film, even by the enemies of the Soviet state, like Joseph Goebbels.

The next was *October*, assigned to Eisenstein for a celebration of the tenth anniversary of the Bolshevik revolution of 1917. The tsar's Winter Palace, even the tsar's throne (there is a photograph of Eisenstein lounging on it), the streets of St. Petersburg (at that time already renamed Leningrad), thousands of sailors armed with rifles and blank ammunition, and the entire populace of the city were put at Eisenstein's disposal.[7]

From the mid-1920s, the period of radical experiments in film, theatre, art, and literature was over; some of the avant-garde artists managed to emigrate, some were forced to change their creative position, some were imprisoned, some were shot, and some committed suicide.

Eisenstein's next film, *Old and New* (1929), was about a new Soviet village. In his words, he set out to turn from the pathos of the revolution to the themes of milking cows and sorting grain. Stalin, after censoring the film, ordered many changes.

The premiere of *Old and New* was in October 1929, two months after Eisenstein had left Moscow for Europe with his assistant, Grigori Alexandrov, and Eduard Tissé. The official reason for the trip was to get familiar with the technique of synchronized sound, still unknown in Russia. Yet more important for the Soviet authorities was the opportunity to disseminate the Communist ideology abroad through Eisenstein's films, lectures, and personal contacts.

The first stop was Berlin. Next they visited the First International Congress of Independent Cinematography in Switzerland.[8]

In Paris, and then in London, Eisenstein met with European celebrities: Pirandello, Brecht, Cocteau, René Clair, Einstein, Joyce, Bernard Shaw, and many others. Eisenstein's lectures in England, France, and Holland and the screenings of his films were successes, but none of the European studios offered him a badly needed contract: when they left Moscow, the three were given only twenty-five U.S. dollars apiece.

The offers Eisenstein did receive and immediately declined looked like mockery: one from a Swiss studio to make a documentary on abortion, another from a Swiss dairy firm to make an advertisement for it. Finally, Jesse Lasky, a Paramount vice president, made Eisenstein an offer to make a film, in six months, the topic to be discussed.[9]

Before leaving for Los Angeles, Eisenstein gave several lectures at Harvard and at Columbia, among other places, and had numerous meetings with members of the American artistic and academic elite. One of the most important encounters was with D. W. Griffith, whose films he so admired.

In Los Angeles it was Chaplin who tried to help them. Several proposals that Eisenstein submitted to Paramount were rejected as too costly. The most promising seemed *An American Tragedy,* a script based on Theodor Dreiser's famous novel. The studio executive David O. Selznick expressed his awe for Eisenstein's script as high art but was afraid that the finished film could not "possibly offer anything but a most miserable two hours to millions of happy-minded young Americans."[10] The contract was canceled in October 1930, five months after Eisenstein's arrival in the United States and eighteen months after his departure from Moscow.

Not one of Eisenstein's numerous biographers could convincingly explain what defeated the projects in Hollywood: some tactical mistakes the director may have made, or the studio's political concerns, or both. Or perhaps it was the innate incompatibility of some non-American directors with the Hollywood system. Maybe Eisenstein experienced the same thing Luis Buñuel did in the 1940s, Kurosawa did in 1960, and Fellini did in the 1970s.

The last hope was to make a film about Mexico, a country Eisenstein had been infatuated with for years. The writer Upton Sinclair (1878–1968), a sympathizer of the Soviet Union, became a sponsor of the film. He raised the money but kept all the rights to the positive and negative copies of the film for his wife and himself. This is how in a couple of years, the Sinclairs were able to sell the material, piece by piece, to various people.

Eisenstein spent over a year in Mexico, from the end of 1930 to the beginning of 1932, during which he shot thousands of meters of film for *Que Viva Mexico* and traveled hundreds of kilometers within the country. The filming was not yet completed when Stalin suddenly demanded Eisenstein's return to Moscow: the director had long outstayed his leave of absence, and a rumor was circulating that he preferred to remain abroad forever. In addition, Eisenstein had overspent the budget and missed the contracted deadline, and the Sinclairs withdrew their financial support at the time when he was finishing the film.

In a letter to a friend, after Eisenstein left, Sinclair wrote, "The Russian government got their great artist back and avoided having him turn into a white emigrant, as Rachmaninov and Chalapin have done. [The Soviets] owe this solely to our efforts."[11]

When Eisenstein returned to Moscow, a campaign against him included even his former supporters. Even Alexandrov turned away from him. Eisenstein was constantly criticized at meetings, conferences, and in the press for intellectualism and formalistic tendencies. Meanwhile he structured programs for The State Institute of Cinematography (VGIK) and was writing his book on montage.

In 1935 Eisenstein started working on *Bezhin Meadow*,[12] a film about a village boy, a young devoted pioneer, who denounces his father, a *kulak,* to the Soviets, because he had hidden his grain harvest for his family and not given it to the state. The outraged father kills his son. In 1937 the postproduction work on *Bezhin Meadow* ceased—the film was banned for ideological mistakes and a lack of political passion and for artistic formalism.[13]

From the beginning of the 1930s, Soviet ideology had changed its focus. Now there was no need for the masses to be shown as a film's hero, as in *Strike* and *Battleship Potemkin.* Now, the Soviet Union had become a totalitarian state and its main hero was the country's leader, the *vozhd'* (as was the *führer* in Germany, *il duce* in Italy, and, years later, the *chairman* in China).

Eisenstein recanted publicly and promised to eradicate his anarchistic thoughts, his individualism, and his formalism. Did he still believe in the revolution, and was he taking his humiliation as his sacrifice to it? Or, perhaps, his urge to be allowed to make films was stronger than anything else.

He was driven out of his teaching and deprived of his salary. But then, unexpectedly, the Soviet government asked him to make a film about Alexander Nevsky, the legendary Russian hero of the thirteenth century.

Of Eisenstein's six completed films, *Alexander Nevsky* (1938) was the most superficial, yet it was a success with the public and the press. The film was also a success abroad. Franklin Roosevelt even asked to see it at the White House. Showing the defeat of the aggressive Teutonic Knights by Alexander Nevsky became an allegorical statement on Nazi aggression. Here at work was the principle of *revealing the present through the past*. There were a few remarkable artistic achievements in the film—for instance, the scene of the Battle on Ice, the incomparable dramatic, rhythmic, and aesthetic unity of visual images, and the music written by Sergei Prokofiev (1891–1953).

At the premiere of *Alexander Nevsky,* in the fall of 1938, Stalin, it is said, embraced Eisenstein and called him "a good Bolshevik." The film brought the director unprecedented official recognition; he was awarded the Order of Lenin and the Stalin Prize First Class and was made the artistic director of Mosfilm, the largest film studio in the country.

In September 1939 the Soviet government signed the Friendship Treaty with Germany. Stalin was delighted and he refused to listen to anyone, from Winston Churchill to the Soviet spies, who warned him of an impending Nazi attack on Russia. He was informed of the details and dates of invasion but still refused to believe it. As bizarre as it might sound, Hitler supposedly was the only man whom Stalin respected and trusted.

After the signing of the treaty and until June 1941, when the Nazis attacked the Soviet Union, *Alexander Nevsky* was removed from Soviet distribution. Stalin did not want to jeopardize his newfound friendship with Hitler. Now Soviet artists were expected to create in the changed political climate. Eisenstein was commissioned to stage Richard Wagner's opera *The Valkyrie* (*Die Walküre*)[14] in the Bolshoi Theatre in Moscow.

As always, in any government assignment, Eisenstein was able to find an aspect of the work that would interest and excite him. Here, it was the epic quality of the opera. He designed and staged it.

*The Valkyrie* opened at the Bolshoi Theatre at the end of 1940. There were only a few rather unsuccessful performances, but the monumental scale of the production, the dramatic use of color, and the interplay of space, sound, and lighting were a foreshadowing of *Ivan the Terrible*.

In January 1941, several months before the German troops crossed the Russian border, Eisenstein was assigned by the Communist Party's Central Committee to make a film about Ivan the Terrible. It was perfectly clear not only that Stalin personally wanted the film to be made but also *how* the vozhd' wanted the tsar to be presented. "I shall wholly devote my personal creativity in the coming year to . . . a film about the great builder of the Russian state in the sixteenth century: *Ivan the Terrible*," Eisenstein wrote in the newspaper *Pravda*.[15] The statement was somewhat puzzling, because Ivan the Terrible had been known for his cruelties, sadism, and fits of rage, in one of which he killed his own son and heir. Eisenstein stated that it was not his intention to turn Ivan the Dreadful into Ivan the Sweet. He believed that it was a historical necessity for Ivan to act in the way he did, with those who wanted to ruin, sell off, or betray their fatherland. Eisenstein, the man who had created the most antitsarist films, was now ready to glorify the biggest autocrat.

Filming started in April 1943 in central Asia, in Alma-Ata, where Mosfilm had been evacuated at the beginning of the war. The local Palace of Culture was used as a studio, and it was decided by the cinema bosses that for reasons of economy two parts of the film would be shot simultaneously.

Eisenstein's group returned to Moscow in 1944 and in less than a year, Part I, a large portion of Part II, and even some scenes from Part III were completed. The premiere of *Ivan the Terrible* (Part I) took place in January 1945 with the war still going on, and the themes of the country's unity, hatred for its enemies, and patriotism were close to people's hearts.

The film was a resounding success. Eisenstein and Nicolai Cherkasov, who played Tsar Ivan, received the Orders of Lenin. Eisenstein was praised to the sky in the press in Russia and abroad.

The awards for Part I were celebrated with a dinner and dance party in early February 1946. It was also the celebration of finishing Part II. "Eisenstein came directly from the cutting room to the party and collapsed on the dancing floor with a serious cardiac infarction. For several months, he was kept hospitalized. During this time, and without his knowledge, Part Two was harshly and publicly criticized by the Communist Party authorities, and banned. Four edited reels for Part Three were destroyed."[16]

The Communist Party Central Committee's resolution, published in all newspapers, blamed Eisenstein for not being serious and responsible in Part II of *Ivan the Terrible*. Stalin accused the director of ignorance of historical facts, depicting Ivan's progressive oprichniks, the tsar's secret police, as if they were members of the Ku Klux Klan, and presenting Ivan, a man of strong character, as weak and indecisive, "someone like Hamlet." So, the most terrifying critic was outraged. Eisenstein learned about all that while he was still in the hospital. A few months later, he and Cherkasov were brought to the Kremlin for a long discussion with Stalin and members of the Politburo of what and how to change the film.

Eisenstein was given time to think everything over. No deadline was mentioned. And he procrastinated as long as he could to start the prescribed cutting and changes; he protected his creation and could not bring himself to destroy it.

Eisenstein died of a massive heart attack while writing at his desk on the night of February 10, 1948. When he was found the next morning, before him was his unfinished essay on color in *Ivan the Terrible*.

*Ivan the Terrible* (Part II) was still banned at the director's death, and it remained so until 1957, the year after "Khrushchev's speech at the 20th Communist Party Congress in which he singled out Stalin's obsession with cinema as a means of self-delusion and self-glorification."[17]

When, in 1958, *Ivan the Terrible* (Parts I and II) was released internationally, it was neither understood nor appreciated by the public, whose cinematic sensibility was influenced by both easygoing Hollywood style and the everyday reality of neorealism. Eisenstein, on the contrary, in his film was grand and theatrical. He even instructed his actors not to act naturally and plausibly, using their everyday life experience. Always remember, he taught them, that you are *performing* a certain role, not *becoming* a certain character.

The monumentality of *Ivan the Terrible* looked archaic and opera-like; the film seemed too stylized with its off-screen choir, like the chorus of classical Greek drama, accompanying, clarifying, and predicting the action. The visual exuberance of the shots was also incomprehensible. In fact, everything about the film seemed alien.[18]

Before the film was shot, it was completed in more than two thousand sketches. No one before Eisenstein had done this. The drawings are not storyboards, but a visual and emotional embodiment of the not-yet-existing film, a certain stage in its creation, the process of thinking over characters, actions, and composition of scenes and shots. As it was for the old masters of European art, for whom drawing was a stage in working on a painting, drawing for Eisenstein played a similar role—it was a stage in his work, and also the "struggle to achieve perfection."[19]

Written by Eisenstein, the script of *Ivan the Terrible* was published as a book and illustrated with his drawings *before* the film was released. In order to convey the flavor of the sixteenth century, it was written in blank verse in stylized, slightly archaic language. The script was self-contained and could be considered an accomplished work of literature.

The music, written by Sergei Prokofiev with Eisenstein's close participation, was as essential to the film as its narrative or mise-en-scènes. As in no other film, music in *Ivan the Terrible* is a *structural component*.

Already before the shooting started, Prokofiev was familiar with Eisenstein's concept of *Ivan the Terrible,* with its dramatic themes, their development, and their transformations. The director and the composer understood each other perfectly, from the time of *Alexander Nevsky*—Eisenstein, who believed in the *musical qualities* of visual images, and Prokofiev, whose music had innate cinematic elements—a quick montage of rhythmic contrasts.

Sometimes, Prokofiev would write the music using only the scenario and drawings. At other times, the composer would receive already edited scenes and, watching the running film, would tap on the arm of his wooden armchair, like Morse code, its rhythms and duration.

In the very beginning of the film, in the overture, the imperious theme of Ivan's struggle for the unified Russia resounds. It is repeated and modified, expressing various aspects of the tsar's image—his determination, his doubts, his sardonic explosions. Eisenstein remarked that Prokofiev's music not only intensifies the impact of the action on the viewers but expresses emotionally what is impossible to express by other means.

As has been already mentioned, *Ivan the Terrible* consists of three parts, each a complete work in itself.

Part III survived only in written form. Forty minutes of its footage were destroyed without the director's knowledge. Only one very short episode was miraculously saved.

Parts I and II have a remarkable stylistic unity in the narration, the visuals, the music, the specific style of acting, the mise-en-scènes, and the editing.

To unify Russia and to reach the Baltic Sea is Ivan's ambition and the main dramatic goal of the film. At the end of the film, in Part III, the waves of the sea "lick the feet of the ruler of all the Russias."[20] All characters in the film are treated by only one measure—whether they are loyal or hostile to Ivan and his mission.

## Part I of the Trilogy[21]

### 1. Ivan's Coronation
*The bells toll frantically. Ivan, the seventeen-year-old archduke, is crowned as the first tsar of Moscow and all the Russias in the Dormition Cathedral in the Kremlin. It is January 1547. Metropolitan Pimen places the royal crown on his head. His bride, Anastasia, is proud of him and happy.*

*Ivan's friends, princes Andrei Kurbsky and Fyodor Kolychev, raise the cups of golden coins over the young tsar's head and empty them over him. The ringing sound of falling coins mingles with the choir.*

*Foreign ambassadors are skeptical. Would Europe recognize Ivan as the autocrat? The boyars[22] are disturbed. Ivan's aunt, Efrosinia Staritsky, his hidden enemy, wants her feebleminded son, Prince Vladimir, to sit on the Moscow throne.*

*Ivan announces the end of the boyars' power; he will now create his regular army to free Russian territories from invaders and will reach the Baltic Sea.*

### 2. The Wedding Feast in the Kremlin Hall

*The guests are sitting at a festive table and the choir is singing a ceremonial madrigal for Ivan and Anastasia. Prince Kurbsky is secretly in love with her and cannot hide his sadness. The ambassador of Livonia incites his envy: why is it that Ivan is on the throne and not Kurbsky?*

*Prince Kolychev cannot tolerate Ivan's disrespect for the boyars and for old traditions; he tells Ivan that he would rather become a monk.*

*A crowd of commoners, incited against Ivan by agents of his aunt Efrosinia, bursts into the Kremlin. Malyuta, the head of the rioters, Ivan's devoted safeguard in the future, is petrified by the tsar's majesty. The scene is interrupted: an envoy from Kazan declares war on Moscow.*

*The scene ends with Ivan's call: "To Kazan!"*

### 3. The Battle at Kazan

*The countryside around the Tartar capital. We see moving serpentine lines of Russian soldiers; each of them throws a coin into a large metal cup (a device for keeping count of casualties).*

The sounds of the coins and the off-screen choir mingle, which reminds us about the "golden rain" at the wedding in the beginning of the film. A thing or action that recurs for a certain purpose—to emphasize similarities or differences, or to establish a rhythm—is called a *motif*. Notice a variation, or rather the contrast, of the "golden rain" motif in the film.

*The Russian army—the heavy ground troops and the cavalry—advance.*

*Ivan emerges from his tent, lit by the rays of the rising sun. Now, after a long siege, Kazan is about to fall. Malyuta, the former leader of the rioters, is the best fighter of all. Prince Kurbsky is not daring or brave in battle but is cruel to the Tartar captives. Ivan restrains him. Kurbsky, furious at being humiliated, almost hits the tsar, but he is stopped by Malyuta's gaze. "The boyars' hatred is even deadlier than the Tartars' arrows," says an old soldier, Alexey Basmanov. Fyodor, Alexey's son, looks at the tsar in admiration.*

*Victory! The Tartars are utterly defeated. "Now I am truly the tsar," declares Ivan. The cannon, bells, fanfare, and music ring out in reply to the tsar's words.*

The transition to the next scene is rather abrupt, and there is no clue about how much time has passed.

### 4. The Tsar's Illness

*The bells toll—Ivan is dangerously ill, or pretends to be in order to find out who plots to take the throne. Metropolitan Pimen holds the Bible to Ivan's face. Anastasia cries quietly. Her baby son, Dimitri, is sleeping in his cradle next to her. Efrosinia rejoices: "Now it is all over!" She begs Kurbsky to swear allegiance to her son, the feebleminded Vladimir, and to be a regent. The boyars' voices are heard: "Long live Vladimir, the tsar of the boyars!" Vladimir, all smiles, tries to catch a fly but doesn't succeed. Ivan, raising himself up, begs the boyars to swear allegiance to the legitimate heir, his son, Dimitri. Kurbsky, in a whisper, asks Anastasia to be his wife, but realizing that Ivan is still alive, swears allegiance to Ivan's son.*

*Ivan returns to his reign. As the reward for Kurbsky's "loyalty," the tsar appoints him to lead the Russian forces against Poland and Livonia, to the west, to the Baltic.*

### 5. The Boyars' Plot and the Poisoning of Anastasia

*Efrosinia, surrounded by boyars, is indignant at Ivan: "He strips us of our hereditary possessions; some boyars have been arrested!" She wants to take revenge on Ivan by poisoning Anastasia and takes charge of this plot. Efrosinia places a cup with poison in the Tsarina's bedroom.*

*Ivan, alone at a chessboard, a chessman in his hands. The gigantic shadow of him and a globe on his desk are projected on the wall.*

The shadow looks like an alarming premonition of betrayals and death. At the same time, it looks majestic, as an indication of Ivan's grandeur.

### 6. The Tsar Mourns

*In the cathedral Anastasia's body is lying in a coffin, surrounded by candles. The widowed Ivan is prostrated with grief on the floor beside the coffin. The metropolitan Pimen, in the darkness of the cathedral, reads a psalm of*

David: "I sink in deep mire where there is no standing." Simultaneously, in the same tone and tempo, Malyuta reads the names of boyars who were executed. Ivan is in despair: Is he in the right in his killing of the boyars? Isn't Anastasia's death God's punishment? In despair he leans against the coffin.

This is the first moment of Ivan's doubt in his actions, the theme of psychological and moral duality of the character, which will bring him to inner defeat and loneliness with hints of madness at the end of the film.

Malyuta tells Ivan that Kurbsky fled to King Sigismund of Poland, and that the boyars are inciting the people against the tsar.

Ivan has no doubts any longer. "The Moscow Tsar is not broken yet!" he exclaims. He wants to have people he can trust, a "brotherhood of iron"—the oprichniks, his guards and his secret police. One of them, Alexey Basmanov, assures the tsar that they will "forge an iron ring" about him and Ivan "would be their iron leader." "I donate [to you] my only son, Fyodor."

### 7. Ivan Leaves Moscow

A herald, in the middle of Red Square, announces that Tsar Ivan is leaving Moscow—he abdicates the throne, blaming the boyars for their dishonesty and treason but bearing no malice against the common people.

The episodic structure of the film excludes the chronological continuity of action. We don't know how many months or years have passed between Ivan's leaving Moscow and his coming back.

### 8. Exile and Recall

The tsar's palace in the town of Alexandrov. Ivan looks much aged and troubled. Next to him stands Malyuta in the long black robe of the oprichniks. He whispers if the tsar is waiting for news from Moscow.

The tsar's ambassador to England brings the news that the first English ships laden with arms and munitions have entered the White Sea. Ivan is delighted that he had outwitted the Germans and Livonians.

Let us not forget that when the film was in production, the English and Americans were Russian allies against the Germans.

In the distance, a procession appears carrying icons and banners. The long line of people winds across the snow-covered plain. Ivan, standing on the steps, bows. The off-screen choir is heard: "O return! O return! . . . O father of us all!"

The unity of the monarch and his subjects is shown graphically, in a harmonious counterpoint shot of close-ups on Ivan's profile and extreme long shots of the people's procession.

*Ivan orders Malyuta to saddle the horses and go back to Moscow to work for the future of the Great Russian State.*

"At the request of his people, Ivan, crowned the lawful Tsar of Russia at the beginning of Part One, is re-crowned as the people's Tsar at the Part's end."[23]

## Part II

### 9. At the Polish Court
*Sigismund II, the king of Poland and the prince of Livonia, and his knights, monks, court ladies, ambassadors, and courtiers, as well as a fanfare of trumpets, greet Prince Andrei Kurbsky. He has surrendered the Russian army to the king. He bows to Sigismund in submission.*

The shot is treated as an accomplished artistic composition with an expressive lighting and aesthetically elaborate mise-en-scène where the courtiers are placed on the palace floor like the chess pieces on a chessboard.

*Kurbsky says that Ivan has taken refuge in Alexandrov and that very soon (the boyars had sent messages to him) the Moscow throne will be free for a more civilized European monarch, a transparent hint to the king.*

*The appearance of a messenger with the news that Ivan is on his way to Moscow interrupts the festivities.*

### 10. Ivan's Return, Recollection of His Childhood
*A snow-covered countryside outside Moscow. Oprichniks in their black robes ride at full gallop. Ivan's coach races by.*

*Ivan appears unexpectedly in the throne hall of the Kremlin. Malyuta and Feodor Basmanov are on either side of him. "Traitors," Ivan says to the boyars. "[My oprichniks] will carry out my orders." Monk Philip (the friend of his youth, Prince Fyodor Kolychev) blames Ivan for being cruel and asks for clemency for the boyars. Ivan replies that the boyars have hated him since his childhood.*

*A flashback: The frightened face of the child Ivan. His widowed mother is dying, poisoned by the boyars. "My son! They have killed me! . . . Beware of the boyars!"*

*Back to the present: Ivan's eyes are dim. "That's how I came to be an orphan, alone and abandoned," says the tsar to Philip.*

Another flashback: *Now, as a boy in the full regalia of a grand prince, Ivan is on the throne. His legs cannot reach the floor. The boyars try to influence his decisions on foreign trade; each wants to pull him in a different direction. One of them insults the memory of Ivan's mother. "Take him!" orders the boy.*

This is the first time that we hear this terrifying order, which will be heard repeatedly in the film.

Return to the present: *Ivan says that he doesn't fear the sword or poison. He only cares and trembles for our great cause. He begs Philip Kolychev not to leave him and offers him the position of metropolitan of Moscow, which he accepts, asking, however, for the right to plea for the accused boyars. Ivan agrees.*

### 11. The Execution of the Kolychevs
*Malyuta talks to the tsar and gets permission to arrest and execute the whole Kolychev family for treason. Ivan hesitates, recalling his promise to Philip. Malyuta reminds him about Kurbsky—all of them are traitors. He says that he will take the tsar's sins himself. "Do what you have to do," the tsar replies. Malyuta hurries out.*

*Ivan is in deep thought: by what right is he the judge?*

*Oprichnik Fyodor Basmanov tries to convince the tsar that Efrosinia poisoned Anastasia, that she brought the cup with poison into Anastasia's bedroom.*

*Malyuta reads the verdict to the Kolychevs that they are to be beheaded for high treason.*

*Ivan looks at the executed men. He takes off his hat and bows, "crosses himself, but suddenly stops and points at the ground . . . a gleam of madness in his eyes. 'Too few,' he exclaims."*

### 12. The Boyars Mourn
*In Philip's cell a group of boyars, among them Efrosinia, are on their knees, asking him to do something to stop Ivan's massacres. The coffins of murdered Kolychevs are there. Metropolitan Pimen charges Philip to excommunicate Ivan. A young novice, Peter, kisses Philip's hand feverishly.*

### 13. The Fiery Furnace Play
*In the center of the cathedral a play is performed: an angel saves three virtuous youths who have been condemned to burn by the Babylonian tsar. Two Chaldeans push them to the burning furnace. With heavenly clear voices,*

*the youths sing about the tsar of Satan, the bloodthirsty torturer—an allu-sion to Ivan—when Ivan and his oprichniks in black monk's robes appear in the cathedral. The youths continue: "Why, O Chaldeans, shameless, a law-less tsar do you serve? Why, O Chaldeans, diabolical, in a tsar of Satan, an outrager, tormentor—do you rejoice?"*

*The tsar sees the smile at Vladimir Staritsky's face and Efrosinia's unrest. He realizes that it was her idea to remind him about the Babylonian tsar, and certainly it was she who poisoned his Anastasia.*

*Philip accuses the tsar of heathen deeds and demands his repentance and that he get rid of the oprichniks; otherwise Philip will not give benediction to Ivan.*

*The youths continue singing about the terrible tsar of Babylon. Suddenly a child among the worshippers asks, pointing at Ivan: "Is that the godless and terrible Chaldean tsar?" "From now on . . . I will be terrible!" roars Ivan.*

It has been observed that the fiery furnace play—a play within the play—resembles *Mousetrap*, performed by traveling actors at Hamlet's request, to mirror onstage the murder of his father, thus revealing the crime of the queen and her husband. In *Ivan the Terrible*, the tsar's adver-saries meant to reveal him through the play but instead were trapped themselves.

### 14. At the Staritskys'

*Efrosinia breaks the news to her party that Philip is arrested and suggests a last measure—to kill the tsar. Otherwise all of them will be executed. Pimen says that only the pure in heart is fit for such a deed, namely, his novice, Peter. Pimen blesses him. Efrosinia places a knife into his hands. Vladimir turns away, frightened. "Why are you pushing me to power? Why do you sacrifice me?" he asks his mother. Efrosinia takes her son in her arms and sings him a lullaby. "Blood is terrifying," worries Vladimir. He doesn't want to be involved in the killing. Efrosinia reassures him that Peter himself will do it.*

*Malyuta enters to invite Vladimir to Ivan's banquet. The tsar wants his cousin Vladimir to be with him there, Malyuta says.*

*Efrosinia agrees to send her son to Ivan; Vladimir will take Peter with him, she says.*

### 15. The Banquet and Vladimir's Death

*In the Kremlin hall the celebration is in full swing. The tsar is sitting at the festive table and watching his oprichniks "dancing wildly and shouting." Among them is a girl in a sarafan with her face covered by a mask with slanted eyes and a frightening sinister smile.*

In this scene Eisenstein infuses the red, blue, and golden colors into the black-and-white film—in his words, he wanted the wild dance of the oprichniks, the explosion of movement, to be expressed in color, and scattered splashes of the red work as symbols of blood and murder.

*Beside the tsar sits tipsy Vladimir Staritsky. Suddenly, under the girl's mask we see Fyodor Basmanov's face. He watches attentively what is going on. Moving the mask back and forth, he sings a song about killing enemies and burning their houses. He notices the novice, Peter, who looks suspicious to him.*

*Vladimir, already drunk, blabs out about the plot to kill Ivan and to put him, Vladimir, on the throne, but he says he doesn't want it at all. Ivan mockingly persuades him to be the tsar. Vladimir is adorned with the tsar's regalia and put on the throne. All bow to him. The naïve fool enjoys the ceremony.*

The mock coronation of Vladimir is a parody on Ivan's wedding and coronation. The joyful celebration now is transformed into a wild and sinister happening. Everything now is reversed and charged with double meaning: the frenzied dancing and singing about robbing and killing instead of a glorious chorus and church bells; black decorative swans instead of white; Fyodor Basmanov in a sarafan covering his oprichnik attire and the mask of a girl on his face—a slight hint that he has now replaced Anastasia in Ivan's life.

*"The end to jesting!" exclaims Ivan suddenly. He orders the oprichniks to go to pray and atone for their sins.*

Now the black color of the oprichniks' attire obliterates the red, gold, and blue. The film returns to black and white.

*Vladimir, frightened, is forced to lead the procession to the cathedral. Ivan becomes indistinguishable from his black-robed guards.*

*Peter, the novice, who hides behind a pillar, takes Vladimir for the tsar, and plunges the knife into his back. Vladimir crashes down on the cathedral floor.*

*Efrosinia comes running, places her foot on the body, and cries out happily that Ivan is no more. But suddenly she realizes that this is her son, and that he is dead. She takes him in her arms and starts singing him a lullaby. She goes insane.*

Eisenstein was asked why the scene of the prince's murder was filmed in a long shot only, and not in close-ups, or at least in medium shots. "Do you want to show guts and blood to the spectators?" asked the director. "They should not see the *physiology of the death but the tragedy of the murder* of an innocent man."[24]

*Ivan lets Peter free—he killed the fool, not the tsar. "As for her . . . ," says Ivan to Fyodor Basmanov. He doesn't finish the phrase, just "drops his hand in a gesture of finality."*

### 16. Ivan's Promise
*Ivan crosses himself at the altar, bows his head, and kneels. The oprichniks behind him also sink to their knees. "Today in Moscow we have struck down the enemies of Russian unity," the tsar says and promises that from now on the sword of justice shall flash against anyone who opposes the great cause of Russian unity and might.*

## Part III (survived only as a screenplay)

17. *Kurbsky sends a signal to King Sigismund to begin the attack on the Russian army.*

*Ivan learns about Kurbsky's and some other betrayals, including that of his confessor, monk Eustace, who is spying on him and plotting his demise.*

*The cities of Pskov and Novgorod are ready to abandon the tsar and join the Livonian kingdom.*

*The Russian army led by the tsar appears at the walls of Novgorod. Ivan in his wrath is "like an unleashed tempest." After all the boyars are arrested and executed, Ivan and his troops leave the city. "Behind are left the snow-covered ruins of houses. Dead bodies lie in the snow. . . . Slaughtered cattle lay around. . . . A dog, dashing away in terror, is struck by an arrow."*

18. *In the cathedral a monk reads: "Remember, O Lord, thy servants who died before their hour." Numerous names follow each other in the monk's rhythmical keening. "Tsar Ivan lies stretched out in the darkness under the fresco of the Last Judgment. . . . [His] lips whisper, as though he were seeking to excuse the terrible deed."*

*The monk continues with the names of executed boyars, their wives and children . . . "Have mercy, O Lord, on the deceased, thy servants, male and female, on those who have gone to rest before their time." Tears flow from Ivan's eyes.*

*Fyodor Basmanov tells Malyuta that the "total of those executed at Novgorod amounts to one thousand five hundred and five." Ivan's lips* whisper, "It's not wickedness. Not anger. Not cruelty. It is to punish trea-son—treason against the common cause." The monk continues reading the names of the dead. Alexey Basmanov tells Malyuta that almost two hun-dred monasteries have been destroyed. "It is not for me," says Ivan at the fresco of the Last Judgment. "It is for the country." He looks at the celes-tial tsar in the fresco. Suddenly, he throws his scepter at the wall and it shat-ters to pieces.

19. In Windsor Castle, the German ambassador asks Queen Elizabeth "to provide no obstacle to a [German] attack on Moscow. England should help the Germans." Jokingly, the queen gives him an ambivalent answer. Meanwhile, she has already started trade with Russia.

20. In a hall the tsar and oprichniks, wearing monks' habits, celebrate All Souls' Day. Above them is a fresco of martyred saints; their golden halos shine brightly.

Fyodor Basmanov with the psalm book turned upside down sings a pro-fane hymn. Wine cups clink against each other.

Ivan sits at the middle of the table, gazing gloomily. Suddenly he interrupts the dancing and singing, saying that he learned that some oprichniks "betray the tsar's confidence [and] barter their holy oath . . . into coin."

He is referring to Alexey Basmanov, who steals from the tsar's treasury and wants to be mightier than the tsar. By Ivan's unspoken order, just a ges-ture, "Fyodor's sword . . . with one stroke severs the gray head of his father, Alexey Basmanov." Now Ivan wonders if Fyodor had no pity for his father, would he pity the tsar? "Take him," Ivan points at Fyodor, and an oprich-nik thrusts his dagger through Fyodor's chest.

A messenger rushes in with the news that the Livonians are coming. "Forward!" Ivan shouts to the oprichniks. "They shed their black robes, revealing the shining gold of their kaftans beneath. The swords, drawn from their sheaths, glitter. All shout: 'On to Livonia!' Malyuta calls out, 'To the Baltic Sea!'" Tsar Ivan and Malyuta gallop at the head of the regiments.

21. Kurbsky's tent. The prince is ready to lead the Livonian army to Moscow. A messenger brings the news that Russian troops, in uncountable numbers, are approaching. A cannonball carries away the top of the tent. It bursts into flames. Kurbsky manages to escape. He gallops through marshes from Russian troops but is mortally wounded.

*22. The Russian army moves victoriously. "Now shall we, like our forebear, the great ruler Alexander Nevsky, drive the Germans from our soil without mercy," exclaims Ivan. The Russians set siege to the last fortress. Malyuta dies under its collapsed wall. At the last moment of his life he catches a glimpse of the sea. The waves roar. . . . Ivan goes down to the waves, and the sea grows calm. "We have reached the sea, and here we will stay."*
*The waves advance to lick the feet of the ruler of all the Russias.*

Eisenstein knew that Stalin's wish was to canonize Ivan the Terrible as a great national hero. It was true that Ivan unified Russia, extended its territory, and created the regular army. He organized Oprichnina, a royal domain, whose members, the oprichnicks, became his secret police. But Ivan never "reached the sea"—that happened only in the film.

Eisenstein kept some facts of Ivan's life: that he was three years old when his widowed mother died, probably poisoned; that as a child he reigned as grand duke of Moscow under the guidance of the boyars; that when he was seventeen, he was crowned the "tsar of all Russias"; that he captured the city of Kazan, the last bastion of the Tartars on Russian territory; that he opened relations with England (this was especially important to emphasize in the early 1940s, when England was Russia's ally against Hitler). However, Eisenstein ignored numerous basic events and downplayed Ivan's cruelty, not even mentioning the tsar's killing, in a rage, of his own son and heir, Tsarevich Ivan, or his nailing with his staff the foot of a messenger from Kurbsky, when the prince defected to Livonia.

From Ivan's life, Eisenstein took only those episodes and those characters that he needed to present his concept of the tsar. More or less close to reality were Prince Andrey Kurbsky (some correspondence between Ivan and Kurbsky after the prince's defection has survived) and Moscow Metropolitan Fyodor Kolychev, who tried to oppose Ivan's terror and was strangled. Real was Anastasia, Ivan's first wife, whose loss he grieved for a long time.[25] But Prince Vladimir Staritsky was transformed beyond recognition, turned into a fictional character.

When Eisenstein was ordered to make the film, he was attracted by the dramatic possibilities of the theme and, first of all, by Ivan's duality and inner contradictions: his leaps from villainy to repentance, from violent outbursts to total withdrawal, from terror and executions to prayers for forgiveness. Eisenstein hoped that he would be able to reconcile what was expected from him by the Politburo and by Stalin with what he himself wanted to do—to show Ivan the Terrible not as a merciless despot, but as a tragic hero and a very lonely man.

Films played an important role in Stalin's life, sometimes more important than reality. He had no understanding of the medium at all; the director, in his judgment, was the one who followed the text of the screenwriter, who, as all Soviet writers, was expected to be "the engineer of human souls."

Stalin was the chief cinema censor; he controlled topics, correcting scripts with his thick blue pencil. He was suspicious of words and of people who wrote them.[26]

From the beginning of the 1930s, the Soviet film was uniformly ruled by the doctrine of Socialist Realism, the representation of a utopian Communist society, though expressed in simplistic, almost primitive cinematic language. It was no longer a cinema of propaganda, but a cinema of totalitarian hypnosis. When untold numbers of people were arrested and murdered, movie theatres showed happy citizens, strong and brave builders of the new life. On the screen there were blossoming fields and joyous peasants singing cheerful songs, while in reality thousands of peasants were being sent to Siberia, executed, or starved to death. While schoolchildren recited poems about "dear and beloved" Stalin, a decree of 1935 extended all penalties, including death, to twelve-year-olds.[27]

Gradually, in film as well as in literature and theatre, the main theme of belief in Communism started to be replaced by the belief in Stalin, the "supreme genius of Humanity." One Soviet writer called Stalin "the unsetting sun of our time, and more than the sun, for the sun lacks wisdom."

From the end of the 1930s two genres became prevalent in Soviet film: spy thrillers[28] and films about Stalin. There was a Georgian actor, Mikhail Gelovani, who was routinely called upon to play Stalin. He was handsomer, taller, and much more impressive than the vozhd'. Stalin was five feet four inches tall, with a pitted face and one arm shorter than the other. Paradoxically, seeing the attractive actor on the screen as himself was one of the cinematic self-deceptions. It is possible that it went even further: in Part I of *Ivan the Terrible* he saw himself as he always wanted to be—tall, royal, and majestic. The party slogan "Stalin is Lenin today" became dated. Now, Stalin understood himself not as the party leader but as *grozny* Tsar Ivan.[29]

From the beginning of the 1940s there appeared a stream of articles, books, and plays that tried to rehabilitate Ivan the Terrible. Eisenstein's film was supposed to do the same.[30] Contemporaries couldn't fail to notice the change in the official perception of Ivan and Stalin's favorable view of him. But only in the 1980s and 1990s did archival materials become available that revealed how deep and intimate were the interest and admiration of one tyrant for the other.

The similarities between them are remarkable: their sinister, erratic behavior, their cunning treachery, their pathological cruelty. Both had paranoid personalities, and both created regimes of unimaginable political terror. The number of Ivan's victims, among whom were also his closest friends and relatives, was staggering; the number of Stalin's victims, among whom were also his relatives, friends, and party comrades, amounted to millions.[31]

After his wife Anastasia's death, Ivan remarried five or six times, and each of his wives either died soon after the wedding or was forced to take a religious vow. Stalin's wife, Nadezhda Allilueva (1902–1932), was found in her bedroom with a bullet in her heart, presumably a suicide, although there were rumors that her husband had shot her. Again, after her death, Stalin became even more cruel, as had Ivan after Anastasia died. Another example: Stalin hated his oldest son, Yakov, who served in the army during World War II and was captured by the Germans. Stalin refused to exchange him for a captured German field marshal, and Yakov was executed—a close parallel to the fate of Tsarevich Ivan. Yet another comparison: Ivan's paranoia was a documented fact. Stalin's daughter, Svetlana Allilueva, wrote that especially by the end of her father's life, he was possessed by fear and suspicion; he mistrusted his devoted guards, servants, and private doctors, and found himself literally alone.

Some archive documents revealed telling details—several of Stalin's private letters were signed *Ivan Vasilievich*, the tsar's first and patronymic names, or their abbreviation—I. V.—the same initials as Stalin's *Iosif Vissarionovich*. Stalin believed this similarity to be of a mysterious nature.

As one critic observed, "Stalin needed Eisenstein's film, because he needed Ivan the Terrible resurrected, rehabilitated and exalted in the Soviet public consciousness as the brilliant forebear of the 'prototype' for himself."[32] Ivan, a powerful autocrat, merciless to his enemies, a conqueror who enlarged and unified Russia, no doubt matched Stalin's own self-image. Stalin saw himself as a modern, glorious Ivan, and Eisenstein initially supported this view and was willing to present the *present through the past*.

Part I of *Ivan the Terrible is an apology* for Ivan's autocracy and, metaphorically, stands for the unlimited power of the vozhd'. It romanticizes the tsar and his oprichniks. The film is nationalistic and patriotic; during the war these feelings, as well as strong hatred for the German expansion, were widely shared by the population. Besides, it was important to show Russian armies victorious in the past.

Eisenstein in Part I glorified the almighty ruler (or, metaphorically, the two rulers) and fulfilled Stalin's unspoken order. We should not forget that Eisenstein "was a man of his country, his time, his generation, and for a while, apparently the figure of Stalin *cast its hypnotic spell on him too, just as it did in various ways . . . on the works and behavior of many artists.*"[33]

From his youth Eisenstein had been enamored with the revolution. Yet it was impossible for him to ignore facts (although the most appalling ones were publicized *after* Stalin's death in 1953; Eisenstein died in 1948). Some of his closest friends, who, he was certain, were not "enemies of the people," were arrested and executed. It was impossible not to see the political terror. And Eisenstein's views changed, and Parts II and III changed as well.

So, Part II blew up the concept of Part I. From a great hero inspired by the goal of making Russia strong, Eisenstein turned Ivan into a maniac, and his oprichniks into pathological killers. Now from an apology, the film becomes the revelation of political nightmare— the price paid for reaching Ivan's goal.

In Part II, the words *treason, betrayal, arrest,* and *execution* are repeated again and again. Those words were the everyday vocabulary of Soviet Russia.

Judging by Eisenstein's various notes, the unmasking of Ivan was not accidental. When working on the script, Eisenstein wrote in his notebook[34] that the atmosphere of the Oprichnina was heavy and dark, today's friends were tomorrow's enemies, and that relationships were based on mutual blackmail and conspiracies. About the tsar's favorite, Malyuta, Eisenstein said that he forgot himself in blood as others did in wine.

This uncanny parallel with the atmosphere of Soviet Russia cannot be a coincidence. Even Ivan's constant talk about enemies echoes Stalin's paranoid speeches about "internal and external enemies."

In Part III, the destruction of inner and outer enemies becomes also Ivan's self-destruction. Although the Russian army reaches the sea, the old and paranoid tsar is left utterly alone. "Alone!" he exclaims at the end in one of the script's drafts, but the word was crossed out either by Eisenstein or by a censor.

In one of the scenes the names of executed boyars are recited non-stop, while Ivan, frightened and horrified, is sitting under the fresco of the Last Judgment. It is hard to believe that this is not a requiem for Eisenstein's contemporaries who were executed; for his friends who disappeared or were arrested, tortured, or murdered, including Meyerhold, who, as Eisenstein said, was the most important person in his life.[35]

In the film, the episodes of Ivan's self-doubts are not long; still these episodes in particular enraged Stalin: why would an autocrat doubt his actions, the vozhd' wondered. "One of [Ivan's] mistakes was to stop short of cutting up the . . . key [boyar's] clans," he said.[36]

The banning of Part II and complete destruction of the forty-minute footage of Part III happened because the *present was shown through the past* not in the way Stalin intended. The past started to throw harsh light on the present, on Stalin's tyranny and the criminal nature of *his* oprichniks, and in a way foretold Stalin's future through Ivan's isolation and loneliness. It frightened and enraged Stalin.

It is very possible that Eisenstein, after justifying Stalin's regime in Part I, risked his life by exposing its true nature in Parts II and III. Certainly, the director went through a period of agonizing thoughts. He wrote in his notebook that the doubts that plagued Ivan were no less torturing than the doubts that plagued him. No one knows whether Eisenstein meant his doubts about the film, about Ivan/Stalin, or about all of his films in general, but it is clear that the question of whether the end justified the means was harrowingly personal for him.

When Eisenstein showed Part II to his close friends, they were scared—the allusions were too close to home. But at that time, proabably, Eisenstein wanted the film to be understood as a contemporary theme. Only his heart attack and the long hospitalization that followed saved him from arrest, and the phrase "Take him!" that was so often repeated in the film was not applied to him.

In his memoirs, Eisenstein recalls an old legend, in which a hero, "to save his strength for future [achievements], obediently spreads himself out in the dust at the feet of his [masters] and mockers and does all [they] required of him. . . . The unprecedented self-control and sacrifice of everything, even self respect, to further his goals, completely captivated me. [Yes] accepting humiliation in the name of our most passionate aspiration. In my personal, too personal, history, I too often perpetrated his deed of self-abasement . . . , too hurriedly, even too willingly, and also . . . as unsuccessfully."[37]

This is the only explanation, evasive and oblique as it is, for the many compromises that Eisenstein made for only one reason—*being allowed to create.*

But despite all the ambiguous standings—and there were quite a few of them in Eisenstein's life and career—he was the only director in the 1940s who, working inside a totalitarian state, showed allegorically, but very pointedly, the true nature of totalitarianism. No German or Italian filmmaker dared to do the same.

## Appendix

### Sergei Eisenstein: "My Drawings for Ivan the Terrible"[38]

There is one process, which starts *from* all sides, *on* all sides . . . the process of making a film.

The finished film is a huge assemblage of the most diverse means of expression and influence that defy comparison with anything else; the historical conception of the subject, the situation in the screenplay and the overall course of the drama, the life of the character portrayed and the performance of the actual actor, the rhythm of the montage and the plastic construction of the shot, the music, the noises and the rumblings . . . the lighting and the tonal composition of the speech . . . In a successful work all this is blended into a single entity. . . .

The dramatic character of the film about tsar Ivan immediately flared up in a scene set . . . around the second half of the screenplay. The first episode to occur to my imagination— . . . the key in stylistic terms—was the confession scene. Where and when it came to me I can no longer say. I only remember that it was the first to do so.

The second scene was the prologue: the death of Glinskaya [Ivan's mother].

In a box in the Bolshoi Theatre. The first sketch of the scene was on the reverse of my ticket. . . .

The epic coloration of the screenplay came about with the third episode: the candle above Kazan. . . . In the movement of the drama: first, somewhere near the end; then, suddenly, the prologue, then, unexpectedly, the middle.

Here Ivan is in one scene in old age, then suddenly, he is in his childhood, and then, in the bloom of youth.

### Serafima Birman's Reflection ("Efrosinia" in the film)

Eisenstein worked with such passion, such spontaneous inspiration, and ultimately with such true comradeship that to distress him unnecessarily . . . was to slap his superb talents in his face . . . [We] loved the man, but with a love that we never expressed in words . . . So we agreed to do the most extraordinary things for him; for instance Cherkasov, in the Kazan sequence, had to wear a very heavy metal costume, and he willingly stood in it on the edge of a precipice, for take after take in a temperature of sixty degrees centigrade. Poor Ludmila Tselikovskaya [she played Anastasia] once spent a whole night in a coffin because Eisenstein refused to let her get out of it. Why did we do these things without protest . . . One reason [was] our deep professional respect for Eisenstein as an artist. But another cause, and of equal importance, was a reflection of the war. Elsewhere in the country, people were fighting and being maimed for something they believed in, and perhaps the only way we could compensate for the privilege of our own safety was to fight a battle for what we regarded as serious and lasting art. For these reasons, and despite our quarrels with him, we eventually did whatever Eisenstein asked us to . . .

## Notes

1. "Mama was, as the Americans say, 'oversexed.' And Papa, in his turn, was 'undersexed,'" recalled Eisenstein in *Immoral Memories: An Autobiography by Eisenstein*, Boston: Houghton Mifflin, 1983, p. 24.

2. At that time the city had been renamed Petrograd.

3. Quoted in You Barna, *Eisenstein*, Boston: Little, Brown, 1973, p. 36.

4. Meyerhold was called the "Picasso of the theatre." His extraordinary productions were closer to circus, puppet theatre, variety shows, and the commedia dell'arte than to traditional theatre of his time.

Among Meyerhold's numerous inventions was a free arrangement of episodes—a theatrical montage, which was the precursor of Eisenstein's cinematic montage.

"I must say, that I never loved, idolized, worshipped anyone as much as I did my teacher [Meyerhold]," Eisenstein wrote in 1947 in his memoirs, at a time when even mentioning Meyerhold's name was dangerous. A faithful Communist, Meyerhold was one of the numerous artists and writers wiped out by Stalin; he was arrested without cause in 1939 and executed as an enemy of the people. Eisenstein, *Immoral Memories*, p. xii.

5. The title and some elements of the action were taken from the drama by the same name, written by the nineteenth-century Russian dramatist Alexander Ostrovsky. The free adaptation was made by Eisenstein's friend Sergei Tretiakov, who some years later was arrested and executed by the KGB.

6. Richard Taylor, "Eisenstein: A Soviet Artist," in *The Eisenstein Reader*, London: British Film Institute, 1999, p. 7.

7. Later on, some of the film's shots were used as documentary photographs and were even included in school textbooks as such. In *October* Eisenstein experimented with so-called *intellectual montage*—juxtaposing images to evoke in the viewers' imaginations the abstract ideas of power, religion, and oppression.

8. One of the congress' participants wrote: "We all knew and admired *Battleship Potemkin* and we regarded Eisenstein as an almost divine figure. And now here they were, three men in boiler suits; Eisenstein himself was short and squat, with the huge head that we already recognized from photographs, eyes that sparkled with an amiable malice. The other two, Alexandrov and Tisse, were extremely good-looking." In Roland Bergan, *Eisenstein: A Life in Conflict*, London: Little, Brown and Company, 1997, p. 158.

9. The salary for the three—Eisenstein, Tissé, and Alexandrov—was five hundred dollars a week for the preproduction period and three thousand dollars a week once filming began—a very modest sum for Hollywood. They arrived in New York with Ivor Montague, a young English filmmaker, as their manager, and Montague's wife as their secretary.

10. James Goodwin, *Eisenstein, Cinema and History*, Chicago: University of Illinois Press, 1993, p. 129.

11. Barna, p. 180.

12. "Bezhin Meadow" is the title of a story by the Russian author Ivan Turgenev, from his collection *A Sportsman's Notebook*. But the main character of the film, Stepok, is modeled on the Soviet hero and martyr Pavlik Morosov, who was killed by his relatives for denouncing his kulak father. *Kulak* is a pejorative term used by Soviet Communists for a peasant "bourgeois," one who is a bit more prosperous than most peasants.

13. The film was destroyed without Eisenstein's knowledge, but during the shooting, the director saved a few individual frames from every shot, and in the 1960s some kind of film reconstruction was made.

14. It was well known that Wagner was Hitler's favorite composer. Simultaneously, the staging of the Russian opera *Boris Godunov* was in production in Berlin.

15. Quoted in Bergan, pp. 320, 314.

16. Jay Leyda, *A History of the Russian and Soviet Film*, Princeton, NJ: Princeton University Press, 1983, p. 349.

17. Ian Christie, "Eisenstein at 90," *Sight and Sound* 57, no. 3 (1998).

18. Eisenstein considered cinema a legitimate descendant of all of the arts, "not just a foundling on their threshold." He was convinced that only cinema could and should unify the arts in a strong homogenous ensemble. In *Ivan the Terrible* one stylistically elevated approach encompasses the poetic text, the music, the visual exuberance of the mise-en-scènes, and color.

19. These are the words of Giorgio Vasari (1511–1574), famous Italian writer and artist.

20. The *Russias* was the archaic form of the word *Russia*.
    All script's quotes are taken from Sergei Eisenstein, *Ivan the Terrible: A Screenplay*, New York: Simon and Schuster, 1962.

21. See Kristina Thompson, *Eisenstein's Ivan the Terrible*, Princeton, NJ: Princeton University Press, 1981, p. 183.

22. *Boyars*, landowners of large territories in medieval Russia, its aristocracy.

23. Yuri Tsivian, *Ivan the Terrible*, London: British Film Institute, 2002, p. 10.

24. The acting style was intentionally old-fashioned. It is in a way like the Russian theatre of the nineteenth century, before the Chekhovian theatre introduced its realism, when actors onstage would drink real hot tea from real samovars. Yet, at the same time, the acting in *Ivan the Terrible*, with its plasticity of movement, expressiveness of body and gesture, and masklike faces, was, in fact, a great homage to Eisenstein's mentor, Vsevold Meyerhold.

25. Historians agree that Ivan's most vicious cruelties began after Anastasia's death.

26. A lot of screenwriters were arrested from the middle of the 1930s to 1953, the year of Stalin's death, and only a few directors were victims of Stalin's terror.

27. At that time, French Communists argued that people matured so quickly under Socialism that by the age of twelve they were already fully responsible citizens.

28. There was literally a spy mania in the country. Through the arts and the press, people were told that because the capitalists and imperialists wanted to destroy their "blossoming country," spies were everywhere. It was a very convenient excuse for arresting and executing anyone as a spy.

29. In Russian the film's title is *Ivan Grozny*. The word *grozny* doesn't have such a negative connotation as the word *terrible*. *Grozny* is closer to *severe, dreadful,* where the meaning of authority is implied, and also *threatening,* but not *terrible.*

30. It was also expected to repeat the patriotic fervor and success of *Alexander Nevsky.* Nikolai Cherkasov, the actor who played Prince Nevsky, was to star as Tsar Ivan.

31. Of the seven Politburo members in 1924 after Lenin's death—Zinoviev, Kamenev, Trotsky, Bukharin, Rykov, Tomsky, and Stalin—only Stalin was alive in the beginning of the 1940s; the rest were either executed on Stalin's order or committed suicide.

32. Leonid Koslov, "The Artist and the Shadow of Ivan," in *Stalinism and Soviet Cinema,* ed. Richard Taylor and Derek Spring, London and New York: Routledge, 1993, p. 112.

33. ibid., p. 114.

34. All one hundred of his *Ivan the Terrible* notebooks survived.

35. Not long before Eisenstein started working on *Ivan the Terrible,* Meyerhold's daughter brought him Meyerhold's archive to hide. Eisenstein buried this archive in the ground at his summer house. This was, probably, his first antigovernment and anti-Stalin action.

36. Richard Taylor, ed. *Eisenstein Writing,* Vol. 3. London: British Film Institute Publishing, 1996, p. 300.

37. Eisenstein, p. xv.

38. Taylor, p. 240.

# NOTORIOUS
## Alfred Hitchcock

|  |  |
|---|---|
| director: | Alfred Hitchcock |
| producer: | Alfred Hitchcock |
| screenplay: | Ben Hecht |
|  | with Alfred Hitchcock |
| cameraman: | Ted Tetzlaff |
| editing: | Theron Warth |
| sound: | John Tribby, Clem Portman |
| art directors: | Albert D'Agostino, Carol Clark, |
|  | Darrell Silvera, Claude |
|  | Carpenter |
| special effects: | Vernon Walker |
| music: | Roy Webb |

### cast

|  |  |
|---|---|
| alicia huberman: | Ingrid Bergman |
| devlin: | Cary Grant |
| alex sebastian: | Claude Rains |
| madame sebastian: | Leopoldina Konstantin |
| paul prescott: | Louis Calhern |
| dr. anderson: | Reinhold Schunzel |

Black and white
*running time:* 102 minutes
*released:* August 1946, Los Angeles

Alfred Joseph Hitchcock (1899–1980) was born in London to an
English Catholic family headed by a small businessman. "I was what

is known as a well-behaved child. . . . I looked and observed a good deal . . . was a loner—can't remember ever having a playmate. I played by myself inventing my own games," Hitchcock recalled.[1]

His first school was St. Ignatius Jesuit College, where "the punishments with hard rubber cane were severe, like the execution of a sentence."[2] The Jesuits, he said, used to terrify him to death, but afterward, he admitted, he was getting himself back by terrifying other people.

For two years he studied at the London School of Engineering and Navigation. He was a good student, always ensuring order and precision in every task he undertook. A schoolmate described him as shy, painfully sensitive, and unattractive. When, in his twenties, he met Alma Reville, his future wife, she was the only girl he had ever been out with.

His first job was at a telegraph company. Next he moved to advertising, and for several years he took art classes at London University. He was a good draftsman, published his caricatures in some second-rate magazines, and wrote stories, one of which in 1919 he signed, "Hitch."

He knew a lot about films, regularly read cinema journals, and was competent in the technical aspect of film. He preferred American movies to British, like many directors of his generation, and was influenced by David W. Griffith's *Birth of a Nation* (1915) and *Intolerance* (1916).

In the 1920s, Hitchcock was hired as a designer of inner titles in silent films by the Hollywood studio Famous Players, a branch of which was opened in London. His work was very simple—adding drawings to the captions of dialogue, sometimes rewriting the captions; gradually he began writing scripts, was promoted to the head of the title department, and rapidly advanced to production management and directing, in which he excelled as if he had known how to do it from his birth.

In 1925 Hitchcock was sent to UFA studio in Germany as a part of an English-German coproduction deal. He worked as an assistant director, designed the sets, and later that year directed his first film, a melodrama, *The Pleasure Garden* (1925). He recalled that in the press he was described as "the young man with the master mind."[3] He was twenty-six at that time.

That year in Germany was truly significant—he met the directors Friedrich Murnau[4] and Fritz Lang[5] and was strongly influenced by *chiaroscuro*, the expressive power of light and shadow, and by the mobility of the camera—the two specialties of the German cinema of the 1920s.

In 1926, back in England, after finishing several films, Hitchcock made *The Lodger*, his most successful work of the silent period, "the first Hitchcock movie," he admitted. In this thriller about Jack the Ripper there was almost everything that would become Hitchcock trademark: suspense and expressive visual language with a minimum of inner titles (there were just some eighty inner titles instead of approximately two hundred for an average film of this length). In *The Lodger* was his first very short personal appearance—the famous *Hitchcock cameo*—in the newsroom and in a crowd. In films that followed, he would emerge carrying a cello, walking with his two white terriers, sitting on a bus, tossing some litter, in a crowd wearing a bowler hat, and in a wheelchair.

In 1926 there was another significant event in Hitchcock's life—he married Alma Reville, his production assistant. Some fifty years later, in 1979, when he received the American Film Institute's Life Achievement Award, he dedicated it to Alma—in his words a film editor, a scriptwriter, the mother of his daughter, and a talented cook. He praised her encouragement and her constant collaboration. As a film critic said, the *Hitchcock touch* had four hands, and two were Alma's.[6] They spent their whole life together (she died two years after him), were completely devoted to each other as a couple, and were happy parents to their only child, Patricia.

With the thriller *Blackmail* (1929), Britain's first synchronous sound feature, he entered the sound era.

In the 1930s Hitchcock made his first classic—*The Man Who Knew Too Much* (1934), based on the director's favorite premise that *an innocent bystander finds himself in a bizarre situation*. With this film he established himself as the master of suspense. According to him, suspense was the most powerful means of holding viewers' attention and making them shiver. Several of his films of the 1930s also became classics: *The Thirty-Nine Steps* (1935), *Sabotage* (1936), and *The Lady Vanishes* (1938), for which Hitchcock won the New York Critics Award for best director.

He had always admired American movies, considering them technically superior to European films. So it was not a surprise when, in 1939, he accepted David Selznick's offer to work in Hollywood and made California his home. He would say that Britain served to perfect his techniques and refine his cinematic instinct, but in America he acquired new offbeat ideas.

In Hollywood he was assigned to direct a film about the *Titanic*, but the project was canceled. Instead Hitchcock made *Rebecca*[7] (1940), a gothic melodrama typical neither of his previous nor of his future works. It was not among his favorites: it had a very romantic theme and was "a completely British picture: the story, the actors, and the director were all English."[8]

Hitchcock bought a house and sent his daughter, Patricia, to an American school. He was making American movies, and with the years he even lost his accent (Alma never did), although still he remained forever an Englishman abroad. He had a typically British sense of humor mixed with macabre, he loved more to conceal than to reveal things about himself, he was more reserved than the Hollywood crowd, and he didn't have much contact with them. He was not interested in anything beyond his work and his family. The Hollywood turmoil—the investigations of un-American activities and Communist influences, purges, blackmail listings—all passed by him.

During the 1940s Hitchcock was fully accepted and loved by American audiences. His films *Suspicion* (1941), *Shadow of a Doubt* (1943), and *Spellbound* (1945) were exciting cinematic events. But his most outstanding work of this decade was *Notorious* (1946), "the very quintessence of Hitchcock," as Truffaut characterized it. "*Notorious* is the first Hitchcock film in which every shot is not only meaningful but beautiful, as beautiful as are Ingrid Bergman and Cary Grant. For the first time in [his] work two great romantic stars are matched against each other, and their romance is wedded to a richly expressive, romantic visual style. [Here] the camera's lush romanticism for the first time is equal and constant partner to [*Notorious*'] wit, elegance, and theatricality."[9] (In *Rope* [1948], one of the film's characters remarks that Cary Grant "was thrilling in that new thing with Ingrid Bergman.")

The 1950s were Hitchcock's even more fruitful period. In that decade alone, he made five of his greatest films: *Strangers on a Train* (1951), *Rear Window* (1954), *Vertigo* (1958), *North by Northwest* (1959), and *Psycho* (1960), not to mention the merely successful *Dial M for Murder* (1954), *The Trouble with Harry* (1955), and the remake of *The Man Who Knew Too Much* (1956).

He took his success very naturally (for many years now he had been a star), without false modesty, rather with laughter. He would say that some movies are slices of life, but his are slices of cake. He openly favored the visual over the verbal; he never looked through the camera during the shooting. All the shots had been planned in advance and prepared by little drawings.[10] "When we tell a story in cinema," he stated, "we should resort to dialogue [the words] only when it's impossible to do otherwise."[11] Structuring the plot, describing it in the script and visualizing it in detail, was for him the most meaningful part of creating his film. The rest, as he said, was just a bore.

In the 1950s, French New Wave critics discovered the unique qualities of Hitchcock's one-style, one-man pictures, calling him the *auteur* and juxtaposing him to Hollywood *filmmakers*.[12] "Hitchcock expresses such a complete control over all elements of his films and imprints his personal concepts at each step of the way. [He] has a distinctive style of his own. . . . [His] screen signature can be identified as soon as the picture begins," wrote Francoise Truffaut, his passionate proponent, who in 1962 conducted a fifty-hour-long interview with Hitchcock.[13]

From 1955 to 1963 Hitchcock produced and hosted a television series called *Alfred Hitchcock Presents* with 365 segments of short mystery thrillers, 20 of which he himself directed. From 1963 to 1965 he produced and directed another program for television, *The Alfred Hitchcock Hour,* which included three hour-long thrillers. Television made Hitchcock a household name in the United States, an identifiable public figure, and brought him a lot of money. Work on television also pushed him to make his film production less time consuming. So, *Psycho* (1960) was shot as quickly as a television show.

Through the last fifteen years of his life, Hitchcock's films were much less impressive, although the director never lost his popularity, neither then nor even today. In his last film, *The Family Plot* (1976), in his cameo appearance, we see his silhouette through a translucent door with the word *death* superimposed on it (this was the office of birth and death registration).

Hitchcock died at the age of eighty, in his house in Los Angeles, in his sleep. According to his wish, he was cremated.

A few months before he died he was knighted by Queen Elizabeth and became Sir Alfred.

*Notorious'* screenwriter, Ben Hecht (1893–1964) started his career at seventeen as a newspaper reporter in Chicago, and in a few years he became a leading columnist on the *Chicago Tribune* and an independent writer. He wrote articles, books (fiction and nonfiction), and plays. For a couple of years he even published the *Chicago Literary Times,* but without any commercial success. In 1925 he moved to New York without money but with a strong conviction to succeed. In less than a year he received a wire from Hollywood from his Chicago friend, a journalist and writer, Herman Mankiewicz,[14] asking if Hecht would accept three hundred dollars per week to work for Paramount Pictures and saying that this money was peanuts—millions were to be earned out there.

For the nearly forty years of his Hollywood career, Hecht wrote scripts for some seventy films (by himself and in collaboration). He was lavishly rewarded but always put down by the well-known Hollywood rule that screenwriters have everything but power. Hecht also directed and coproduced several films, but he always felt that his real call was writing novels: he was the author of more than thirty published books. Nevertheless, his legacy, to a large extent, has been in screenwriting, in his remarkably inventive and highly professional contributions to the films of such directors as Ernst Lubitsch (1892–1948), Josef von Sternberg (1894–1969), Howard Hawks (1896–1977), William Wyler (1902–1981), and Otto Preminger (1905–1986), among many others. His script coauthorship with "the gentlemanly . . . portly Hitchcock beaming amid his nightmares"[15] on *Spellbound* (1945) and especially *Notorious* was among the highlights of his writing career.

From his first film, Hitchcock realized that dramatic suspense is something to which people relate easily: the thrill, the anticipation of the worst, and the feverish desire for the best. More than any other filmmaker, Hitchcock contributed to the understanding of how cinematic suspense works. He knew how to perplex, how to thwart his viewers' expectations and, at the same time, feed them new premonitions and new surprises, how to completely sweep people up with his suspenseful curves. He gave his definition of suspense, making a careful distinction between *suspense* and *surprise*:

> We are now having a very innocent little chat. Let us suppose that there is a bomb underneath this table between us. Nothing happens, and then all of a sudden, Boom! There is an explosion. The public is *surprised,* but prior to this surprise, it has been an absolutely ordinary scene, of no special consequence. Now, let us take a *suspense* situation. The bomb is underneath the table and the public *knows* it, probably because they have seen the anarchist place it there. The public is *aware* that the bomb is going to explode at one o'clock and there is a clock in the decor. The public can see that it is a quarter to one. In these conditions this same innocuous conversation becomes fascinating because the public is participating in the scene. The audience is longing to warn the characters on the screen, "you shouldn't be talking about such trivial matters. There's a bomb beneath you and it's about to explode."[16]

In the first case the public is given fifteen seconds of *surprise* at the moment of the explosion. In the second case they are provided with fifteen minutes of *suspense*.

In 1943 David Selznick, a powerful Hollywood producer, gave Hitchcock an issue of *The Saturday Evening Post* with an article about a young actress who fell in love with a high-society New Yorker. He wanted to marry her, but she had a secret in her past: she was asked by the government counterspy service to become a lover of a foreign agent to get very important military information. Now she worried that her boyfriend and especially his mother would learn about her spy affair. Unexpectedly, when the mother was told about it, she said she had always hoped her son would find the right girl, but she never expected him to marry a girl as fine as this.

Hitchcock and Ben Hecht decided to take only one thing from the article: *a girl is to sleep with a spy in order to get some information.*

In three weeks they completed the first draft of the film treatment.[17] The title, *Notorious,* was found already at that point. "Our original intention had been to bring into the story government officials and police agents. They discover groups of German refugees training in secret camps in South America with the aim of setting up a new Nazi army. But we couldn't figure out, what they were going to do with the army once it was organized."[18]

So, they dropped the army idea and focused instead on the neo-Nazi organization in Brazil and on its very active agent, Alex Sebastian, and his mother (although at that point, Madame Sebastian wasn't as vicious as the one in the film).

In this treatment an American intelligence officer, Walt Boone, and his civilian recruit, Alicia Wyman, are trying to penetrate the Nazi organization. Alicia, in her recent past a playgirl, now is in love with Walt, but she has to marry Alex Sebastian. Soon after their wedding, Alex discovers that she is a spy and, with the help of his mother, starts putting arsenic in her milk to poison her. Walt rescues Alicia. She returns to the United States, to the home of Walt's parents to await Walt's return from the war. So, Alex Sebastian and his mother had been invented as well as the name Alicia, the love between her and Walt, and the marriage to Sebastian.

Hecht and Hitchcock met several days a week from nine in the morning until six at night, Hecht either paced or lay on the floor; Hitchcock would sit primly on a straight-back chair, his hands clasped across his midriff, his round button eyes gleaming. Hecht dealt in narrative structure and development, Hitchcock in visual pyrotechnics. During the days between conferences, Hecht would type out the story-to-date, then return to Hitchcock for reconsiderations, alterations, revisions.[19]

The next treatment starts with Alicia Sebastian, an actress, singing in a bar in Germany. She meets, unexpectedly, her former FBI boss, Prescott, who came to this bar. They recall what happened years ago. The narration unfolds in a flashback: In Brazil, Alicia, an American daughter of a well-to-do father, falls in love with Wallace, an intelligence officer. She learns about her father's participation in a neo-Nazi group. Confused and disturbed, Alicia becomes an FBI recruit (notice—she herself does it). Because of her father, she is ashamed to see Wallace and, without telling him a word, marries Alex Sebastian, a high-ranking Nazi and her father's friend. Sometime later, Alex realizes that his wife Alicia is a spy and starts to poison her. Wallace unexpectedly meets the Sebastians at an outdoor restaurant in the mountains, provoking Alex into a fight, and they both fall against a railing and die. Back in the bar, Alicia finishes her story. Prescott bids farewell and leaves the bar. Alicia rises to sing another song.

This treatment wasn't satisfying either, but some important elements of the future film were found here: the father who was a spy and Sebastian's friend and Alicia's marriage as a patriotic sacrifice.

The next treatment eliminates the bar-frame story and the deaths of Sebastian and Wallace. It starts, as the film does, with the sentencing of the traitor Huberman, Alicia's father. Also, as in the film, there is a party at Alicia's, with Wallace among the guests, and there is the same speeding-car episode. Wallace convinces Alicia to work for the FBI. Alicia and Wallace are in love with each other, but Alicia has to marry Alex Sebastian, her father's friend, a sentimental Nazi agent who raises orchids in his hothouse. Alex's strong-willed mother, when she learns that Alicia is an FBI agent, starts poisoning her. Wallace rescues Alicia, but at the last minute she dies in his arms.

The small changes in the next treatment include the new name for the FBI agent—Devlin. He rescues Alicia with more difficulties and even with gunfire; in the last scene, the couple Alicia and Devlin are before a judge, exchanging marriage vows.

Neither the authors nor the producer was satisfied with this treatment either. At that point Hitchcock introduced the so-called

*MacGuffin*—the director's invented term for a secret whose discovery is essential for the story. It can be a letter, a suitcase with documents that someone needs to get, a stolen diamond ring, or a shady past that might be discovered. Hitchcock recalled: "I introduced the MacGuffin—samples of uranium concealed in some wine bottles. The producer said, what in the name of goodness is that? I said, this is uranium, it's the thing they're going to make an *atom* bomb with. And he asked, what *atom* bomb? This, you must remember, was before Hiroshima."[20]

In April 1945, four months before Hiroshima, Hitchcock and Hecht brought uranium and atomic warfare to *Notorious*. At that time the *Herald Tribune* wrote about the film Hitchcock was working on and its unfamiliar term *atomic bomb*. Somewhere it was called *automatic bomb*. Hitchcock recalled: "Ben Hecht and I went over to the California Institute of Technology to meet Dr. Millikan, at that time one of the leading scientists in America. We were shown into his office. The first question we asked him was: 'Dr. Millikan, how large would an *atom* bomb be? He looked at us and said, 'you want to have yourselves arrested and have me arrested as well?' "[21]

Hitchcock liked to tell this story and usually would add, probably for a dramatic effect, that later he learned that after his uranium research, an FBI agent followed him for several months.

Selznick did not like the uranium *MacGuffin*. He lost interest in the project and sold the production package—the director, the screenwriter, the stars Ingrid Bergman, Cary Grant, and Claude Rains—to RKO.

*Notorious* starts with a sign on the screen: *"Miami, Florida, 2:30 pm, April 24, 1946,"* which locates the action in precise time and place and gives a feeling of authenticity to what is going to happen, although Hitchcock was never inclined to be too realistic. He used to say that his films presented life, but cleansed from its stains of boredom.

*1. Reporters with cameras and lights are waiting at the closed doors in the courthouse: a judge sentences a Nazi agent, John Huberman, to twenty years in prison for treason against the United States. The door opens; his daughter, Alicia, appears. She is young, attractive, stylish. Her face is expressionless; she is silent. The reporters besiege her.*

Flashlights explode over Alicia. The camera focuses on her face in a close-up. Hitchcock believed that the size of the image had power over the viewer's emotions, especially if the audience identifies with that image.

2. *At a small gathering in Alicia's Miami Beach bungalow, most of the guests are drunk, as is the hostess. The commodore, an older gentleman, keeps reminding Alicia of a cruise they are to take the next day. But she is more interested in a new guest, Devlin. She sends the rest of her guests away.*

For most of the scene we don't see Devlin's face, only the back of his head and shoulders—an unusual close-up. The director prolongs our wondering who this man is, showing his face only at the end of the scene. This is a typical example of Hitchcock's control over audience perception, his love of intriguing, even teasing, the viewer.

3. *Alicia, quite drunk, suggests a late-night drive with Devlin. It is windy and he ties his scarf around her bare waist.*

The scarf is an important detail in the curve of the Alicia-Devlin relationship (see scene 42).

4. *Alicia drives recklessly, increasing her speed to frighten her passenger. His casual mood is unchanged. The police pull the car over. Devlin hands the cop his identification. "Sorry, but you didn't speak up," the policeman apologizes before saluting and leaving. Alicia is furious. She has figured out that Devlin is an agent and orders him out of her car. He clips her in the jaw, knocking her unconscious, and takes over the wheel.*

The policeman's remark sounds prophetic: *not speaking up* is Devlin's characteristic trait and something that almost ruins his relationship with Alicia.

*The scene fades out, goes to black; a short pause before the next scene fades in.*

5. *The next morning, Alicia wakes up in her bed, severely hung over and still in the clothes she was wearing the night before. Devlin has already made a remedy for her, a glass of juice, and urges her to sip it. Close-up on the glass—an emphasis on it* [see scenes 40 and 43 where Sebastian urges Alicia to drink coffee with poison]. *Later we see Devlin through Alicia's hungover gaze, sharply inclined to one side; then he moves like the hand of a clock almost the entire circle and stops in a straight position.*

At work here is the *subjective camera*—the audience sees the actions through Alicia's eyes and not through an objective, impersonal point of view.

*Alicia is sobering up. She is still furious at Devlin for deceiving her. He explains that he has been assigned to recruit her for intelligence work, to "smoke out" Nazis hiding in Brazil. Her father's past will make it easy for her to infiltrate this group. But she claims to have no interest in the work whatsoever. "I don't go for patriotism . . . or patriots."[22] Devlin refutes this by playing back a recorded conversation between Alicia and her father, who is trying to persuade her to work for the Nazis. But she tells him that she hates him and what he stands for and that she loves America and would never do anything against it.*

*The screen fades to black.*

6. *On a plane over Rio de Janeiro, Devlin tells Alicia that he has just received news that her father committed suicide. She feels sorry. However, now, she says, she no longer has to hate him.*

From the very beginning of the film Alicia is its center. This is *her* story. Only fifteen minutes of the screening time have passed, but we already know so much about her, and the title of the film is hers. She is the notorious woman. At the same time, we know next to nothing about Devlin and never will learn more.

*From the plane, Rio is seen in a quick shot—far away, immense, a metaphor for the excitement of the unknown. A few views of the city follow each other through dissolves.*

7. *In Rio, Alicia and Devlin are waiting for their assignment. They are sitting in a sidewalk café. Alicia has not been drinking for eight days, nor has she "met any new boyfriends." Devlin does not give her much credit for these accomplishments. She can sense he is attracted to her, yet he is afraid of falling in love with her. "Why won't you believe in me, Dev?" she asks.*

8. *Paul Prescott, Devlin's boss, and several American officials are discussing Alicia's mission. Prescott says that she is perfect for the job that they have planned for her because "she knows how to make friends with gentlemen." Furthermore, Alex Sebastian, one of the men they are after, was a good friend of her father's and was once infatuated with her. Devlin, someone mentions, knows nothing about Alicia's assignment.*

In some respect, Alicia is condemned by the CIA just as Emil Hupka was by the Nazis (scene 19) and Alex Sebastian will be at the end of the movie (scene 48).

*9. Devlin and Alicia have fallen in love. In Alicia's apartment they exchange what has been called the "longest kiss in screen history." It is interrupted by Prescott's telephone call. Devlin must go to the office but promises to come back soon and bring a bottle of wine, and they will have their first dinner together.*

It has been said that Hitchcock would involve the viewer in a relationship of his characters to such an extent that it could be called a *ménage à trois.*

*10. In Prescott's office, Devlin is confronted with a plan that he could never have anticipated. He doesn't want to believe that Alicia will agree to it and tries to protect her. Prescott's aide facetiously suggests that Devlin has fallen in love with Alicia. Prescott argues that Devlin is "not the sort to associate with a person of Miss Huberman's reputation." They tell Devlin that Sebastian was once in love with Alicia. Devlin leaves, forgetting the bottle of wine on a desk.*

The camera observes the bottle in a close-up. It is one of the film's motifs—along with the keys, the cup of coffee, the doors, and the scarf.

New questions lure the audience deeper into the story. Will Devlin deliver this message to Alicia? If so, will she accept the assignment? What does this mean for their romance, which just a short time ago seemed so perfect? The dramatic tension of the plot starts to rise.

*11. A troubled Devlin returns to Alicia. He tells her that she is to infiltrate Sebastian's life and, through him, gain access to the rest of his Nazi circle. She is quite hurt that Devlin did not protest. "Down the drain with Alicia . . . I suppose you knew about the pretty little job all the time," she says and pours herself a drink.*

"The significance of Alicia's act of pouring the drink is that it indicates her resignation to her degrading role."[23]

*12. The next morning in a taxi, Devlin tells Alicia that she has to remember that they met on the plane to Rio and that he is a public relations man for Pan Am.*

*13. Alicia and Devlin are riding horses along a path when they see Alex Sebastian and a companion, also riding. At first, Sebastian does not notice Alicia, so Devlin sneaks a kick at her horse, sending it off wildly. Sebastian sets off to the rescue, and when he stops the horse, he is quite taken with the rider.*

Alicia and the speeding horse bring to mind the scene with Alicia in the speeding car with Devlin.

*14. Devlin is lonesome and worried in the café, where he and Alicia had sat earlier.*

This is a very short one-shot scene, five seconds only.

*15. In a restaurant with Sebastian, Alicia claims that she idolized her father and that Devlin is just someone who has been "pestering" her. "It's off, but I feel at home with you," Alicia says. Sebastian is very touched and invites her to a party at his house.*

Sebastian is openly in love with her, something she wanted Devlin to be; she wanted him to radiate it. Sebastian even asks what they shall have for their "first dinner together," which reminds Alicia that her first dinner with Devlin never took place.

*16. At his office, Prescott tells Alicia to memorize the names of all the men that she will meet at the party. "Just use your eyes and ears," he instructs her.*

*17. Alicia is at the door of the Sebastian mansion, not knowing what to expect. The butler, Joseph, lets her in. The splendor of the space frightens and intrigues her. Madame Sebastian, Alex's severe-looking mother, glides down the grand marble staircase to meet Alicia. She tries to intimidate her by asking why the daughter did not testify at her father's trial. Alicia quickly replies that her father asked her not to do it, for her own safety.*

Madame Sebastian's gliding down the stairs is shown in a long duration shot to get a deeper response from the viewers when they see "the witch of the castle [converge] upon the victim."[24]

Another point to notice—the staircase. Several times in the film it will be a setting for various dramatic situations. This time is the first.

*18. Sebastian introduces Alicia to the guests, four German men (including Dr. Anderson, the guest of honor) and a Brazilian couple.*

We see all of the guests through Alicia's eyes, in close-ups of the *subjective camera*. The camera stays just a few seconds longer over each of them to reveal something unpleasant and frightening in their faces.

*During the dinner, Emil Hupka, one of the Nazis, becomes exceedingly alarmed when he notices the bottle of wine to be served. Sebastian calms him down.*

The camera stops in a close-up on the bottles. Now the bottle motif appears in a different context.

*19. After dinner, all of the men, except Hupka (he is waiting at the closed door), discuss the seriousness of his blunder. No one pays attention to Hupka's apology, and it is clear that he is going to be executed by his accomplices. One of them will "escort" him home.*

This scene is important not only by itself but also as an insight into what will happen later, when Alex Sebastian will face, as Hupka does, his heartless accomplices.

*20. The next day at the racetrack, Madame Sebastian observes, "Miss Huberman has been gone a long time." Sebastian wishes that his mother would be more cordial to his girlfriend. Meanwhile, Alicia and Devlin are trackside, pretending to have just bumped into one another. She tells him about Hupka's nervousness over the wine bottle. She is angry at Devlin for pushing her into the situation. He reminds her that she accepted the job on her own. He feels like a fool for ever having believed that Alicia could change her routine. Alicia is crying behind her binoculars. Sebastian's arrival breaks the conversation. Devlin leaves. Sebastian is jealous, but Alicia claims that she detests Devlin. Sebastian asks if she would care to prove that his rival means nothing to her.*

*21. In Prescott's office, the intelligence men are conferring. One of them makes a slur against Alicia, arousing Devlin's anger. Alicia arrives in a state of confusion about what to do: Sebastian has asked her to marry him. Prescott considers it a wonderfully useful opportunity; Devlin keeps silent.*

Knowing the nature of Alicia's assignment, one expects to see her efforts to get into Alex Sebastian's house, to see scenes of his seduction, and so on. Instead, there is an unexpected plot turn—a *surprise* and a dramatic paradox—Alex Sebastian asks Alicia to marry him. Surprise dismisses previously held anticipations and gives the action new lift. This is what Hitchcock called the "rising curve of the story," an expression of the director's love for the unexpected and disconcerting. It always was very important for Hitchcock that the public would not be able to anticipate what was going to happen.

Notice how sparse the dialogue is here and how revealing the facial expressions are.

*22. At the Sebastian estate, Alex firmly announces his and Alicia's wedding date to his mother, much to her chagrin.*

Notice that Alex is presented not as an entirely negative character. He is sincere in his feelings—there is no disparity between the apparent and the real; he doesn't have the evil air that his mother and his associates do. He genuinely loves Alicia. Besides, it is *he* who is betrayed.

*23. Alicia and Sebastian return, after the honeymoon, to the mansion. The butler, Joseph, opens the door. Madame Sebastian is not there to welcome them. The couple ascends the elegant stairs.*

We have seen neither the wedding nor the honeymoon. Here Hitchcock uses the so-called *elliptic* structure, when a large piece of action is omitted without breaking the straight development of the plot.

*24. Alicia gets familiar with the Sebastian household and asks Joseph for the keys to some of the locked closets. He informs her that Madame Sebastian keeps them all. Alicia coaxes Alex to get the keys from his mother, and he does, except the one for the wine cellar, which only he himself carries. She cannot open the wine cellar door, and the camera stays, in a close-up, at the keyhole, with the meaningful name* Unica.

The motif of the key starts at this point before we even see the key. Later Alicia learns that she must get the key to the well-guarded wine cellar.

*25. Alicia meets Devlin in the park. They decide that there must be something of great importance in the wine cellar. Devlin tells her to persuade her husband to throw a party so that he can get into the house to inspect the wine cellar himself.*

*26. Before the party, in the dressing room, Alicia sees Alex's keys on the chest. The sound of a shower comes from the half-open door of the bath—he is there.*

Alicia is looking at the keys. Here the suspense starts. The close-up on Alicia's face makes her emotions totally open to us and makes our closeness to her more intimate. From this moment, every action, every line of dialogue serves *to delay* the relief of tension.

*Alicia's fingers sort the keys and find the needed one, and she begins to detach it. Over this we suddenly hear Sebastian's raised voice.*

The fact that Sebastian might at any moment discover what she is up to is a threat to her and tension in progress for us. Hitchcock makes us Alicia's accomplices.

*Now Alicia has the key in her possession. She looks at it in her palm. Sebastian is talking about his surprise that Devlin is coming to the party.*

Stretching out the dangerous moment has made the scene particularly suspenseful.

*While Alicia is wondering where to hide the key, Sebastian's voice tells her cheerfully that he is coming* [the danger is reinforced], *and he asks Alicia not to "get impatient" waiting for him.*

In light of what is happening, the irony of this phrase only underlines the gravity of the situation. We are glad that Sebastian does not realize what is going on. The question is what will happen if and when he discovers it.

*The camera pans to Sebastian in the bedroom. Now the camera itself stretches out the time, and there is another delay: Sebastian talks at length about his love for Alicia and about his trust in her.*

Here is yet another twist to make the situation more tense and to remind Alicia and the audience that the more he loves her and trusts her, the stronger will be his reaction when he discovers the truth.

*Sebastian is taking her clenched hands in his, opens one hand to kiss it, but before he can open the other, which contains the key, Alicia slips her arms around his neck. . . . We see Alicia's right hand lower itself behind his back. She opens it and drops the key onto the soft carpet.*

The audience breathes a sigh of relief, but the director takes full advantage of the challenge he put to Alicia. Even after she has dropped the key from her hand, she still must get it out of Alex's range of vision, and she does.

*In her embrace, Alicia slowly turns Sebastian away as though in a kind of ecstatic sway. . . . Her feet approach the key. She kicks it just under the bureau. Close-up on the key, resting almost out of sight underneath the bureau.*

The camera takes time to emphasize this shot. The key becomes almost a character in the film. The danger has passed for the moment. The expectation that Sebastian will be deceived is unreasonable, but Hitchcock was convinced that film should be stronger than reason.

*27. The party is a crowded, yet elegant affair—distinguished guests, music, loud happy chatter.*

Here comes the famous crane shot—an uninterrupted long take—which starts at the top of the stairs, taking in the view of the whole party scene, moves down from a height, and closes in at the bottom of the stairs in a close-up on Alicia's hand hiding the key. Hitchcock loved it when the camera took over to tell the story and sustained the tension throughout.

*Alicia's hand and handkerchief are shown in a close-up. She is anxious—Devlin is not among the guests. When he does arrive, she promptly slips the key into his hand.*

It seems that all the grandeur of the reception becomes the background for the small key.

Among the guests is Hitchcock himself—he appears in his cameo shot taking a goblet of champagne from a tray.

As Hitchcock stated quite clearly in his example of the bomb underneath the table, suspense and time are interrelated, and suspense nearly always concentrates on a race against time. Whenever the audience is aware of a clock ticking, the sense of danger is increased and the suspense is therefore intensified.

*Holding the key, Devlin waits for Alicia to go to the wine cellar. But she, fearful of arousing suspicion, cannot leave Alex and the guests too suddenly.*

*Alicia is sipping some champagne. She glances down behind the buffet. There is a group of eight bottles of unopened champagne.*

The ticking need not necessarily come from a clock. In the following episode, the sense of time running out is not only from the butler, who is about to go down to the wine cellar, but also from the bottles themselves, whose number is ever diminishing. A new wave of suspense takes the tension to a higher pitch.

*28. Joseph tells Alicia that he will need more champagne soon.*
The "clock" has been set.

*On his way to the cellar, Devlin stops at the bar. He sees that there are now only four bottles of champagne. The butler takes another one, leaving only three.*

The clock is ticking and the rising curve of the story becomes trickier.

*Alicia is with Sebastian and a group of guests. A servant arrives with a tray of drinks.*

The glasses are a persistent reminder of the time running away. Alicia's gaze is directed to the laden tray with hands exchanging empty glasses for full ones.

Now the camera itself emphasizes that the wine is running out. Now glasses are a so-called *cataphor*[25]—something that warns that some event or action can occur, in this case, when Alicia and Devlin are at risk, that they might be caught.

*29. After slipping away from Alex, Alicia stands guard while Devlin inspects the wine cellar.*

*30. In parallel action, Joseph, serving at the buffet, glances down at the bottles and counts out what is left.*

*31. Devlin accidentally upsets one of the many bottles on the shelf. It topples to the floor and to great surprise spills a metal ore instead of wine. Alicia joins Devlin. He scoops some of the ore into his pocket and replaces the broken bottle with another one, almost identical but with a different date on it, which Sebastian will notice very soon.*

The public always likes to be one jump ahead of the story, Hitchcock would say. They like to feel they know what is coming next, but the director should keep the viewer really far from what's going to happen. At the same time he often stated that pure suspense is "where the audience knows what the characters do not."

*"In the medium shot, Devlin is finishing off the bottle. The camera moves in until only the neck of the bottle fills the screen. He is putting on the tinfoil cap, squeezing it tightly between his fingers."*

Notice how detailed and focused the description of the action was in this episode, not only telling about the action but also predetermining the stretching of the time.

*32. While Devlin and Alicia are still in the cellar, Sebastian and Joseph are nearing it.*

The action moves closer to the "bomb explosion." In Hitchcockian suspense, as we know, the audience is provided information that the characters of the film do not have: the audience knows that Joseph and his master have started for the cellar; Alicia and Devlin do not. With bated breath the viewers try to figure out at which moment Alex and Joseph will reach the cellar.

*33. With a grunt of satisfaction Devlin puts the bottle on the shelf among the others. The camera pulls back as Devlin steps down and with his handkerchief gives a few final swishes to the floor. The camera pans to the door over Alicia and Devlin.*

The suspense surrounding the wine cellar is over. But the audience's tension is relieved only for a moment.

*34. As Alicia and Devlin turn into the main corridor, they hear footsteps. Alicia, as does the audience, sees Sebastian and Joseph coming down. She hurries Devlin through the glass door. Sebastian sees them. He sends Joseph away so that he will not be a witness to this embarrassing scene.*

Notice how unpredictable the action is in the following episode.

*Devlin and Alicia are outside a glass door as they see Sebastian and the butler coming downstairs to the cellar. Devlin tells Alicia that he is going to kiss her so that Sebastian will think that this is a love scene. He embraces her tenderly and they kiss. "Slowly, the kiss which has started merely as a trick to fool Sebastian, turns into the real thing for both of them." Devlin whispers to Alicia to push him away and act as if they've been caught.*

The thrill of the wine cellar scene—the emotions that we have gone through with this couple—has made the viewers even more devoted accomplices to Alicia and to Devlin too. Now, being closer to them, viewers are more prepared to empathize with their situation: Sebastian, their mutual adversary and an enemy of their country, has marital rights to Alicia; she and Devlin have to tolerate his sarcasm and his jealousy; she has to explain herself to Sebastian; and what's more, Devlin must tell him something that is necessary at the moment but, at the same time, is paradoxically a very personal, painful truth—he loves Alicia.

*Sebastian says that he is sorry to intrude on this scene. Alicia asks him to discuss everything later, without Devlin, who, she says, is hopelessly drunk. "You love him," Sebastian says. "No, absolutely not." She tells Devlin to go.*

*Before leaving, Devlin tells Sebastian: "I knew her before you—loved her before you—but wasn't as lucky as you. Sorry, Alicia." He leaves. Sebastian hides his rage from her and sends her to the guests, and he also returns to the party.*

It would seem that things are calming down, that the danger has passed.

*35. Suddenly Sebastian remembers the champagne and summons Joseph to go to the wine cellar with him. At the cellar door, he puts his hand in his pocket, but does not find the needed key. He tells Joseph that champagne is not necessary—they have plenty of whiskey and wine. Joseph agrees. They leave.*

But the camera stays on the wine cellar door. There is no key to open it. This is a specific feature of Hitchcockian style—the camera itself not only tells the story but makes its remarks. And also, there's another variation on the door motif, something intriguing *behind* the door.

Although in *Notorious* the suspense is focused on the key and on the fake wine bottle that contains uranium, it is not these scenes that are the highest point of dramatic tension.

Hitchcock has emphasized many times that it is wrong to attach too much dramatic importance to the uranium in *Notorious*. This specific MacGuffin could be changed. It could be industrial diamonds instead or something else. He stated that *Notorious* was simply the story of a man in love with a girl who, in the course of her official duties, had to go to bed with someone else and even had to marry him. That's the story. The main conflict here is not between the neo-Nazis and the FBI. It is between *love and duty*.

*36. The last guests are leaving. Sebastian doesn't want to show to Alicia that he is enraged, but he realizes what happened to the key.*

Until this point, his suspicion has been that Alicia loved Devlin, never that she could be a spy.

*37. In the morning, Sebastian discovers the key on his chain.*

*38. Sebastian notices the disorder in the wine cellar, finds the pieces of broken glass, some grains of uranium, and stains around the drain. Now he fully realizes what is going on, and his jealous suspicion becomes irrelevant.*

*39. Sebastian wakes up his mother to tell her that he is married to an American agent, and that Devlin is her accomplice. Meanwhile, Alicia wakes up in the morning quite relieved, believing that Sebastian never noticed the key was missing.*

We, the viewers, know what Alicia doesn't. "You should let the audience, from time to time, 'play God'" was Hitchcock's opinion.

*Sebastian is certain that his associates will murder him (as they did Emil Hupka) if they discover the truth. His mother calms him: his Nazi compan-*

ions will never find out about Alicia, but he must let her mastermind his young wife's demise. She will be poisoned, but very slowly.

40. At lunch that afternoon, Alex gently persuades Alicia to drink her coffee.

41. In Prescott's office, Alicia is painfully sensitive to the light. Prescott informs her that the ore found in the wine bottle was uranium. Now her job is to find out where it comes from. He also tells her that he will be changing her contact: Devlin has requested a transfer to Spain. Prescott calls her "Mrs. Sebastian," showing unexpected indifference to her, even some cruelty.

42. Alicia meets Devlin in the park. He notices that she looks ill. She lies that it is a hangover. Rather bitterly, she returns a scarf that he gave her, says goodbye, and staggers off.

The scarf is a meaningful detail for the plot—it measures the beginning and the end (as both of them imagine) of their relationship.

At this point of the film all the main characters are insincere: Alicia lies about the hangover, Devlin doesn't tell her about Spain, Sebastian gives poisoned coffee and never has mentioned the key.

43. Madame Sebastian is pouring more coffee for Alicia—we see the poison cup in a close-up. Dr. Anderson takes notice of Alicia's physical deterioration. He suggests that she see a doctor and tells her that he is going to the Carioca Mountains and suggests that perhaps a trip there might help Alicia's condition. Alicia casually gets him to admit exactly where he is going in the Cariocas. Alex quickly interrupts before Dr. Anderson can divulge any more information. Dr. Anderson mistakenly reaches for Alicia's cup instead of his own, alarming the Sebastians, and Alicia suddenly realizes that the coffee is poisoned. She politely excuses herself and begins to make her way out of the room. Her vision is impaired [again, the subjective camera, as in scene 5]. She collapses in the hall. Dr. Anderson and the Sebastians carry her to her room against her feeble protests. Sebastian orders Joseph to have her phone disconnected.

44. Prescott and Devlin cannot figure out why Alicia has missed all of her meetings for five days. Devlin decides to pay a call on the Sebastians. Prescott finds it unnecessary.

45. Devlin arrives at the Sebastian estate when Alex is having a meeting with his associates. Joseph announces Devlin just as Dr. Anderson reports that he

*has been followed on several recent occasions. Sebastian is caught between the importance of Anderson's news and Devlin's arrival.*

*46. Devlin sneaks up the luxurious stairs to Alicia's bedroom and discovers her on the verge of death. "They are poisoning me—slowly," she whispers. "I thought you'd gone away to Spain." She sinks back, exhausted. Devlin props her up. "I had to see you," he says. "I love you." "Oh, Dev, if you'd only said it before!" The camera circles them.*

Once again, as in the beginning of the film, he saves her from intoxication—this time from a deadly one.

*47. Alicia cannot walk. She asks Devlin to go alone, hurry up, because all of them—all of Alex's Nazi associates—are in the house. Devlin carries Alicia downstairs.*

Again we see the magnificent rounded staircase of the mansion. Several times it served as the set for dramatically charged episodes, and every time the content and mood of the mise-en-scène was different: the dreadful Madame Sebastian descending the stairs to meet Alicia; Alicia and Alex Sebastian ascending the stairs after coming back from their honeymoon; the gliding of the camera itself downstairs to find the key in Alicia's hand; Sebastian slowly climbing the stairs while realizing that his wife is a spy; and now the final episode with Devlin carrying Alicia downstairs to rescue her from the Sebastians and, it seems, from everything that can harm or bother her.

*"You are never getting rid of me," Devlin says. "I'm going to crawl after you on my hands and knees for the rest of my life. And I'm beginning right now."*

Although the danger has by no means passed, this scene is the climax of *Notorious* in which, according to Hitchcock, a man is in love with a girl who, for her official duties, had to go to bed with another man. Now only the two of them matter; this is the *climax* of the film, and even if the Nazis were to kill them now, this romance would still have ended with the lovers united. In the conflict of love versus duty, love has been victorious.

*Sebastian is approaching them on the steps, wondering what is going on. "I'm taking her to a hospital to get the poison out of her." Devlin challenges Alex to tell his friends who Alicia is and promises to keep his "mouth shut. So will the department. Is it a deal—or do we start shooting?"*

If Alex's associates learn about Alicia's mission in his home, they will kill him. We wonder which force is stronger in him, the will to live or the desire to see Alicia and Devlin killed. His choice is unpredictable.

There is no clock ticking in this scene, although perhaps the business associates, who may at any moment burst upon the scene, are analogous to the ticking clock. There is no hidden bomb here; the audience knows no more than do the protagonists. In other words, there is no real suspense in the master's classic definition. But this scene is of such emotional intensity that it is difficult not to describe it as full suspense.

*Madame Sebastian appears from her room. She tells Alex to pretend to help Devlin to take Alicia downstairs and to make sure Alex's associates see it.*

Again an unexpected twist—Sebastian and his mother become partners with Alicia and Devlin. Sebastian's associates see him helping Devlin to support Alicia on the stairs—indeed, this act is his defeat; he gives in. Devlin and Alicia prevail as Sebastian's associates watch what is going on.

*48. Devlin carries Alicia to his car and leaves Alex Sebastian in the hands of his Nazi conspirators. "Alex, will you come in, please? We wish to talk with you," says one of them. Sebastian turns and walks back to his home. The camera dollies after him. He is condemned. The tall wooden door closes behind him.*

The film ends at this point. We don't see Sebastian's confrontation with his associates or his immediate execution. But we know that this will happen.[26] The imaginary scene of Sebastian's trial in a way balances the court scene at the beginning of the film when another Nazi, Alicia's father, was sentenced to prison. At that point the door of the courthouse opened (scene 1), and now a door is closed (scene 48). The *door* signifies the beginning and end of the film, like a theatrical curtain that would rise up and fall down.

Look at the scene diagram in Figure 4–1. The sign of *the door* is repeated several times. Sure, there are plenty of doors in the film, but the emphasis here is only on those that play an important role in the plot: scene 17—Alicia enters into the frightening unknown; scene 19— Emil Hupka waits at the door for his death sentence, as the premonition of what is coming for Sebastian (scene 48); scene 24—the locked door of the wine cellar increases the suspense of what is behind it;

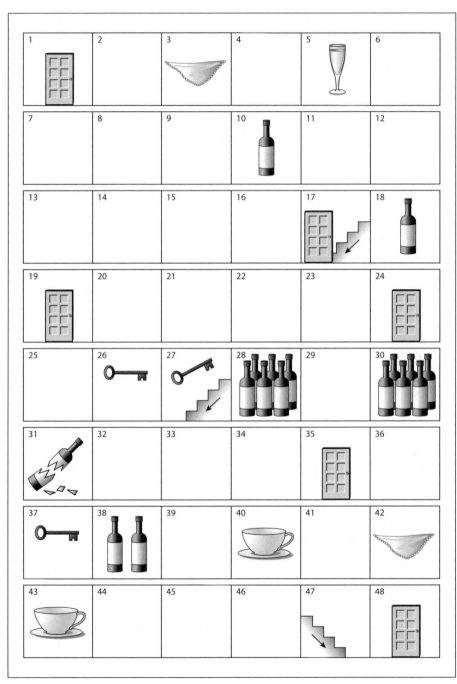

*Figure 4–1. Scene Diagram for* Notorious

scene 35—when Sebastian discovers that the wine cellar key is missing, the camera stays long on the door as if making a sarcastic statement or even teasing the deceived man. And certainly scene 1 when the door opens and the main character—Alicia—appears.

*The scarf* marks the beginning of Alicia and Devlin's closeness (scene 3) and what seems its end (scene 42).

*The glass* of juice and *cups of coffee* represent a contrast between Devlin's remedy (scene 5) and Sebastian's poison (scenes 40 and 43).

Hitchcock likes to present the same object in different light (the pun is unintentional). Consider the splendid marble *staircase* in the Sebastians' mansion, for instance. It looks uninviting when the vicious hostess descends it to meet Alicia (scene 17), but it appears festive when the camera glides down at the party (scene 27); it looks suspenseful when Devlin rushes up to Alicia's room to find her deadly ill (scene 46); and the staircase looks intensely dramatic when Devlin, with Alicia in his arms, comes down, being watched by the Nazis (scene 47).

You can see on the chart how the *wine bottle* motif develops: a bottle that Devlin forgets in the CIA office (scene 10)—the wine for dinner with Alicia, which never took place; a wine bottle with uranium, which causes Hupka's hysterical fit—it presumably leads to his execution (scene 18); the wine bottles at the grand party (scene 28), which represent time and suspense—the fewer of them that are left, the sooner Devlin will be discovered in the wine cellar; the bottle that falls and reveals uranium (scene 31); the missing uranium bottle, which makes it clear to Sebastian that the Nazis' secret is discovered (scene 38).

*The key* is the source of various reactions: fear when Alicia steals it from Sebastian's chain (scene 26); tension and satisfaction when she manages to pass the key to Devlin (scene 27); Sebastian's humiliation (scene 35) and the horrifying revelation that Alicia is a spy (scene 37).

From his youth, as a man, and later in his life, as the director, Hitchcock was a social outsider. He was indifferent to politics and to the elite world of his artistic contemporaries. His life was self-restricted to his work, his family, and his daily rituals, which he followed religiously. His schedule for work almost never changed; he always wore, at any season, even in the California summers, on the set and everywhere else, a dark business suit with white shirt and tie; he stayed at the same hotels, ate at the same restaurants, read only *The London Times*. In his life he exercised "perfect and total control, almost as if to make life his own creation. . . . [He loved] the triumph of artifice over accident, a kind of daily victory over chance."[27] He lamented even about nature's "lack of design." He did not like any changes in his daily schedule, just as he did not accept any improvisation in the process of shooting. According to Hitchcock, one creates a film *before* shooting: to create it while standing behind the camera is similar to writing music while standing in front of the orchestra, which is waiting to play it. He prepared everything. He never took a shot that was not preplanned. Even his editing was, in some way, done ahead of time; he called it "precutting the film inside the camera." He never shot a scene from a variety of angles—just from one angle for the shot he needed.

Hitchcock was witty, ironic, sometimes sarcastic. When a woman angrily complained to him that her daughter was so frightened by the shower scene in *Psycho* that she would no longer shower, he replied: "Then, madam, I suggest you have her dry-cleaned."

Humor and irony in his films could be expressed not only by film characters but, as we've seen, by the camera itself. In *Notorious* when the camera stayed for an extended time on the closed door of the wine cellar, it was a sarcastic remark about a frustrated, jealous husband.

Hitchcock was a born storyteller. He was genuinely puzzled when critics tried to present him as an explorer of metaphysical anxieties, Freudian complexes, or the Catholic doctrine of original sin. He was master of action. Philosophical meditation and intellectual discourses were not part of his universe. He would have been perplexed to hear some recent academic interpretation of his films and often irresponsible analysis of his own inner world. He would be in total disbelief, for instance, to read how cruel he was to Alicia, his favorite radiant heroine of *Notorious*.[28]

An artist, a showman, the master of cinematic form of expression, Hitchcock never pretended to do more than enchant and entertain. He did not divide films into commercial and artistic. His commercial films *were* artistic.

## Appendix

### *Alfred Hitchcock: "Film Production"*[29]

In a play, the action is moved forward in words. The film director moves his action forward with a camera—whether that action is set on a prairie or confined to a telephone booth. He always must be searching for some new way of making his statement, and above all he must make it with the greatest economy and in particular the greatest economy of cutting; that is to say, in the minimum of shots. Each shot must be as comprehensive a statement as possible, reserving cutting for dramatic purposes. The impact of the image is of the first importance in a medium that directs the concentration of the eye so that it cannot stray. In the theatre, the eye wanders, while the word commands. In the cinema, the audience is led wherever the director wishes. In this, the language of the camera resembles the language of the novel. Cinema audiences and readers of novels, while they remain in the theatre or continue to read, have no alternative but to accept what is set before them.

Then comes the question of how they are to see what they are shown. In a mood of relaxation? Not relaxed? It is how the director handles his images that create the state of mind, of emotion, in the audience. That is to say, the impact of the image is directly on emotions. Sometimes the director goes quietly along in a mood of simple, normal photography, and the eye is pleased as it follows the story. Then suddenly the director wishes to hit hard. Now the pictorial presentation changes. There is a bursting impact of images, like a change in orchestration. Indeed, orchestration is perhaps the best simile for a film, even to the parallel of recurrent themes and rhythms. And the director is, as it were, the conductor.

Perhaps the most significant and individually important thing about a director is his style. This style is evidenced by both his choice of subject and his manner of directing it. Important directors are known for their style. . . .

## Notes

1. Francois Truffaut, *Hitchcock*, New York: Simon and Schuster, 1966, p. 17.

2. Truffaut, p. 18.

3. David Freeman, *The Last Days of Alfred Hitchcock*, New York: Overlook, 1984, p. 23.

4. Friedrich Murnau (1888–1931), celebrated German filmmaker, made *Nosferatu—The Symphony of Horror* (1922) and *The Last Laugh* (1924), two classics of the world cinema.

5. Fritz Lang (1890–1976), outstanding German director, author of the famous *Metropolis* (1927), *M* (1931), and numerous other films made in Germany and the United States.

6. Pat Hitchcock O'Connell and Laurent Bouzereau, *The Woman Behind the Man*, New York: Berkeley, 2003, p. 1.

7. That film won the Oscar for best picture in 1940, but for the producer, David Selznick, not the director.

8. Truffaut, p. 92.

9. William Rothman, *Hitchcock, The Murderous Gaze*, Cambridge: Harvard University Press, 1982, p. 24.

10. Hitchcock executed his drawings remarkably fast.

11. Truffaut, p. 335.

12. Directors who don't have distinguished cinematic style are called metters-en-scène.

13. The largest part of the interview was published in Truffaut's *Hitchcock* (1966).

14. Herman Mankiewicz (1897–1953) came to Hollywood in 1926 and soon became a celebrated writer and producer. The author of *Citizen Kane's* screenplay, he shared the Academy Award for the film with Orson Welles.

15. Ben Hecht, *The Child of the Century*, New York: Simon and Schuster, 1954, pp. 396, 482.

16. Truffaut, p. 52.

17. A film treatment is a summarized description of a film plot written in the present tense.

18. Truffaut, p. 120.

19. Leonard Leff, *Hitchcock and Selznick: The Rich and Strange Collaboration of Alfred Hitchcock with David O. Selznick*, New York: Weidenfield and Nicolson, 1988, p. 179.

20. Truffaut, p. 121.

21. Truffaut, p. 121.

22. All quotes are from Ben Hecht and Alfred Hitchcock, *Notorious* (script), Los Angeles: Script City, 1969.

23. William Rothman, "Alfred Hitchcock's *Notorious*," *Georgia Review*, 1975 (Winter), p. 897.

24. Albert La Valley, ed., *Focus on Hitchcock*, Englewood Cliffs, NJ: Prentice Hall, 1972, p. 12.

25. Read about the *cataphor* in Deborah Knight and George McKnight, "Suspense and Its Master," in *Alfred Hitchcock Centenary Essays*, eds. Richard Allen and S. Ishii Gonzales, London: British Film Institute, 1999, p. 108.

26. In *Notorious*' script, a finale was added: In a government office, two secretaries are working on Alicia's file. It reports that her mission was accomplished successfully. One of the secretaries changes the last name on the file from Sebastian to Devlin.

27. Richard Allen and S. Ishii Gonzales, eds., *Alfred Hitchcock Centenary Essays,* London: British Film Institute, 1999, p. 5.

28. See Tania Modleski, *The Women Who Knew Too Much: Hitchcock and Feminist Theory, 2d ed.,*.New York: Routledge, 2005.

29. Sidney Gottlieb, ed., *Hitchcock on Hitchcock*, Berkeley: University of California Press, 1997, pp. 216–218.

# IT'S A WONDERFUL LIFE
## Frank Capra

|                   |                                         |
|------------------:|-----------------------------------------|
| director:         | Frank Capra                             |
| producer:         | Frank Capra, for Liberty Films          |
| screenplay:       | Frances Goodrich, Albert Hackett, Frank Capra (additional scenes by Jo Swerling; based on a short story by Philip Van Doren Stern) |
| cinematography:   | Joseph Biroc                            |
| art direction:    | Jack Okey                               |
| music:            | Dimitri Tiomkin                         |
| editing:          | William Hornbeck                        |

### cast

|                  |                    |
|-----------------:|--------------------|
| george bailey:   | James Stewart      |
| mary bailey:     | Donna Reed         |
| mr. potter:      | Lionel Barrymore   |
| uncle billy:     | Thomas Mitchell    |
| clarence:        | Henry Travers      |
| mrs. bailey:     | Beulah Bondi       |
| ernie:           | Frank Faylen       |
| bert:            | Ward Bond          |
| violet:          | Gloria Grahame     |

Black and white
*running time:* 132 minutes
*first release:* December 25, 1946

Francesco Capra was born to a lower-class, rural family on May 18, 1897, in Bisacquino, a small village outside Palermo, Sicily. His mother, the daughter of a prosperous Sicilian shoemaker, was disowned when she married his father, a farmer of citrus trees (a skill that would serve him well when the family relocated to Southern California). The son inherited his father's intuitive love for beauty and his mother's determination and "ability to survive under any circumstances."[1]

The Capras saw no need to invest in the education of their seven children, who were expected from a very young age to do farm work for local landowners. But young Francesco wasn't satisfied with these prospects. He had what he called a "mania for education"[2] that he hoped would deliver him into a better life.

Help also came from the Capras' oldest son, Ben, who with similar ambitions had fled Sicily for America and welcomed the family to come to stay with him in Los Angeles. In the spring of 1903, the Capras joined millions of other Italians who had left for America. Partway through the thirteen-day sea voyage, cramped in steerage with more than fourteen hundred people, Francesco Capra turned six years old.

The family members took whatever jobs they could find in Los Angeles. As a teenager, Frank was playing the guitar and banjo in a downtown café and working graveyard shifts as a janitor to get himself through high school and to save money for college. He was a bright, hard-working student with an admirable work ethic.[3]

In 1915 Capra enrolled in Pasadena's Throop College of Technology, from which he graduated in 1918 and enlisted in the army. After being demobilized, he worked various jobs—tutoring, hustling, traveling—until finally, he bluffed his way into a job at a fledgling movie studio near San Francisco's Golden Gate Park.

He made a short film adaptation of Rudyard Kipling's poem *The Ballad of Fulta Fisher's Boarding House*, which opened in April 1922. It was distributed nationally and was well reviewed. Capra took on small-scale movie work, including a stint in a San Francisco film-processing lab. Gradually, he learned the filmmaker's craft, working his way up the motion picture totem pole, as an editor, prop man, and writer.

Between 1924 and 1927 Capra found a niche as a gag man, writing scripts for film comedians. He moved to Los Angeles to work for the famous producer Mack Sennett. (Sennett's Keystone Company, a decade earlier, as we know, had also been an important career stepping-stone for Charlie Chaplin.) The bullish Sennett was accustomed to giving orders and having them followed without questions. Capra recalled challenging his rules often and even brazenly demanding a raise his first day on the job.

He worked as a gag writer for comedian Harry Langdon (1884–1944), one of several silent film sensations at the time. He wrote and codirected Langon's debut, his classic comedy *Tramp, Tramp, Tramp* (1926). Capra later recalled that it was an important educational experience to see that the fragile illusory world of creativity "is built on and supported by a heavy industry that *has* rules and tangible costs. Labor, materials, equipment, film, time and overtime, are all real and calculable. . . . Making up your mind is the hair-tearing part of film production."[4]

After a few more increasingly successful collaborations, Langdon left Capra behind. Meanwhile, Capra began work on another project, a comedy, *For the Love of Mike*, which would be the film debut of the popular French stage actress Claudette Colbert (1905–1996). It would also be a disaster. Colbert found the process of film acting alien and hopelessly uncomfortable, and Capra found that it was too difficult to work with her.

Dissatisfied with filmmaking and uncertain about his future, he considered a return to Caltech for an advanced degree. He returned instead to the Sennett studio. Then, in October 1927, came a turning point: he was hired by Columbia Pictures, at the time only a shabby, impoverished upstart of a film studio, whose reputation Capra would help to establish. He directed several films in various genres, earning a good reputation among the actors with whom he worked and among audiences, who appreciated his uplifting and diverting stories during the Great Depression. His comedy *Lady for a Day* (1933) got four Oscar nominations, but Capra's real breakthrough success came with the screwball comedy classic *It Happened One Night* (1934), about the romance between a precocious heiress (played by Colbert, with whom Capra this time had better results) on the run from her controlling family and a reporter (Clark Gable) hoping to scoop her story. It won Academy Awards in every major category: best picture, best screenplay (adapted), best actor, best actress, and best director. Capra's *Mr. Deeds Goes to Town* (1936) and *You Can't Take It with You* (1938) were also nominated for Oscars.

In 1932, Capra married Lucille Reyburn, a charming and wholesome woman who'd grown up in California, graduated from the University of California–Berkeley, and been widowed at twenty-six. Frank had been unhappily married before and parted bitterly with his first wife, Helen. But he and Lu, as everyone called her, would stay together until her death, in 1984. They had four children.

After *It Happened One Night*, Capra found his stride and the theme that infused his most significant work: "a simple, honest man, driven into a corner, will come up with courage, wit, and love to triumph over his environment."[5] He also found the ideal leading man to represent this worldview. Upon seeing James Stewart (1908–1997) in Sam Wood's 1937 film, *Navy Blue and Gold*, Capra recalled, "I sensed the character and rock-ribbed honesty of a Gary Cooper, plus the breeding and intelligence of an Ivy League idealist."[6] He put that character to memorable use; Capra and Stewart's collaborations were fruitful for both, encapsulating Capra's human touch and helping Stewart's self-effacing everyman become a populist icon of American cinema. Donna Reed, Stewart's costar in *It's a Wonderful Life*, observed that he was the most demanding actor with whom she'd worked, and he was so natural that she never knew when he was acting.

Stewart recognized what he had in Capra, too: "He brings out the best in an actor. He doesn't *demand* effects; he coaxes them out of you; I wouldn't call his direction subtle so much as evocative, gently guiding. You fall in with his spirit, and before you know it you are acting in accordance with it, naturally, effortlessly. I think his approach is a unique one among directors. Certainly, it worked magically for me."[7]

The films they made together—*You Can't Take It with You* (1938), about a farcically awkward meeting between the very different families of a woman and her fiancé; *Mr. Smith Goes to Washington* (1939), about an idealistic young senator who takes on political corruption in Washington; and *It's a Wonderful Life* (1946), have been noted for their affirmation of American values.

To some, Capra had become the plain-language film-poet of the common man, to others he was too sentimental and oversimplifying. What to some was the *Capra touch* or *Capra-esque* was to others *Capra-corn*, a derisive term the director himself jovially adopted.

By the start of the 1940s, Capra became the leading American director; he had been adored by the public and honored by Hollywood with three best director Oscars. In April 1945 he formed his own short-lived company, Liberty Films, with William Wyler, Sam Briskin, and George Stevens. Capra believed that a film should be identifiable as the product of a single vision, and, as his autobiography reminds us, he was the first director whose name appeared above the title in the credits.

Yet unquestionably he owed part of his success in the 1930s and early 1940s to his regular screenwriter, the former playwright Robert Riskin.[8] Their first shared studio effort was 1932's *American Madness*, about a banker nearly done in by the Depression after making good-faith loans to people in his community, who collectively come to his rescue—a classic Capra-corn plot that would recur in *It's a Wonderful Life*. The last Capra-Riskin cooperation was on *Meet John Doe* (1941).

As we know, on December 7, 1941, while the United States–Japanese diplomatic negotiations were going on in Washington, Japanese warplanes conducted a sneak attack on Pearl Harbor, Hawaii, destroying the United States Pacific fleet and killing thousands of American servicemen. The most devastating assault in American history, the attack became a wake-up call for the nation. Before Pearl Harbor, numerous Americans resisted being drawn into the war, which had started in 1939, considering it a European affair. Now the situation changed dramatically—America itself was no longer a safe place, and the war came to the United States not from Europe but from the Pacific. The United States declared war on Japan, and Frank Capra returned to army service. On February 5, 1942, he was ordered to Washington, D.C. The American immigrant from war-ravaged Europe would join the fight on America's behalf. As he observed his fellow citizens enlisting, Capra wrote, "I had a guilty conscience . . . besides, it gave one a superior aura of patriotism and self-sacrifice—qualities one rarely has the chance to flaunt in the faces of his peers."[9] From the outset, Capra observed, being a military man took away all the privileges of being a famous filmmaker, and it came with infuriating army bureaucracy.

Capra became an invaluable part of the newly created Office of War Information. He had a personal meeting with General George C. Marshall, who told him that America's young men in uniform had to know what they were fighting and dying for. Capra was instructed to make a series of training films to provide those answers. He hedged a little—he'd never made a documentary before, but he was reminded that the bulk of his audience had never been soldiers either. What's more, he shortly thereafter saw Leni Riefenstahl's Nazi propaganda film, *Triumph of the Will* (1935), which was both ideologically vicious and cinematically superb. Capra later stated that Riefenstahl's film was a "classic, powerful propaganda . . . as a psychological weapon aimed at destroying the will to resist, it was just as lethal."[10]

As Capra contemplated the task before him, his determination and personal involvement grew. It seemed impossible "to allow the inspirational *Why We Fight* films to be made by Signal Corps colonels," he wrote.[11] He decided to incorporate clips from *Triumph of the Will* and other Nazi propaganda into his own work—they would be self-incriminating.

The Why We Fight series contains seven fifty-minute films, released from 1942 to 1945: *Prelude to War, The Nazis Strike, Divide and Conquer, The Battle of Britain, The Battle of Russia, The Battle of China,* and *War Comes to America.*

Capra called himself the executive producer of these projects, many of which did not require shooting much new footage. He supervised writers, helping them develop structural outlines and narration based on available documentary footage, some fiction film clips, and the reused Nazi documentary films. There was a lot of debate about the series but eventually the Why We Fight films were screened all over the world. General Marshall personally gave Capra the Distinguished Service Medal, and for *Prelude to War,* Capra won his fourth Oscar.

*It's a Wonderful Life* (1946) was Capra's first feature film since returning from military service. It was again about the difference a common man can make, but in a special and somehow more personal way. The result was darker in tone and more intimate than all of his previous work. Like James Stewart,[12] Capra would later call it his favorite film; he described it as the picture he waited his whole life to make. After his wartime experiences, he was keen to express the notion of appreciating what you have and of knowing you're appreciated, of having a home and family to come back to.

Like some of his Hollywood contemporaries, Capra seemed unable to keep pace with changing attitudes among the American public and studios in the postwar world. As his son, Frank Capra Jr., observed after his father's death, the positive, wholesome, and sentimental qualities of Capra's films were rare even in his heyday of the thirties and forties and mostly nonexistent in later years. Capra's *State of the Union* (1948), with Spencer Tracy as an industrialist who with help from his wife, played by Katharine Hepburn, earns his party's nomination for president, was another box-office failure. His last feature was 1961's *Pocketful of Miracles,* a remake of his *Lady for a Day* and a final, resounding disappointment. His earlier films, however, had begun to take hold in academic circles, where the value of their social criticism was and continues to be debated.

In 1971 Capra published his autobiography, *The Name Above the Title,* which became a bestseller. Meanwhile his politics were scrutinized from the left and the right: while the modest underdogs in his films were taken as heroes of conservative American values, the greedy bankers and other "predatory sophisticates" were seen as anticapitalist; while the House Un-American Activities Committee kept files on him (as early as 1951), Capra volunteered to work for the Department of Defense on projects relating to the wars in Korea and Vietnam.

When Capra made a much publicized return to Sicily in the spring of 1977, he was described in a paper as an American in Sicily, not a Sicilian coming home, and was challenged by students from Italy's national film school for his strong affinity for the American way of life. It had been "hammered into their heads" that America was a lousy place, Capra recalled.

In 1982, the American Film Institute gave Capra its Life Achievement Award. In 1985, a year after his wife died, he suffered a stroke. Frank Capra died on September 3, 1991, in La Quinta, California.

*It's a Wonderful Life* originated from a Christmas story, though it wasn't conceived as a Christmas film per se. In 1943, the novelist and historian Philip Van Doren Stern included his short story "The Greatest Gift" in two hundred Christmas cards sent to family and friends. He had submitted a version of the story to several magazines, but none had been interested in publishing it. Among the recipients of Van Doren Stern's card was his Hollywood agent, Shirley Collier; three months later the story had found its way to RKO, which bought the option to film it, with Cary Grant, for ten thousand dollars. As it turned out, Grant was busy, and the several writers RKO hired to develop the project couldn't produce a satisfactory script, so "The Greatest Gift" languished until it was discovered by Frank Capra, who loved it and bought it himself in 1945.

James Stewart, who had served as a bomber pilot during the war, flew numerous missions over Germany, and came home a full colonel,[13] was eager to work with Capra again and immediately said yes to the project before he even knew all of the details.

When the film was released, some critics called it a human drama of essential truth[14]; others felt it was too sentimental, "a figment of simple platitudes." The film was also a box-office failure—possibly because there was no more faith in small-town values or because it seemed too dark a picture for the holiday season. *It's a Wonderful Life* was gone from movie houses within a few weeks.

Many years later, in the 1970s, the film lost its copyright protection and became a public domain property. As a result, television stations could broadcast the film at their leisure and at no cost, so they did. From the early 1970s, *It's a Wonderful Life* began earning a loyal TV audience, which ironically made it into a national Christmas ritual. Capra and Stewart were both delighted that their favorite film had finally become the favorite film of many American families too. They were less delighted when it was colorized.

After the war, Capra was anxious about how to assimilate a view of the new world. America had emerged victorious and prosperous from the war, but not without losses of human lives and of some optimism, which had been considered a specifically American quality.

He thought the story of "The Greatest Gift" contained what he needed for his first postwar film and assigned husband-and-wife screenwriters Albert Hackett and Frances Goodrich to adapt the story. He worked with them very closely to make the movie *his*; he had a natural sense of being an *auteur* even before the French New Wave critics developed this concept. He worked with the dialogue, making the language more colloquial and finishing off scenes with memorable "cappers"—swift and unexpected changes of tone and surprise punch lines. His personal touch was a powerful and proven tool.

Capra's only choice for the film's protagonist, James Stewart, told the press that he didn't pick stories, he picked directors. He was happy to work with Capra once again.

In early 1946, Capra sent the script to RKO's legal department for approval. The Hollywood Production Code aimed to keep films' content within the careful limits of good taste. The legal department would not permit words like *nuts, dang, lousy, jerk,* and *impotent* in the *It's a Wonderful Life* screenplay. One memo even went so far as to say that the expression "garlic eaters" can be offensive for some people.

The shooting began in April 1946. "There was a growing excitement among all of us as we strove day and night . . . we threw everything we had into our work . . . after three months, shooting some 68 miles of 35-millimeter film, we completed the filming and had a big wrap-up party for everyone."[15]

It was observed that Capra's technical education gave him a strong attention to every detail in his work. His script notes also attest to his sensual, artistic outlook: "the differences between the sound of rain in summer and winter. Rain on leaves makes a different sound than rain on bare limbs."[16]

In fact Capra loved the participation of weather in movies. The snowy scenes of *It's a Wonderful Life* are very deliberately memorable. Until then, most Hollywood movies had used falling corn flakes to simulate snow, but they were notoriously too noisy for the shooting of close-ups. Capra's special effects supervisor, Russell Shearman, invented a new kind of snow from soap, water, and the foam used in fire extinguishers, blown through a wind machine. This innovation, which later earned an Honorable Mention from the Motion Picture Academy for its contribution to film effects, proved mercifully quiet, photogenic, and very convincing. It is hard to believe that the snowy scenes in *It's a Wonderful Life* were shot during a record heat wave, with temperatures in the high nineties (these oppressive conditions were responsible for the crew's single day off during the whole shoot).

The small-town set, built in Encino, California, was at the time one of the largest sets ever constructed for an American film. Its three city blocks covered four acres and required, in addition to the construction of several buildings, transplanting twenty oak trees.

Unlike some other directors, most notably the obsessive preplanner Alfred Hitchcock, Capra did not know in advance how he would direct each scene. He rehearsed it several times, exploring various ideas and moving people around until he'd found what he wanted. "His editing of a picture was unique. . . . Nowadays, directors wait till the end of shooting and then start editing. . . . Capra would run the picture as he went along."[17] The film was edited in the fall of 1946.

Capra hosted a private screening for a few hundred people in early December, eight months after the shooting started, and *It's a Wonderful Life* was then rushed to a Christmas-day release in fifty theatres across the country. The film, as mentioned earlier, didn't do well at the box office, and despite five nominations, it didn't win any Academy Awards. But to this day, it's considered typical Americana and remains popular even among generations for whom the life of Bedford Falls hardly resembles anything they know.

*It's a Wonderful Life* is set in the fictional American small town of Bedford Falls, presumably in upstate New York, and spans roughly from the 1920s to the mid-1940s. In Capra's words, "It's a movie about a small town guy who thinks he is a failure and wishes he had never been born. He's surprised to learn that he was not a failure, that he fitted into the scheme of life and actually contributed much to the happiness of several people."[18]

Capra's cinematic style is direct and unadorned. He is strong in narrative skill; generally we're not aware of camera placement or lighting effects or editing. The film's muted technique reflects a quiet moment in Hollywood history, before the storm of the 1950s, which liberated the camera to become a character in its own right.[19]

*It's a Wonderful Life* is built of forty scenes.

*1. The opening credits are presented as a series of pages in a Christmas storybook. A sign appears: "You Are Now in Bedford Falls."[20] Snow is falling and has started to pile up. We see a celebratory banner that reads: "Welcome Home Harry Bailey."*

There is a direct thematic and emotional significance in the words *welcome home* and a direct connection with the time of the film's release right after the war, when American soldiers were returning home and were greeted with similar banners.

*A wide shot of the typical small-town center: a row of oaks, the snow-covered street, some car and pedestrian traffic, and Christmas lights. It cuts to a series of shots of various locations we will come to know later. We hear the voices of the inhabitants, praying for George Bailey.*

This short exposition ends with a shot looking down on the Bailey house through the falling snow. This house will play a significant role throughout the film.

*2. The camera dissolves to the stars, moving through space. It focuses on a cluster of galaxies, which flicker as we hear a conversation among heavenly voices. "Looks like we'll have to send someone down. A lot of people asking for help for a man named George Bailey."*

We hear the protagonist's name before we see him—a device to attract our attention and to intrigue us.

*"George Bailey?" the voices continue. "Yes, tonight's his crucial night. We'll have to send someone down immediately." Clarence, a bumbling angel, second class, is summoned: a man on earth needs help. "Splendid! Is he sick?" the angel asks. "No, worse," comes the response. "He's discouraged." To get his wings, Clarence must keep George from taking his own life. From this point, he becomes George Bailey's guardian angel.*

*3. Flashback to George's childhood. He and his friends are sliding down a snowy hill onto a frozen pond. George's younger brother Harry slides onto thin ice, which breaks, and falls into the pond. George pulls Harry from the water and saves his life but gets an ear infection and loses hearing in that ear.*

*Mr. Potter, the richest and meanest man in the county, is passing by in an ornate carriage.*

Potter is the antagonist in the film, a grotesque, wicked individual.

*4. Another flashback: The young teenager George works at Gower's drugstore. Two little girls, Mary and Violet, watch him with admiration. Violet says to Mary that she likes George.*

*"You like every boy," Mary replies. She asks George which ear is his bad one, and whispers in that ear that she'll love him forever.*

Here is the exemplary Capra touch—in one phrase or detail, he reveals the core of a character. Mary whispers about her love in the ear that *does not hear*. This at once discloses her angelic and decent nature and marks the starting point of her love, patience, and hope. George doesn't hear her, of course, and starts right in on his plans to become a world explorer.

*George's boss, Mr. Gower, meanwhile, is drunk and teary—he has learned that his son has died of influenza. Inadvertently, he puts a poisonous drug in a customer's pillbox. George tries to tell him about the mistake, but Gower gruffly shouts at him to deliver the pillbox right away. George doesn't know what to do. He notices a poster on the wall: "Ask Dad, he knows."*

With a touch of humor, here an important theme is initiated: George will grapple with several difficult decisions through his life and will defer finally to his father's social and moral values.

*5. In the office of the Bailey Brothers Building and Loan Association, Peter Bailey, George's father, talks with Potter. He sits in a thronelike wheelchair, demanding that Peter Bailey foreclose on the families indebted to him. When George hears how Potter describes his father and his uncle Billy as failures, he shouts that Potter can't say that, and gives Potter a shove.*

This naïve confrontation lays the groundwork for George's future rivalry with Potter.

*Mr. Bailey doesn't have time for his son now. The boy himself decides not to deliver the pillbox. Gower is outraged; he slaps George but soon realizes how right the boy is. George swears he won't tell anyone what happened. As they embrace, the camera zooms in, and the image fades out.*

6. *Fade in to the inside of Mr. Gower's luggage shop years later. George, now a young adult, wants to buy a suitcase for his travel, but someone has paid already. George's plans are ambitious. Clarence's off-screen voice asks, "Did he ever tell anyone about the pills?" "Not a soul," is the answer. "Did he ever marry the girl? Did he ever go exploring?" "Well, wait and see."*

7. *A slow wipe brings us to the drugstore, which hasn't changed much. George has come to thank Mr. Gower and to say good-bye to him. He sees the old cigar lighter and again, as years ago, makes a wish for a million dollars.*

This old-fashioned ritual is an important motif in *It's a Wonderful Life*, where wishes—some frustrated, some fulfilled—have an important function in the plot.

8. *George is walking briskly down the main street, with his relatives and friends wishing him well on his trip. The policeman, Bert, and the cab driver, Ernie, greet him amicably. As does Violet, who has grown into a coy and flirtatious woman. It is clear that everyone around here knows and likes George.*

9. *The Baileys' dining room that evening. When asked by his father if he'd consider coming back to the building and loan business after college, George replies that he couldn't, he wants to do something important. "I feel that in a small way we are doing something important," his father says. He explains that people want their own "roof and walls and fireplace, and we're helping them get those things in our shabby little office." Yet he understands George's feelings and encourages him finally to get his education and get out. "I think you're a great guy," George says gratefully to his father.*

Remember the "Ask Dad, *he* knows" poster on the drugstore wall? Now it has lost its humorous meaning. Mr. Bailey really knows about life what his son doesn't yet.

10. *The festivities at the high school gym. George and his brother Harry say hello to friends. Mary's date, Freddie, is in the middle of a boring story when George steals her away for a dance. They join the crowd for a Charleston contest. The jealous Freddie opens the floor and the full-sized swimming pool underneath is revealed. George and Mary fall in the pool, but they simply laugh it off and keep dancing in the water. The other dancers dive in the pool to join them.*

Capra uses water symbolically in this film. Crucial moments hinge on how people emerge or are rescued from getting drenched—from the young Harry Bailey to the older George—and the water itself is a jolt, both threatening and purifying.

11. *George walks Mary home, under a bright moon. They pass an old-fashioned, two-storied house almost ruined but once was splendid. Each throws a rock, breaks a window, and makes a wish. Mary tells him she'd like to live here; George doesn't seem to understand. He says that he wants to leave their crummy little town and to see the world, then go to college, and then he is going to build things. Mary won't tell him her wish. George offers to lasso the moon for her. "I'll take it," she says.*

*Suddenly, with a flash of headlights, a car appears. Uncle Billy tells George his father's had a stroke. George makes hasty exit. Mary watches him go in a sad, longing close-up.*

This is a crucial turning point in *It's a Wonderful Life*, the first deep dent of reality into George's cloudless poetic dreams of the world, or of giving Mary the moon. The scene also introduces the house, the gloomy image that in the course of the film will be transformed into "home sweet home."

12. *There is a group of people in the Bailey Brothers Building and Loan. We learn that George's father died and that George did not go to Europe, in order to straighten things out.*

*Potter is here; he wants to destroy the building and loan business. He cannot stand that when he turns people down, the Baileys grant money for buying houses. Potter speaks disapprovingly of the late Mr. Bailey's business strategies. "What does that get us?" he says. "A discontented lazy rabble instead of a thrifty working class."*

*George rebukes Potter most eloquently, telling him that those people do all the working—they live and die here—in the town. The board of directors votes to keep the building and loan going—with the single provision that George himself takes over as executive secretary. If he doesn't, they'll all vote with Potter.*

13. *Again the field of stars that appeared in the beginning of the film. Clarence's voiceover informs us that George did not go.*

George's moral obligations turn out to be stronger than his wish to get away to school. The dramatic conflict of the film is George's obligations as his father's son and a citizen of his town versus his own dreams and aspirations, and, in a more general sense, we can say that the conflict of the film is the reality of life placed against wants and wishes.

14. *Dissolve to the railroad station, four years later. George and his uncle Billy wait to meet Harry, George's brother, who's back from school. Now George is ready to start his travel; he has some guidebooks, and he tells Uncle Billy that the three best sounds in the world are anchor chains, plane motors, and train whistles.*

*Harry surprises them by introducing his new wife, Ruth. George is deflated to learn that her father has offered Harry a good job in a city far away from Bedford Falls.*

Here George is given a chance to pursue his dream, but he feels that his obligation is to not stand in the way of his younger brother's happiness.

15. *George throws his travel guidebooks away. He restlessly roams the town's main street. Violet spots him and they say hello, but George huffs and walks away. He finds himself pacing outside Mary's house. She invites him in and puts on a record of "Buffalo Gals"—their song from the dance. George asks why she didn't go back to New York; she says she was home-sick. He could not believe it.*

*Mary's mother expresses her dismay that her daughter invited George Bailey, especially when Sam Wainwright, a very successful friend of Mary and George's, will call from New York. George, feeling unwelcome and frustrated, leaves.*

*As Mary answers the phone, George returns for his hat. Mary tells Sam that George is there, and Sam asks to speak with him. Sam offers George a job in New York. He wants to talk to both of them, so George and Mary get closer and closer to share the receiver, and finally they embrace and kiss, ignoring the phone. Mary's mother, watching from atop the stairs, is aghast. She helplessly clutches her robe and flees* [a device Capra used to cut through the sentiment with humor].

George loves Mary, and will marry her, but now his last chance to leave Bedford Falls is lost. The film conflict gets more convoluted— George's dreams are dented, are challenged by his love for Mary.

16. *George and Mary, the newlyweds, proceed through a throng of relatives and well-wishers. Mary throws her bouquet and Violet catches it. Ernie, the cab driver, asks where they're going for the honeymoon. George pulls out a stack of bills—they are going to see the world. When the cab passes the building and loan office, they see a crowd of depositors. Potter scared them, telling them that their money is lost. Panic is in the air. Mary saves the situation by offering the honeymoon money to the depositors.*

*Some hours later, when the customers have gone and only two dollars remain, George gets a call from the new Mrs. Bailey, who tells him to come home and gives him an address that he doesn't recognize.*

17. *George walks through the rain. He sees the old house where he and Mary broke the windows. Now a glow of light shines out from them. George strolls up the path. Inside, he looks the place over, and we get a wide shot of what he sees: in this deserted, cobwebbed house, Mary is waiting for him, smiling, a fire crackling in the fireplace behind her, a candlelit table set for two. The phonograph is playing, and the leaky roof and the crumbled rafters don't matter. "Welcome home, Mr. Bailey," Mary says.*

Indeed, it is one of many of George's homecomings in this film. Now is the first time George starts to realize that home is something to be honored, respected, and nurtured.

Capra doesn't hesitate to make a final reach for the emotions here.

*Outside, George and Mary's friends Bert and Ernie stand in the rain, singing a duet of "I Love You Truly." The silhouettes of George and Mary can be seen inside the window.*

*Mary says this is what she wished for when she broke the window in this house all those years ago. George tells her she's wonderful.*

18. *George and Mary help a family, the Martinis, move to a new home. Hanging from a tree, a handmade sign reads, "Welcome To Bailey Park." The camera pulls back and down from the sign to reveal "a district of new small houses. . . . New lawns here and there, and young trees." A happy crowd has gathered at the Martinis' new home.*

19. *In Potter's bank office, a rent collector tells Potter that many of his former renters have moved to Bailey Park. The homes, he says, are worth more than they cost to build and he might soon be asking George Bailey for a job. Potter impatiently sends the man away.*

20. *Sometime later, in his office, Potter lights a cigar for George and tries to convince him to become a Potter employee, at twenty thousand dollars per year, and to sell him Bailey Park. George is tempted by the offer. But "as they shake hands, George feels physical revulsion . . . he knows he could never be associated with this man."*

21. *Mary is sleeping in their modestly furnished bedroom when George comes*

*in. He is upset and confused. He tells Mary she could've married anybody else in town. She says she never would, besides she wants her baby to look like him. George is delighted to learn that he'll be a father.*

22. *A montage of scenes shows the Bailey family growing, over which we hear the heavenly voices telling that now it is clear that George never leaves Bedford Falls. We see and hear also about how various Bedford Falls characters served during the war, including Harry Bailey, who shot down several planes and saved some fellow soldiers' lives. As for George: "Four-F on account of his ear, George fought the Battle of Bedford Falls." He works as an air-raid warden and conducts drives for paper, scrap, and rubber.*

23. *The montage ends on the day before Christmas. George shows Ernie a newspaper in which the front-page story is about Harry winning the Congressional Medal of Honor. In the town square, some folks raise a banner: "Welcome Home Harry Bailey."*

The flashback comes to an end—it is close to the point that the film started, the day before Christmas 1945.

24. *George's partner, Uncle Billy, is in the bank. A close-up reveals the large sum of cash he is preparing to deposit. Potter, wheeled in by one of his goons, looks at the old man, who proudly shows off Harry's portrait in the newspaper—his nephew, Harry Bailey, is a war hero.*

*Unwittingly, Uncle Billy folds his envelope full of cash into the newspaper and hands it over to Potter. When he goes to make his deposit, he can't find the money. Potter discovers the error and peeks through the door to see Billy in a frantic search for the money.*

25. *In the building and loan office, George is talking to Violet. She is ashamed to have to come to him for money. George explains warmly that this is fine, that this is just a loan.*

*George learns that Uncle Billy lost the money and realizes how serious the situation is.*

26. *Night, inside Uncle Billy's shabby living room. Uncle Billy is sobbing. "Where's that money?" George screams. "Do you realize what this means? . . . Bankruptcy and scandal, and prison. . . . One of us is going to jail!" George storms out, kicking a trash can on his way. The camera pulls back to watch him leave.*

*27. George, covered with snow, comes home to Mary and their four children. His daughter Janie is working carefully through "Hark the Herald Angels Sing" on the piano. Mary trims the tree. George doesn't tell Mary what happened, but he angrily complains about everything, about the house, calling it a drafty old barn, about having all these children, about Janie playing the piano, about being stuck in Bedford Falls. He is almost out of his mind, screaming, insulting his daughter's teacher on the phone, yelling at the children, kicking things over, overturning his models of bridges and buildings. Mary and the children are horrified. George looks around and sees them staring at him "as if he were some unknown and wild animal." He rushes out.*

*28. Potter's office. Shrunk again in the chair before Potter's desk, George resorts to asking for help. Potter enjoys his predicament. He refuses him a loan of eight thousand dollars, knowing full well that the loss was Billy's fault—and his own. Potter asks for collateral, and all George has is five hundred dollars' worth of equity in his life insurance policy. "You're worth more dead than alive."*
    *Potter plants an insidious thought about suicide in George's mind.*

*29. At Martini's bar, George, totally discontented with his life, with reality in general, is drunk, and he prays.*
    James Stewart recalled:

> In agony I raised my eyes and, following the script, pled, 'God . . . God . . . Dear Father in Heaven, I'm not a praying man, but if You're up there and You can hear me, show me the way. I'm at the end of my rope. Show me the way, God . . . ' As I said those words, I felt the loneliness . . . hopelessness of people who had nowhere to turn, and my eyes filled with tears. I broke down sobbing. This was not planned . . . but the power of that prayer, the realization that our Father in Heaven is there to help the hopeless . . . reduced me to tears. Frank, who loved spontaneity in his films, was ecstatic.[21]

*Mr. Martini in his bar gently encourages George to go home. Next to him, we discover, is the husband of the schoolteacher George admonished earlier on the phone. He punches George in the jaw. "That's what you get for praying," George says bitterly.*
    A sudden comic relief—Capra's favorite device.

*30. A wide shot of a dark street. George's car crashes into a tree. A man comes out of the nearby house. He is not happy with the damage done to his tree, but George waves him off and staggers away through the snow.*

*George walks to the bridge. The snow is heavy, and the night is very dark. He follows a catwalk out to the center of the bridge. The churning water below is filled with chunks of ice. Someone is watching him silently.*

*George seems to have taken to heart Potter's poisonous suggestion that his family will be better off financially without him and also would not have to face the scandal and his imprisonment. Just as George is ready to jump, a body falls in the water with a very loud splash. The man in the water calls for help and flails his arms. George takes off his jacket and dives in.*

Here is the repetition of the jumping-in-water motif. But the dance party in the swimming pool is its happy version. This one is an act of despair. At the same time it is the rescue of drowning Clarence—something that happened in the beginning of the film when George rescued his brother Henry.

*George swims out to the man. Cutting to a very wide shot, we see the full span of the bridge and the two people in the water, with a bright beam of light shining down on them.*

*31. Inside the tollhouse. The old man whom George rescued is the angel Clarence. He and George are warming up while the toll keeper watches them suspiciously. Their clothes are drying on a line. Clarence says that he jumped in the water to save George from suicide. "It's against the law to commit suicide around here," says the toll keeper. "Yeah, it's against the law where I come from too," Clarence replies. "Where do you come from?" "Heaven." When Clarence, who couldn't be further from the traditional image of an angel, finally describes himself as "angel, second class," the toll keeper falls over in his chair. "I wonder what Martini put in those drinks," George says. He retreats into his own gloom: "I suppose it would have been better, if I'd never been born at all." This phrase gives Clarence an idea, and he grants George's wish.*

What is going to happen next is an extraordinary dramatic twist.

*32. The snow stops, and a gust of wind blows the door open. George and Clarence rush through the town, now called Pottersville. No one recognizes George—it is the nightmare of being a stranger.*

*In Martini's bar the cozy Italian feeling is gone. The barman Nick himself is unfriendly, even rude. George is puzzled why Nick doesn't* recognize him. Even the druggist Mr. Gower doesn't recognize George. George learns that Gower spent time in jail for poisoning a young boy. Clarence says that George was not there to stop Gower.

George and Clarence get shoved through the door and land outside, face-down in the snow. Clarence explains that George was given a great gift: a chance to see what the world would be like without him.

The earnestness of this moment is leavened with a touch of some-what corny humor: Clarence looks heavenward to ask how he's doing and then says, "No, I didn't have a drink."

33. George continues into the town square. "Where before it was a quiet, orderly small town, it has now become . . . a frontier village . . . [with] night clubs, cafes, bars, liquor stores, pool halls and the like. . . . Gower's drug-store is now a pawnbroker's establishment."

George finds what used to be the building and loan office, now a dance club being raided by the police. A cop tells George that his family's company went out of business years ago. George also sees Violet, "arrayed as a tart, being dragged into the patrol wagon." He hails Ernie's cab, but Ernie doesn't recognize him either.

George approaches his house. "Windows are broken, the porch sags, one section of the roof has fallen, doors and shutters hang askew on their hinges."

George runs up to his mother's house and notices a sign: "Ma Bailey's Boarding House." His astonishment and horror come to the highest point: his mother opens the door, but "she gives no signs that she knows him" and slams the door in his face. "Strange, isn't it?" Clarence asks. "Each man's life touches so many other lives, and when he isn't around, he leaves an awful hole, doesn't he?"[22]

34. George and Clarence head off for Bailey Park, which is now a cemetery. The wind ruffles their clothes. George sees the tombstone of his brother Harry. Clarence explains that Harry died when he fell through the ice because George wasn't there to save him and that the men whom Harry saved during the war have died too. George grabs Clarence and demands that he reveal what has become of Mary.

35. Mary exits through the door of the Pottersville Public Library. She looks almost unrecognizable. George calls her, but she tries to get away. He chases her down the street, grabs her. She screams and runs away into a nearby bar, and faints.

Policeman Bert arrives on the scene, but George knocks him down and *runs away, shouting for Clarence. Bert gets up and pursues George in his police car.*

This action has moved swiftly. George's revelations get worse and worse, and George becomes more desperate to get his life back than he was to give it up.

*36. Wipe to the bridge. George, still calling Clarence but getting no answer, hurries back out onto the catwalk where he first saw him. George is beyond despair now. He folds his hands together and begs that he wants to live again!*

*37. As the police car pulls forward, the camera tilts up to reveal Bert getting out. "Hey, George," he calls. "You all right?"*

*George is amazed and delighted that Bert recognizes him and bursts into ecstatic laughter, jumps into Bert's arms, shouts, "Merry Christmas," and runs off. He passes the sign in the town common, which is back to normal: "You Are Now in Bedford Falls."*

*38. The camera follows George as he calls out to others on the street, "Merry Christmas," and they reply. He even peers in Potter's window and wishes him a merry Christmas. Potter looks out at the ecstatic face in his window. "Happy New Year to you—in jail," he snaps.*

Potter is even worse than Scrooge.

*39. Inside the Baileys' entrance hall, the bank examiner waits with a reporter, a photographer, and a sheriff, looking stern. They hear George shouting and the door bursts open. George comes charging in, covered with snow. It is his final and most triumphant homecoming. "Isn't it wonderful? I'm going to jail! Merry Christmas!" George shouts. The camera follows as he looks for Mary. He is delighted to be back. "Merry Christmas, Daddy!" call the children. George sees them at the top of the stairs.*

Jimmy Stewart wrote that he was playing James Stewart, some variations of himself.

*As George runs to greet his children, the banister knob comes off in his hand, as we have seen several times before. It had irritated him, but this time he laughs, kisses it, and puts it back.*

Through this seemingly unimportant detail we are shown enormous changes in George's character and his situation. He charges up to embrace the children.

*At the base of the stairs, the bank examiner, the sheriff, and the reporter watch and wonder. The photographer takes aim. The children run to George. Mary comes through the front door. She races up the stairs and into George's arms. She has something to tell him, but they're both so overjoyed that they can barely speak.*

*"It's a miracle!" Mary says. She runs to the front door, where Uncle Billy appears, carrying a big laundry basket filled with money, followed by a crowd of Bedford Falls townspeople. Billy dumps the money on a table and frantically explains that the locals went around town collecting on the Baileys' behalf. Others come in and add their money to the pile. George and Mary, surrounded by the crowd, show their emotion. A telegram has come from a friend in London saying he will advance George up to twenty-five thousand dollars.*

*Everyone cheers. Janie starts her carol on the piano, and the crowd sings along. The bank examiner finally makes his own donation and proudly joins the chorus. The sheriff tears up the warrant and begins singing too.*

*40. Brother Harry arrives and receives warm welcomes. He offers a toast to his big brother George and calls him the richest man in town! More cheering. On the pile of money, George sees Clarence's copy of* Tom Sawyer, *with a note: "Dear George, remember, no man is a failure who has friends. Thanks for the wings. Love, Clarence."*

*A bell rings on the Christmas tree. George looks up at the ceiling, smiles, and winks. "Attaboy, Clarence," he says.*

So George is saved. But let us not forget that it was not only Clarence's effort that helped him. George's neighbors also came to his rescue.

*The singing builds to a crescendo. The camera moves across the singing crowd and then back to George and Mary and one of their little girls. Fade out.*

It's a Wonderful Life has all the qualities of a classic Hollywood picture: its action is based on a cause-effect chain; it has a protagonist and an antagonist; the plot is unified, with a clearly defined closure; the meaning of every scene is easy to comprehend; there is no alienation of the viewers from the action, no interruption in the viewers' involvement in the lives of the characters (something that would be successfully challenged in the 1950s); the gaze of the camera is unobtrusive and doesn't draw attention to itself, nor does the so-called invisible editing; the cinematic style of the film can be defined as a style without style.

The genre of *It's a Wonderful Life* (something about which Hollywood always was very particular) is melodrama: the film is sentimental, has an emotional appeal; the characters are divided into good and bad; the issues are simplified; there are some sensational moments, a romantic atmosphere, and a happy ending.

But the happy ending of *It's a Wonderful Life* is not conventional and not just a necessary fixture of the genre. The happy ending here is earned from inside out, in a long dramaturgical way with twists and turns, and with relations, thoughts, and transformations more meaningful than a melodrama could have afforded. But the most important thing here is a dramaturgical device that Capra brought into development of his story.

*It's a Wonderful Life* consists of forty scenes that unfold in three different times: present, past, and imaginary time (see Figure 5–1).

1. scenes of the present (1, 2, 23–31, 37–40)
2. scenes of the past (3–22)
3. scenes of imaginary time and situations (32–36)

The scenes of category 3 are crucial to the story. We witness the shocking revelation of George's journey when he is nonexistent, and people and places are degraded and barely recognizable because he

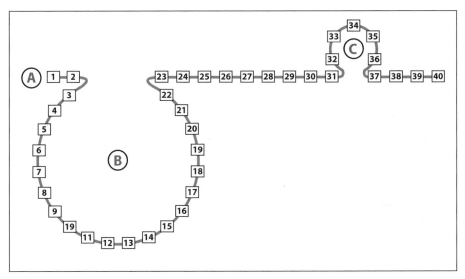

*Figure 5–1. Scene Diagram for* It's a Wonderful Life

wasn't there to do, to say, or to help in the ways he had in "reality." He comes to realize that small things in life can add up to something bigger and more important than they might seem. So he accomplished "something big and something important," as he'd dreamed in youth, although not in the way he had imagined it. The journey Clarence sends him through is a sudden flash of insight, an epiphany of how precious life is. His revelation elevates the story from the ordinary (the story "about a local boy who stays local"[23] and about small-town values) to the exceptional and universal. It is clear that Capra's span is much broader than the local territory. He is after life values in a parable sense, and he tells a story with a strong human and social message: George's story would seem insufferably moralizing were he not so painfully punished and beaten down before being rewarded with a happy ending.

Some scenes of It's a Wonderful Life resemble paintings of Capra's contemporary Norman Rockwell: all those immediately recognizable Americana types, executed with sympathy and humor, the middle-class Americans with their traditional values of family responsibilities, home, patriotism, and self-reliance. "I do ordinary people in everyday situations," wrote Rockwell, "and that is about all I can do." What is the final artistic goal for Norman Rockwell—to show ordinary people in their everyday life—is the starting point for Frank Capra. In other words, it seems that where Rockwell ends, Capra begins.

There are clearly some fairy tale elements in It's a Wonderful Life: the stars; the heavenly voices; an incarnation of evil, Mr. Potter, who is more a symbol than a character; an incarnation of goodness, Mary, who is like the gracious beauty of a fairy tale. But she, unlike Mr. Potter, is also a real character, and she loves and needs George as he loves and needs her; we see what could have happened to her without him.

At one point, George wants to get the moon for Mary—a gesture of a fairy tale hero rather than a young man from Bedford Falls. "Just say the word, and I'll throw a lasso around [the moon] and pull it down . . . and the moon-beams would shoot out of your fingers and your toes, and the ends of your hair."

There is also Clarence. Capra presents an image of the guardian angel with supernatural power and simultaneously (almost in a destructive postmodernist fashion) makes fun of that image. The irony here is overwhelming: the angel is a little old man who strives to get wings. He saves George's life and his dignity, and he pronounces Capra's weighty statement: "Each man's life touches so many other lives, and when he isn't around, he leaves an awful hole, doesn't he?" George's understanding of this wisdom happens gradually, in front of us.

The main pattern of the plot is duality, ambivalence, but it is always well balanced. For every hope and good cheer, there is an outburst of rage and cruelty; for every whitewashed sweet spot, there's brutal bitterness.

There is idealism and cynicism, comedy and drama, reality and fairy tale, heaven and hell (how else can we describe George's plunge into the nightmarish alternate past?). Sometimes the same things and people are presented in their opposite qualities; for example, Mary is shown as a beautiful wife and mother and, in the world without George, as an unattractive, angry loner.

You can see in Figure 5–2 that the house (what becomes George's house) is presented in six scenes.

> Scene 1—The house is seen from outside, in good shape, with lights in the windows (the present).
>
> Scene 11—The house is gloomy and deserted (the past).
>
> Scene 17—The house is beginning its rejuvenation (the past).
>
> Scene 27—The inside of the settled-down house before Christmas (the present).
>
> Scene 33—The house is again a neglected ruin, as in scene 11 (the imaginary situation).
>
> Scenes 39–40—The house finally becomes home sweet home, and reality becomes like a dream in George's eyes.

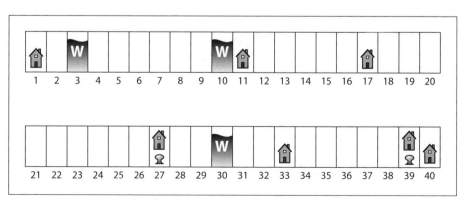

*Figure 5–2. Key Motifs in* It's a Wonderful Life

Every change in the image of the house accentuates a new stage in the development of the story.

No less meaningful is the water motif, which also indicates stages of story development:

In scene 3 George rescues his brother Harry, who has fallen through the ice.

In scene 10, a happy George and Mary fall into the water of the swimming pool.

In scene 30 George jumps into the river to rescue Clarence.

Two times repeated, the banister-knob motif reveals George's changing attitude toward the house: in scene 27 he throws the falling knob in disgust (he hates the house); in scene 39 he kisses the knob as the expression of happiness for coming home. Those two gestures reveal the enormous change that has happened within George Bailey.

In the course of the film, we have seen George, alternatively, as the most fortunate and the most unfortunate man. The rhythm of the change from one to another repeats the pattern of the plot built on contrasts and transformations. So, subconsciously we feel that the ecstasy of the film's finale could, to an extent, be perceived as a happiness doomed to be short-lived (don't forget, the evil Mr. Potter is still alive and unpunished) and therefore only more precious.

Even the title of the film is ambivalent. On the one hand, it has a strong positive meaning: Yes, life is wonderful—look at all the happy faces of the Baileys and their supporters. At the same time, after witnessing George's hardships and disappointments, we sense a certain irony in the title, as if someone is sarcastically saying, "Life is wonderful, isn't it?"

It's a Wonderful Life, with its bells, snow, holiday spirit, decorated trees, and greetings, is justifiably canonized as a Christmas movie. But what happened to its protagonist, George Bailey, in December 1945 could have happened in October or May of any year.

## Appendix

### Frank Capra's Recollections[24]

On April 8, 1946, I began shooting It's a Wonderful Life. All that I was and all that I knew went into the making of it. The pace was that of a four-month nonstop orgasm. . . . Then we previewed *Wonderful Life* for the press:

> . . . one of the most efficient sentimental pieces since *A Christmas Carol.* —James Agee, *Nation*

> . . . a masterful edifice of comedy and sentiment. —*Life*

> . . . Sentimental, but so expertly written, directed, and acted that you want to believe it. —*Newsweek*

> . . . *It's a Wonderful Life* is a pretty wonderful movie. It has only one formidable rival (Goldwyn's *Best Years of Our Lives*) as Hollywood's best picture of the year . . . —*Time*

But some other Manhattan critics sprayed it with bladder juice:

> . . . for all its characteristic humors, Mr. Capra's *Wonderful Life* . . . is a figment of simple Pollyanna platitudes . . .
> —*The New York Times*

> . . . so mincing as to border on baby talk . . . —*The New Yorker*

But I thought it was the greatest film I had ever made.

### From Frank Capra's 1968 Interview with a Student[25]

I suppose the most difficult scene and I think one of the best scenes in the picture—actually the most difficult—is the little scene where he comes in and raises hell with his kids there while she's playing and just before he runs out and tries to throw himself in the river. That whole little scene in there with the kid playing the piano—it's a very dramatic scene and yet it can get laughs. The action . . . the little girl pounding on the piano is funny and the little kid asking those silly questions is funny. Here you're playing with dynamite. *You're playing with laughs in a dramatic scene.* Which to you want to do? So that particular scene is probably one of the most difficult to stage because if it becomes too funny the drama will not come over and they'll laugh at the drama too, and the audience will think they have to laugh at everything. I suppose that was the hardest scene to stage.

## Notes

1. Joseph McBride, *Frank Capra: The Catastrophe of Success*, New York: Simon and Schuster, 1992, p. 18.

2. Frank Capra, *The Name Above the Title: An Autobiography,* New York: Macmillan, 1971, p. 3.

3. Capra's 1971 autobiography, *The Name Above the Title*, like many self-told Hollywood stories, is hardly the epitome of factual and historical accuracy, but it ably demonstrates Capra's storytelling skills and gives the correct impression of an enterprising and indefatigable young man, whose combination of gall, street smarts, hard work, sensitivity, and stubbornness forecast his broad-ranging success.

4. Capra, p. 65.

5. Capra, p. 64.

6. Lawrence Quirk, *James Stewart: Behind the Scenes of a Wonderful Life*, New York: Applause, 1997, p. 98.

7. Quirk, p. 100.

8. Robert Riskin (1897–1955), native New Yorker, playwright, and screenwriter. After Riskin's great success working with Capra in the 1930s, they parted ways in the early 1940s. Perhaps Riskin became fed up with Capra's being credited for everything in their films. Capra and Riskin worked together on *Lady for a Day* (1933), *Mr. Deeds Goes to Town* (1936), and *You Can't Take It with You* (1938), which were all nominated for Oscars, and *It Happened One Night* (1934), which won several Oscars. Riskin also wrote *Broadway Bill* (1934) and *Lost Horizon* (1937). *Meet John Doe* (1941) was their last film together.

9. Capra, p. 330.

10. Capra, p. 327.

11. Capra, p. 328.

12. *It's a Wonderful Life*, DVD, Artisan Home Entertainment.

13. Later Stewart earned the rank of brigadier general in the air force reserve.

14. Prominent film critic James Agee wrote in *The Nation* on February 15, 1947: "Much too often this movie appeals to the heart at the expense of the mind . . . at still other times the heart is simply used, or the mind, as a truncheon. The movie does all this so proficiently, and with so much genuine warmth, that I wasn't able to get reasonably straight about it for quite a while."

15. "Jimmy Stewart Remembers: *It's a Wonderful Life*," *Guideposts* magazine, 1987 (December).

16. Jeanine Basinger, *The It's a Wonderful Life Book*, New York: Alfred Knopf, 1986, p. 20.

17. Basinger, p. 90, from an interview with the cameraman, Joseph Biroc.

18. Basinger, p. 44.

19. Shortly before his death in 1997, Jimmy Stewart said in an interview: "After some fifty years, I've heard *It's a Wonderful Life* called an American cultural phenomenon. Well, maybe so, but it seems to me there is nothing phenomenal about the movie itself. It's simply about an ordinary man who discovers that living each ordinary day honorably, with faith in God and a selfless concern for others, can make for a truly wonderful life." James Parish and Ronald Bowers, *The MGM Stock Company: The Golden Era*, New York: Arlington House, 1973, p. 676.

20. All screenplay quotations are from the screenplay as it is printed in *The It's a Wonderful Life Book*, by Jeanine Basinger.

21. *Guideposts,* 1987 (December).

22. This thought is very close to a famous quotation from a John Dunne sermon: "No man is an island, entire of itself; every man is a piece of the continent. . . . And therefore never ask for whom the bell tolls; it tolls for thee." Not long before the film, in 1940, Hemingway took the poet's words as an epigraph to his new novel *For Whom the Bell Tolls.*

23. James Agee's expression.

24. Capra, pp. 382–383.

25. Basinger, pp. 253–254, from Frank Capra's 1968 interview with a student at the Academy of Motion Picture Arts and Sciences.

# BICYCLE THIEVES
## (LADRI DI BICICLETTE)
### Vittorio De Sica

| | |
|---:|:---|
| director: | Vittorio De Sica |
| producer: | Vittorio De Sica |
| script: | Cesare Zavattini |
| | with Vittorio De Sica |
| | from the novel by Luigi Bartolini |
| photography: | Carlo Montuori |
| cameraman: | Mario Montuori |
| editing: | Eraldo Da Roma |
| music: | Alesandro Cleognini |

### cast

| | |
|---:|:---|
| antonio ricci: | Lamberto Maggiorani |
| maria ricci: | Lianella Carell |
| bruno: | Enzo Staiola |
| balocco: | Gino Saltamerenda |
| the thief: | Vittorio Antonicci |

Black and white
*running time:* 87 minutes
*released:* November 1948, Rome
*awards:* Special Oscar for the most outstanding foreign film, 1949

A few years after *Bicycle Thieves* was released, international film critics, polled by *Cahiers du Cinema,* voted it one of the best three films
ever made (the other two were Eisenstein's *Battleship Potemkin* and
Chaplin's *The Gold Rush*).

Vittorio De Sica (1902–1974) was born in Sora, a little town south of Rome, into a prosperous middle-class family. Soon after his birth his parents moved to Naples, four years later, to Florence, and in a couple years after that, to Rome. It was said that De Sica absorbed the humor and temperament of Naples, the cultural refinement of Florence, and the noble charm of Rome. He was an innate singer and actor and even as a teenager was successful in music hall performances. His father, a passionate admirer of theatre and music, encouraged his son to become a professional entertainer. Meanwhile, the son studied accounting as a more secure career. Yet during World War I, he toured the hospitals in Naples with an amateur troupe, singing Neapolitan songs.

At twenty-one, De Sica was drafted into the army, and for his good looks and six-foot height, enlisted in the grenadier's regiment. When the service was over, he joined a professional theatre company.

He played in sentimental romantic comedies, initially in supporting roles and very soon, as the first lead. His theatrical persona was an Italian "little man," striving for social success but constantly missing the opportunities. "I [often] played comic parts with my ideas of tragedy deeply hidden," he recalled.[1] From 1926 he starred in films, was adored by the public, and was called the Italian Cary Grant by the critics. He also acquired national fame as a popular singer; some of his songs became the biggest European hits of the 1930s. In 1937 he married the actress Giuditta Rissone, with whom he had a daughter. His second wife, Spanish actress Maria Mercader, was the mother of his two sons, Manuel, a composer, and Christian, a pop singer and film director.

De Sica usually is described as an artist "with an unfailing sense for images, an ability to move audiences,"[2] a person who loved romance, was one of the most elegant men in Rome, lived in a fashionable Paroli district, and loved to be called *commendadore* (commander), but above all, he was a hardworking professional.

In 1940, he started directing films. "Only by directing can I express what is within me,"[3] he stated years later. He had a unique talent in working with actors, and he himself continued acting in films until the final years of his life. All together he starred in more than 150 Italian and foreign films, among them such hits as Roberto Rosselini's *General Della Rovere* (1959), Charles Vidor's *Farewell to Arms* (1958), and Max Ophuls' *Madam de . . .* (1953). "I must act to pay my debts," he wrote. "I am worth more commercially as an actor than director."[4]

The debts he acquired were not only for habitually overspending his meager production money but also for his obsessive card gambling.

The most important of De Sica's early films was *The Children Are Watching Us* (1942). "In those difficult times, my thoughts turned more to the children than to adults who had lost all sense of proportion. This was truly the moment when the children were watching us. They gave me the true picture of how our country was morally destroyed."[5]

In the early 1940s his collaboration with screenwriter Cesare Zavattini started. Ten years later Andre Bazin[6] wrote that in the history of cinema there had not been a more perfect example of symbiosis between screenwriter and director. It was a creative closeness only. They were different in temperament, lifestyle, and worldview: De Sica rejected any political or religious affiliations, trusting only his conscience and sensibility; Zavattini was a political fighter and a convinced Communist.

During the Nazi occupation of Rome, De Sica was brave enough to refuse Goebbels' proposal to make a film, with the excuse that he was too busy with a commission from the Vatican.

After the end of the war and the liberation of Rome, De Sica and Zavattini made *Shoeshine* (1946), a tragic story of two contemporary street boys. The film had an immediate international success but was widely criticized in Italy for showing the country's postwar poverty and devastation, so-called *rags for abroad*. The title of the film came from "Shoeshine, Joe?"—an expression used by Italian street boys who followed American soldiers around, hoping to earn a couple of coins.

In the United States the film was awarded a special Oscar. Released two years after *Shoeshine*, *Bicycle Thieves* (1948) was considered a classic of *neorealism*—a powerful though short-lived artistic movement. Zavattini predicted that the rich would turn up their noses at the film. But the opposite happened. The intellectual elite and the rich patrons of the arts were ecstatic. At the opening night at the Barbarini Theatre in Rome, they screamed, "Long live De Sica!" and didn't let him leave the podium, and when ten-year-old Enzo Staiola, the little Bruno in *Bicycle Thieves*, arrived in his father's uplifted arms, the public was in a frenzy.

Paradoxically enough, it was the Italian mass audience who did not like the film. De Sica described how during one of the first showings of *Bicycle Thieves* in Rome, a working-class man asked for his money back: he wanted to be entertained, not reminded about the misery of his life, he said. The director, who considered himself *an artist of the poor*, was deeply disappointed and hurt.

Outside Italy, *Bicycle Thieves* was a big hit, although in the United States (it is hard to believe now), distributors asked to cut two "offensive" episodes: one where little Bruno wants to urinate and the other where Ricci pursues the thief into a bordello. But the film was presented at a United States premiere in December 1949 without any cuts and was shown with great success all over the country.

Almost as triumphant was De Sica and Zavattini's *Miracle in Milan* (1951), which the director called "a fairy story." There, he wrote, "Men and angels are to be found living on good terms together. . . . In this style I had two masters, René Clair and Chaplin, towering above me with all the forces of their genius."[7] *Umberto D.* (1952) was De Sica's favorite film. "[It] was made absolutely without compromise, without concessions to spectacle, the public, the box office," he said.[8] He dedicated it to his father, whose name was Umberto. De Sica described how Chaplin cried "like a baby" when he saw the film. But he predicted that *Umberto D.* would not be as successful as *Shoeshine* or *Bicycle Thieves*— the films accessible to any kind of public, intellectual or illiterate. ("Double narrative," as we would say now.) *Umberto D.* was the director's last neorealist film.[9]

After De Sica and Zavattini's cinematic victories, their films *Indiscretion of an American Wife* (1953) and *Gold of Naples* (1955) were harshly criticized, and the writer and the director were accused of betraying neorealism by going away from the dramas of the poor to light comedies and melodramas. They were made with professional actors and stars and frequently shot in the studio. They were less inspired than earlier films. "All my good films, which I financed by myself, made nothing. . . . My bad films made money. Money has been my ruin."[10] Only De Sica's *Garden of the Finzi-Continis* (1971) reached the height of his best early films.

De Sica's last project was a film about Italian immigrants in America, which he planned to shoot in Brooklyn. It was his answer to *The Godfather*. The project was never realized: De Sica died on November 13, 1974, in Paris on the day of the opening of his last completed film, *The Voyage*.

Novelist, publicist, and screenwriter Cesare Zavattini (1902–1989) was the central figure of the neorealist movement. A dedicated Marxist, he believed in Communism as the supreme goal of history and considered it his obligation to always side with the poor and to attract attention to their needs. He believed in the Communist revolution.

He was loved by the rulers of the former Soviet Union and was one of the first foreigners who visited Cuba after the revolution. He befriended Fidel Castro and called Cuba his "second homeland."

De Sica called Zavattini the tireless inventor of film stories and highly appreciated his gift of cinematic vision; the director said he had a camera in his mind.

They met in 1935 on location for *I'll Give a Million,* a sentimental comedy with an ironic view of the Italian middle class—Zavattini the screenwriter and De Sica the leading man. Their real work together began in 1942 with the film *Children Are Watching Us.* This time De Sica was the director. They understood immediately that their film ideas worked hand in hand, Zavattini said. They both had a "hunger for reality," genuine compassion for their characters, and active rejection of what they called the Hollywood gloss over life as it is.

Although politically very active, Zavattini in his work with De Sica followed the director's principle that Communist propaganda should be left to newspapers, posters, and election speakers, not to films.

Aside from his more than twenty films made with De Sica, Zavattini wrote scripts for others, mostly Italian directors. He is the author of such neorealist classics as Luchino Visconti's *Bellissma* (1951) and Giuseppe De Santis' *Rome 11 O'Clock* (1952).

Zavattini's voluminous writing brought him money, but he lived very frugally with his wife and four children in a middle-class neighborhood on the outskirts of Rome. His indulgence was collecting art and books on art. He himself was an amateur painter.

In the middle of the 1950s, Zavattini's screenwriting changed to more traditional dramas and comedies, but he didn't want to admit that neorealism had become a rigid dogma and a serious obstacle to the further development of Italian cinema. With age, his political fervor grew stronger. In his articles and speeches he called for a crusade against capitalist elitism in both society and cinema.

Zavattini lived a long life. He died at the age of eighty-seven, and until his last days he wrote books and screenplays and made documentaries. But *Bicycle Thieves* remained his highest artistic achievement, overshadowing everything else in his oeuvre.

It was Cesare Zavattini who, in the immediate postwar years, when the country was in poverty with unemployment, black markets, and housing and food shortages, called on Italian filmmakers to turn their cameras to the everyday life of ordinary people and to show it without embellishment or dramatization. He called this new cinema *neorealism*—the term already being used in discourses on Italian film.

Zavattini formulated the basic principles of neorealist films: they have to have social content, historical actuality, realistic treatment, rejection of theatrical and cinematic conventions, popular settings, and political commitment on the part of the filmmakers. But neither in those years nor in the years to come was there a clear definition of *neorealism*. Was it a school, a genre, a movement, a style? A moral position rather than an artistic stand? A form of social criticism? The Italian Communist party, very influential during the postwar period, defined *neorealism* as an ideology, one of both antifascism and anti-Americanism.

After the war, film stock was limited, and studios and most of their equipment were destroyed. But neorealist directors[11] were shooting their films on location, using natural light, recording sounds during actual shooting (instead of using prerecorded studio material), and turning the technical deficiencies of the postwar period into stylistic advantages. There were no movie stars in those films; instead, there were nonprofessional performers who did not look or talk like actors. The neorealists used to say that the very need for reality forced them out of the studios. But the studios were partly destroyed anyway or were occupied by refugees.

As a movement, neorealism lasted from the mid-1940s to the mid-1950s. In that period, more than eight hundred films were produced in Italy (mostly melodramas, adventure films, and sentimental comedies), and among them only about ninety were neorealist. Of those, no more than a dozen received wide recognition. But despite its brief lifespan and small output, neorealism turned out to be very significant for the country's prestige. The Italian public in general was more impressed with the success of neorealist films abroad, especially in the United States, than with the films themselves. The first love of the Italian spectators remained the Hollywood films, which caused worry for both the church and the Communist Party, who considered Hollywood the Trojan horse of capitalism.

Neorealism was esteemed and imitated by filmmakers in England, Spain, France, India, Japan, and Russia. The deep humanity of the Italians fascinated the world's audiences. Never before had spectators experienced such pain and such joy for film characters.

The movement played a significant role in film history, being the first break from the practices and values of Hollywood, which had been considered the norm at that time: the studio system, the genres, the movie stars. Neorealism was even a departure from the traditional organization of cinematic stories, with an Aristotelian plot gradually ascending to the climax and then descending to the finale.

Toward the middle of the 1950s, neorealism turned into a set of ideological conventions. Because of the economic boom resulting from the Marshall Plan, poverty was no longer the burning topic of Italian life, and the loss of a bicycle would not have been so devastating.

Later on, contemplating the fate of the movement, De Sica stated: "Neorealism was born after a total loss of liberty, not only personal, but artistic and political. It was a means of rebelling against the stifling dictatorship [of Mussolini] that had humiliated Italy. When we lost the war, we discovered our ruined morality."[12]

Benito Mussolini's dictatorship, which lasted from 1922 to 1943, created an atmosphere full of ambiguity. Il Duce, as he preferred to be called, a former orthodox Marxist who was in the past praised by Lenin, a National Socialist, wanted his subjects not only to follow him but also to love and venerate him. In contrast to Hitler and Stalin, Mussolini was a pragmatist rather than ideologue and had no agenda of racial discrimination or extermination of certain classes or groups. There were no concentration camps in Italy. His subjects were permitted to travel abroad. For those who were or appeared to be adversaries to the regime, the primary punishment was the notorious castor oil.[13] The repressions started after Mussolini's alliance with Hitler in the middle of the 1930s, something unexpected, because Il Duce regarded Hitler as a "vulgar and dangerous gangster." Hitler, on the other hand, needing Mussolini's support, called him "the greatest son of Italian soil since the collapse of the Roman Empire."[14] The praise was irresistible to Il Duce, and Italy and Germany formed the Axis alliance in 1936. The real cruelties of Mussolini's Black Shirt Squads (the forerunners of Hitler's Brown Shirts) started after Italy entered the war on the German side in 1940, and thousands of Italians, who fought in the war, especially in Russia, "froze to death, died of hunger, of wounds, or were taken prisoners."[15]

At the core of the Fascist regime was radical nationalism and hatred of democracy and capitalism. On the surface, Italy under Mussolini appeared to be secure and even making progress—there were government projects; no strikes; no violence in the streets; and even the mafia's activity was quieted down. As Fellini said in his film *Fellini-*

*Roma* (1972), under Mussolini all the flies disappeared and the trains started running on schedule.

Like any other dictatorship, Italian Fascism was against individualism and was anti-intellectual by its very nature. But Mussolini's policies were built on his moods and whims. Although he was an enemy of American capitalism, he allowed publications of American authors and even tolerated some praises of America in the Italian press. The former Marxist, he now hated Communists, yet some notorious Marxists still taught in Italian universities, and at the Rome Film Institute, students watched and analyzed Soviet films.

Mussolini knew how to deal with writers, artists, and all sorts of intellectuals, how to "buy them off rather than persecute them." Italian writer Cesare Pavese wrote that most of them cynically accepted the game and status quo.[16]

Mussolini loved cinema. In his private screening room he enjoyed watching Laurel and Hardy films and American musicals. He knew that cinema was "the strongest weapon" of propaganda, but "the best propaganda for the fascist Italy was a successful Italian film at the box office."[17]

In his cinema policy Mussolini was guided by his son, Vittorio, an ardent film enthusiast and a founder and editor-in-chief of the surprisingly progressive journal *Cinema*. It was associated with intellectuals, writers, poets, artists, and filmmakers. Vittorio spent some time in Hollywood and made no secret that he loved the spirit and energy of American films and that he wanted filmmakers of his country to learn from them, and he did not hide his disdain for Italian sentimental comedies, called *white telephones*.[18]

In 1935, Mussolini founded Centro Sperimentale—the Experimental Center for Cinematography—a school for education and training of directors, screenwriters, actors, cameramen, and all sorts of film technicians.[19] He needed highly professional filmmakers, like Eisenstein and Pudovkin, who would glorify Italy as those Russians had been glorifying Soviet Russia, *his* Italy—because he strongly believed that the country belonged to him. His popular slogan was *"A chi l'Italia? A noi!"* ("To whom does Italy belong? To us!"). But everybody knew he meant "To me."

In 1937 Mussolini built the famous Cinecitta,[20] the largest cinema studio in Europe. He himself conducted the opening ceremony and talked about highly nationalistic and patriotic films that would be made at the Cinecitta.

Italian filmmakers did not have the same sort of censorship as those in Germany and in the Soviet Union. But still there were some restrictions: no moral or political aberrations on the screen, no themes concerning social matters, no sabotage of religion, no unhappy life, and, certainly, no suicides. According to Il Duce, Italy had to appear in films flourishing, healthy, and forever young.

Mussolini also loved to be shown on the screen. Vain and comfortable with his dictatorial power, he regularly appeared in newsreels and documentaries as an aviator, an athlete, riding a horse, planting a tree, laying brick for a public project, or as a family man, surrounded by his wife and children. He loved to appear in a variety of military uniforms. Cinema was more than anything else instrumental and successful in creating his political persona.

Once, Mussolini appeared on the set of *Scipione Africano,* the film about the victorious Roman general of the third century BC. Hundreds of extras, costumed as soldiers of ancient Rome, saluted him with worshipful cries of "Duce, Duce!" This was filmed and shown all over the country. No one at that time could have imagined that in less than ten years, he would be overthrown by his own party, rescued by German paratroopers, and run, under Nazi protection, a small "republic" called Salo; and shortly thereafter, he would be captured and shot, along with his mistress, Claretta Petacci, by Italian partisans and hanged, upside down, in one of Milan's public squares.

The title *Bicycle Thieves* (*Ladri di Biciclette* in Italian), is often wrongly translated as *The Bicycle Thief*. This mistake somehow takes away the dramatic irony of the story, because in the film there is not just a thief who steals a bicycle. The man whose bicycle is stolen—Antonio Ricci, a decent family man—does the same. So there are two thieves in the film.

The plot of *Bicycle Thieves* is straightforward, and it unfolds smoothly, step-by-step. This is a *linear* plot, where everything happens in chronological continuity: it starts on a Friday in the early afternoon and ends the following Sunday at twilight. This is also a *circular* plot— the film ends with Ricci not having a bicycle, as it was in the beginning of the film.

There is a clearly defined *dramatic goal* in the film—to find the stolen bicycle. There is no deviation from it, no flashbacks, no subplots, no hidden information that we don't know. One dull-witted viewer exclaimed that it was nonsense: A man looking for a bicycle for the entire film, and in the end he doesn't find it.

The simplicity here is deceptive—it has deep dramatic density. Within the plot, closely interwoven with the search for the bicycle is the theme of the relationship between Ricci and his son Bruno. This is the most powerful part of the film, which touches and moves to tears. The action is too close to us, too real. We hardly notice the use of the camera or cutting.

*Bicycle Thieves* consists of thirty-five scenes, each characterized, as scenes usually are, by the same place (a scene at the pawnshop, a scene at the church, a scene at the market, etc.), or by unbroken time (in one scene Ricci runs from one street to another—here the space changes, but the time is unbroken). Each scene moves the plot forward.

We easily identify several sequences of the film—groups of scenes bonded to each other by many apparent and hidden ties. Every sequence is a unit complete in itself, and, simultaneously, it is part of a larger whole, the film, the way a chapter of a novel is a part of the whole novel. The only difference is that chapters are openly delineated by writers.

In films the spectators don't consciously register the sequences as well as scenes. Only for the sake of film analysis is it necessary to note the structure.

The film starts with the *exposition*[21]—an introduction to the characters and the place.

*In a pan shot we see a government project on the outskirts of Rome, a vast, dusty, treeless space with monotonous buildings. At an entrance of an employment office is an official "with a little cigar in his mouth, holding a handful of papers standing in front of a group of unemployed men."[22] An official shouts, "Ricci . . . Ricci . . ." A worker in the crowd is looking for Ricci running and shouting, "Ricci, Ricci." The camera tracks with him in a long shot.*

The name *Ricci*, rhythmically repeated a number of times, functions almost like a bell, attracting attention and arousing curiosity: who is this man?

*We see Ricci in the merciless light of noon, a handsome, decent-looking man. He sits outside the crowd, on the ground, at the foot of a small public fountain; he doesn't expect a job to be offered to him. But he gets a job pasting street posters. However, his delight is immediately shattered: he is expected to have a bicycle for this job. Unfortunately, his bicycle is at the pawnshop, and there is no money to redeem it.*

With the opening of the film, "an emotional, orchestral theme which returns in many dramatic moments throughout the film" starts. This is not just a background accompaniment. The theme hints at deeper meaning, to something that is not shown but is going to happen. The music forecasts the action and makes us more perceptive and melancholy in a bittersweet way.

## Sequence 1

Sequence 1 includes seven scenes, each about redeeming the bicycle:

1.  Ricci tells his wife, Maria, of the job's requirement.
2.  Maria finds the solution to the problem of how to get the bicycle.
3.  Ricci and Maria pawn their bed linen and on this money redeem the bicycle.
4.  Ricci and Maria ride to the poster office to get his uniform.
5.  Maria tries to catch a glimpse of the office through the window, but someone closes the shutters.
6.  Maria pays her debt to a fortune-teller who, some time ago, predicted that Ricci would find a job.
7.  Ricci and Maria happily ride home.

An escalation of emotions runs through the whole sequence, from Ricci's despair ("*Oh, why was I ever born?*") and his only consolation ("*I can always throw myself into the river*") to hope ("*It's all o'kay. The pay [will be] good*"), and finally, to sheer happiness when the couple ride home—Ricci has the job!

The action in this sequence is pointed: Everything people do and say is about the bicycle. Yet through the details, various facts about the time and the place are communicated to us. For example, a small communal area where we first see Maria has piles of barbed wire—a reminder of the recent war. And in the pawnshop an employee tries to find a space for Maria's bed linen. He climbs up and up "*until he reaches a beehive of shelves filled from floor to ceiling with sheets.*" The camera, in a long, slow tilt, follows him, revealing more and more bundles identical to Maria's, as if replicating more and more situations similar to hers. Here things represent the reality of people's lives, the poverty of postwar Italy. We learn about the disaster in the national economy through small things, without ideological topics or social statements.

In the pawnshop scene, De Sica uses close-ups (which he doesn't use often) in *reaction shots*, going back and forth between Maria asking for more money and the clerk who hesitates to give it. The close-ups make this exchange expressive.

Pay attention to the fact that in the pawnshop scene, the brand of the bicycle, *Fides,* is mentioned for the very first time here, for a practical reason: to identify it. Throughout the film the word will be repeated, sometimes teasingly, sometimes symbolically, playing on the meaning of this Latin word: "worthy of belief and trust, reliability, good faith, honesty, and honor." All of these terms stand in ironic contrast to what the particular Fides represents in the film.

Notice also how casually the motif of a theft appears in the film: Ricci leaves his bicycle virtually unattended at the entrance to the fortune-teller's place. The title of the film already has aroused our apprehension for the bicycle. We suspect that it can be stolen, but we don't know when. But now this is only a tease—no one takes the bicycle. The director is only playing with our suspicions. And somehow, after this episode, they fade.

In one of the scenes of this sequence we see Ricci astonished that his wife could seek the advice of a fortune-teller. *"How can you, a woman with two children and with a head on your shoulders, be taken in by this foolishness. . . . It's just idiotic,"* he says to Maria. The psychological and structural importance of the scene will become clear much later, when Ricci himself turns to Signora Santona for help.

However, into the full-of-hope atmosphere of this sequence there sneaks a premonition: Ricci lifts Maria up to admire the inside of the bill-posting office through a barred window. But someone in the room slams the shutters closed. Metaphorically, this is what is going to happen: the couple will only glimpse a moment of happiness before it will be abruptly snatched away from them.

In this sequence, as well as in the rest of the film, the work of the camera is unnoticeable. In De Sica's opinion, nothing should interfere with the flow of the story. He could state, like his famous contemporary, Luis Buñuel, that when watching a film, if he noticed the work of the camera, he immediately left the room. (How different that is from Jean-Luc Godard, for whom, some years later, the camera's performance was of paramount value.)

In *Bicycle Thieves,* the shots seamlessly follow each other without any deviation from the story line. This is *consequential* editing.[23] The scenes of the film in their turn do the same. They smoothly blend into each other through dissolves, rarely separated by a black screen. But now to indicate the end of this sequence, there is a short pause before sequence 2.

## Sequence 2

The sequence includes eight scenes, running from a very happy Saturday morning to a heartbreaking Saturday evening. In the previous sequence the dramatic line of the plot ascended from despair to happiness; here, on the contrary, happiness descends to despair. (See Figure 6–1.)

> Scene 1 to scene 7—the ascent from despair to happiness
> Scene 8 to scene 15—the descent from happiness to despair

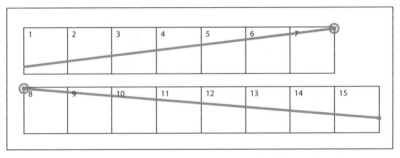

*Figure 6–1. Scene Diagram for Sequences 1 and 2 of* Bicycle Thieves

*The sequence starts with a close-up on the wheel of the bicycle. Through the spokes, we see Bruno, Ricci's ten-year-old son. He is polishing the bike with great care, almost tenderly. The father, in his new uniform, enters the room. It is six-thirty in the morning, and they have to hurry up. But Bruno is still busy.*

The following dialogue is about the bicycle, but its real function is to introduce Bruno and to reveal the particular father-son, older-younger relationship. Throughout the film we will see the pattern of change in these roles: from time to time Bruno takes on the part of the more experienced and more thoughtful one and even scolds his father for his irresponsibility.

> BRUNO: *Papa . . . did you see what they did?*
> RICCI *(off): No. . . . What?*
> BRUNO *furiously points to the pedal: A dent!*

RICCI: *Perhaps it was there before.*
BRUNO (enraged): *No . . . it wasn't . . . I'm sure. You don't know how they look after things in there? You should have been more careful. . . . It's not them who pays for repairs, you know.*
RICCI (laughing): *Shh . . . keep quiet.*
BRUNO (cleaning and sulking): *I'll keep quiet, but I'd have complained to them.*

Everything Bruno says shows a sensitive, responsible child, devoted to his family, mature before his time in the difficult postwar years in Rome. He even works at a gas station while his father hasn't had a job. And now, in this scene, it is he, not Ricci, who closes the shutters so the morning light will not disturb the sleeping baby.

Bruno adores his father, looks at him with admiration, and imitates him. He even puts his sandwich in the front pocket of his overalls with the same gesture.[24] Through the film, different aspects of Bruno's attitude toward Ricci are shown: he follows his father; criticizes him lightly; protects and even saves him; is offended by him; but is also treated as his father's equal; for a moment loses faith in his father, when he sees him as a thief; feels sorry for him; cries with him; forgives him; and no matter what, keeps in step with him. (De Sica recalled that, when working on the film, in his imagination, he always saw the father and son together.)

The film was an adaptation of a novel of the same title by Luigi Bartolini, but the protagonist there was childless. Bruno was Zavattini's invention, and the boy's presence, his *point of view*, gave a story about a stolen bicycle the quality of drama, almost a tragedy. Bruno brought to the film a moral dimension.

From the very first moment the boy appears on the screen, he captivates us. Enzo Staiola, who stars as Bruno, is not even for a moment a child actor. Implanted in the *Bicycle Thieves* world, with De Sica's remarkable guidance, the boy is totally authentic, just continuing to be himself. The director recalled that Enzo, when invited by him to a café, would eat only one-half of a cake, carefully wrapping the rest in a napkin to take home to his family.

The sequence has diversity of events, moods, and locations:

8.  The happy morning at home.
9.  Ricci riding the bicycle in the early morning with Bruno on the handlebars.

10. Getting the posters and a lesson in postering.
11. The awkward attempt to paste the Rita Hayworth poster, and the theft.
12. The unsuccessful chase after the thief.
13. Disappointment at the police station—they can do nothing for Ricci.
14. Ricci getting on the overcrowded bus.
15. Meeting Bruno at the bus station and walking home—Ricci cannot bring himself to tell his son what happened.

Ricci riding the bicycle with Bruno on the handlebars is a very happy scene, although nothing but riding is going on. The whole atmosphere, the light, the huge sky, the energy of movements, the tempo—everything appears lively.

Most of the film's action takes place outdoors. But the city isn't shown traditionally, as the imperial Rome, with its immediately recognizable, world-famous sites. De Sica did not want to take attention away from the story.

In the scene of Ricci and Bruno riding, all the surroundings are so harmonious that it is hard to believe anything bad could happen. What a contrast this is to everything we have seen previously—the depressing view of the project buildings, the crowded pawnshop, the poor small apartment. Lively music, full of ringing bells, enhances the feeling of the father and son's happiness.

The scene where a poster man teaches Ricci how to paste a poster with Rita Hayworth[25] (*"For this job, you've got to be intelligent, have a good eye, and be alert,"* he says) is a good example of the film's mise-en-scènes, where the unity is based on a variety of images and on dramatic and visual contrasts. What can be further apart than the image of elegant and frivolous Rita Hayworth, the *erotic queen* of Hollywood, and Ricci with a bucket of glue up on the ladder? While Ricci struggles with the wrinkles on the poster, a well-to-do man using an umbrella as a cane strolls by. He is followed by a boy, Bruno's age, asking for a coin; another boy standing close to the ladder plays on his accordion. We are reminded that this is postwar Italy, where children often have to earn money, as Bruno does. The accordionist is playing an uplifting circus-type melody. But the poster man, annoyed by it or maybe by Ricci, who cannot grasp the skill of postering, gives the boy a quick boot. All of these—the wrinkles in the poster, the strolling man, the accordion, and the kick—happen simultaneously, in one shot, filmed from the same position of the camera, but we feel a wider world outside the frame.

The man with the cane doesn't spare a coin. The theme of the rich and the poor, the adults and the children (one boy wasn't given a coin, the other one was kicked) unobtrusively announces itself and immediately disappears. The humorous, playful passages of the music try to remove melancholy from our feelings.

*On another street, in the center of Rome, when Ricci is up on the ladder, struggling again with another Rita Hayworth poster, his bicycle is stolen, seized and ridden away before his eyes, by a young man in a German forage cap (the cap later becomes the identifying mark of the thief).*

This is the beginning of losses for Ricci—from this point he will gradually lose self-confidence, his moral convictions, his self-respect, and his idealization of his son.

*The chase after the thief, both on foot and by car, is diverted by the thief's accomplice and ends fruitlessly.*

Notice how the tempo of the chase accelerates, not by means of the editing (in most films after Griffith, this was done by splicing together shorter and shorter pieces of film) but by speeding up the tempo within the mise-en-scène. First Ricci, then the car simply accelerate their speed in the chase. These shots are of a long duration, De Sica's favorite format, so the spectator can follow the uninterrupted action.

The scene was shot with multiple cameras from various angles—something not typical for neorealist films.

*In the police station scene, a journalist is talking to a constable, Failoni, to whom Ricci has just complained of the theft. The journalist asks about some news. "No, nothing . . . just a bicycle," the constable answers.*

On the social scale, Ricci's misfortune is "nothing"; society is totally indifferent to his loss.

## Sequence 3

Sequence 3 has two scenes, both located in a *"vast but dimly lit cellar"*—the Communist Party headquarters. The unchanged lines in Figure 6–2's scene diagram suggest the stagnation of the hope of finding the bicycle.

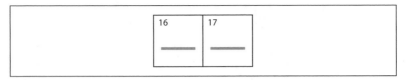

*Figure 6–2. Diagram for Sequence 3*

*16. Ricci's tension and despair continue; he edges his way toward someone familiar and whispers an unheard question. A speaker who addresses a small group of people asks Ricci to be quiet and go somewhere elese if he is not interested in what they are interested in.*

We will see that crowds and masses of people are always menacing rather than supportive forces for Ricci: a crowd here, at the headquarters; another at the employment office; one at the bus station; one at the market; another in the church; and the one that captures him.

Contrary to Zavattini's ideology, proletarian solidarity doesn't reveal itself at the Communist Party headquarters. Ricci doesn't even dare to ask for help. The Communists care for masses, not for individuals.

*17. On a tiny stage some amateurs are rehearsing a number, "Cabaret": a man is singing off-key about love. The "producer" Biacocco, a heavyset, comical man, to whom Ricci bewails his loss, suggests they go to the market together the next day; he is sure they will find Ricci's bicycle there, or "its parts." Biacocco himself, along with the clumsy, grotesque movements on the stage, and the ridiculous lyrics of the songs, create an absurd world that is so extraneous to Ricci.*

*Maria comes to the basement to talk to Ricci. "Is it true?" she asks in tears.*

Maria appears in only a few scenes. It is clear that her role was marginalized so as not to take attention away from the interaction between Ricci and Bruno. But whenever she is in the shot, her presence is perfect. Lionella Corell, a journalist, had come to see De Sica for a newspaper interview. He offered her the role of Maria on the spot—she looked exactly the way he had imagined Ricci's wife.

The entire cellar sequence has no music, except the songs performed on the stage. The emotional atmosphere here is expressed in the labyrinth of corridors of the cellar (a hint on Ricci's situation—no way out!), in the oppressive low ceilings, heavy arches—everything like the misfortune that weighs upon him.

Another important ingredient of the mise-en-scène is the light. This is one of the film's few scenes where artificial lighting is used and where the shadows on the walls express Ricci's disturbance.

Notice that the funny part of the scene, the stage performance, doesn't function as comic relief. Ricci's tension is so immense that everything funny, by contrast, only reinforces his drama.

At the end, the scene fades to black, and there is a long pause of darkness before the action resumes.

## Sequence 4

Sequence 4 consists of eight scenes.

18. *The early hours of Sunday morning, at the Piazza Vittorio, "in the cloudy, dawn light." In a deep focus shot we see, far in the background, Ricci and Bruno descending from a bus. Day is breaking with all the morning activities: street sweepers, garbage trucks, cars. With Biacocco and two other men, the search has begun—the vain and pathetic expedition.*

*In a tracking shot we see countless bicycles and bicycle parts, as if the camera is remarking on how hopeless their day is.*[26] *Bruno reminds his father that the brand name of the bicycle is Fides. Repeated several times, the word here sounds ironic. For a moment it seems that they have found their Fides but it turns out to be a mistake. The search ends in failure.*

19. *It seems as though nature itself has turned against them—at another market, at the Porta Portese, the torrential rain scatters the vendors. The father and son find shelter on the sidewalk. A group of Austrian priests, in long gowns and round hats "cackling in German, shelter themselves on either side of Bruno and Ricci." The boy is almost squashed between them and completely baffled by strange words he cannot understand*

Another unpleasant experience in this day, and another glimpse by Bruno into the world of adults.

20. *The sun breaks through. Suddenly, in the distance, Ricci notices the thief. He talks to an old man and instantly vanishes. Ricci and Bruno follow the old man. They catch him, but he denies knowing the thief. He slips away from them and disappears into a church. They follow him.*

21. *The scene in the church is full of restless activities. Rich volunteers are*

*directing the poor parishioners—sending them to the barber, showing them to the dining room, leading them to Mass. Ricci doesn't need any of those, thus causing a great irritation among the volunteers. Ricci explains that he is looking for an old man who had been here. A volunteer tells Ricci to get out immediately.*

*Bruno and Ricci head toward a little door and go out.*

So, in scene 18, there was an instant of hope that quickly vanished; in scene 20, it seemed that Ricci and Bruno would catch the thief, but it was rather a tease of fate that not only diminished what little had been left of their hope but dented, indirectly, the father-son closeness. From scene 22 to 25, the curve of their relationship and celebration of life (after threat of Bruno's death) is of such an importance that the theme of the bicycle disappears for a while. (See Figure 6–3.)

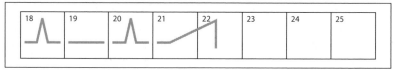

*Figure 6–3. Diagram for Sequence 4*

22. *Outside the church, they realize that they have lost track of the old man.*

> BRUNO: *God knows where he is now!*
> RICCI (stopping): *Oh, be quiet . . . he couldn't have flown away.*
> BRUNO: *I wouldn't have let him go . . .*
> RICCI: *Oh . . . shut up, will you!*

*Distressed and irritated, Ricci raises his hand and slaps Bruno. The boy is stunned. "Why did you hit me?" he repeats, in tears. He wants to go home and complain to his mother.*

From Bruno's reaction we realize it is unusual for his father to be unjust and harsh with him. It is against Ricci's principles, and we consider this moment as the beginning of his downfall.

23. *In the next scene Ricci leaves Bruno at a bridge while he goes to look for the old man. Walking along the river, he hears screams that someone has drowned. Ricci, and we along with him, imagine that this is Bruno. [Again, just a tease.] Ricci runs down to the bridge, short of breath, hysterically murmuring his son's name. But it isn't Bruno.*

Throughout the film, the camera has been at eye level. But at this point we see Bruno from a low angle in a long shot. He is sitting at the top of a stone stairway. From Ricci's point of view, he is high above everything, like a vision or a dream. But he is real, and he is alive, and this is the first time that Ricci looks up to his son.

24. *The father-son reconciliation is conveyed through Ricci's words and Bruno's proud and silent sulking. They walk together again. Bruno is dragging his feet. Ricci eventually stops walking. The father asks if he is tired. Bruno looks down and nods his head, feebly. He looks over to a large stone block. Ricci tells him to sit down there—there is nothing else to do.*

Notice the nuances in the father's new behavior. Now he is attentive to Bruno; he tries to start a conversation.

*To appeal to his son's expertise, Ricci asks if Modena is a good soccer team. Bruno only shakes his head slightly. "Are you hungry?" the father asks. "Could you manage a pizza?" The child in Bruno succumbs. He smiles.*

25. *In the restaurant Ricci treats his son as an equal and discusses with him the most vital family matters. Just a short while ago Bruno, the child, had wanted to go home and complain to his mother about Ricci, but now we see him as his father's partner.*

*Nibbling on mozzarella, Bruno writes on a paper napkin what Ricci is dictating: "12,000 basic, 2,000 overtime, plus family allowances 800 by 30 . . . what does that come to?" While the numbers make for rather a dry language, here they stand for Ricci's dream.*

*A Neapolitan musical group plays a popular song about fate: A young woman can give her newly born son any beautiful name, but that would not change the reality of his being black. Bruno with curiosity and pleasure looks at the musicians, and the father celebrates his son's "resurrection." He pours wine into Bruno's glass. ("If your mother only knew I was letting you drink!")*

A profound revelation descends upon Ricci: *"Everything sorts itself out except death."* And he is overwhelmed with Bruno's being here with him, alive. He realizes how deeply he treasures him and how insignificant the loss of the bicycle is in comparison to what could happen to Bruno. For a short while he forgets about the disaster. Nowhere else do we see him smile so blissfully. He is happy.

*Only death is final, everything else will sort itself out and will change.* This is the bittersweet optimism that balances the dramatic crisis at the conclusion of *Bicycle Thieves*, but the finale is given to us now, at the sixtieth minute of the ninety-minute film (almost at the golden section), instead of at the end.

Notice the comparison of Bruno and a rich boy at the restaurant, a social statement that De Sica, as always, makes lightly—just a hint, a reminder that there are the poor and the rich, and the imperious rich boy with his purposely silly hairdo (here De Sica's comic spirit comes out) looks ridiculous.

## Sequence 5

Sequence 5 consists of just one scene, in which there is no action in finding the bicycle (see Figure 6–4).

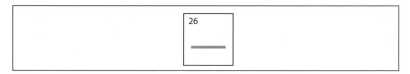

*Figure 6–4. Diagram for Sequence 5*

*26. In his misery Ricci turns to the fortune-teller, Signora Santona. She says that either he will find it immediately, or will never find it.*

Ricci's coming to the fortune-teller is a sign of his helplessness. Her prophecy only contributes to the feeling that any effort is futile. The very fact that Ricci consults her is significant: not long ago, he had told his wife how foolish and idiotic it was to listen to the fortune-teller's nonsense. It is a continuation of Ricci's fall, which began when he hit Bruno, and the abandonment of his principles, something that will culminate in his theft of a bicycle.

Notice a nuance in the scene:

*In the waiting room, Bruno jumps the line of patrons. Now he is the force rejuvenating his exhausted father. "Over here, Papa. Here's a seat free."*

But no one can understand that they are really in a hurry, no one wants to help, like that constable who said earlier, "nothing . . . just a bicycle." The world is indifferent to Ricci. But the touches of humor here and there prevent the film from being sentimental.

This entire sequence develops without music, and only at the very end do we hear a distant bell ringing—a familiar sound of Rome—summoning people for prayer.

## Sequence 6

Sequence 6 consists of six scenes. Hope appears again, more real than ever, in scene 27, but then it gradually fades (see Figure 6–5).

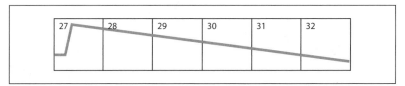

*Figure 6–5. Diagram for Sequence 6*

27. *Ricci and Bruno suddenly notice the thief in the street and chase him.*

28. *The thief escapes into a bordello and they follow him inside.*

Again, in a suspenseful moment, De Sica inserts a comic detail: it seems that the old woman–guard takes Bruno for a client. *"A child! You are not coming in here! Get out . . . now!"*

*The prostitutes try to protect the thief from Ricci, but he grabs the thief by the collar, and in a moment they are out.*

29. *In the street, Ricci holds the thief tight. "My bicycle," he demands. "What bicycle? I'm no thief," the thief says. While they argue, a long shot of the street shows that their shouts have attracted a crowd of people who are approaching in silence; they are the thief's neighbors.*

30. *The hostile crowd is turning dangerously against Ricci; Bruno worms his way out and brings a policeman. Meanwhile the thief falls down and shakes uncontrollably in an epileptic attack.*

31. *A policeman, Ricci, and Bruno search the place where the thief lives, with no results. "You have no witnesses . . . no proof . . . nothing can be done,"* the policeman says to Ricci.

But in a way, the situation is ambiguous. We see the thief's over-crowded rooms, his mother, his sister, the shabby poverty of all of them. And although we despise the thief for what he has done to Ricci, still his action becomes in some way if not forgivable, at least explainable.

On the film's opening night Vittorio Antonucci, the only professional actor in the crew, who played the part of the thief, was greeted with silence, without any applause.

*32. Outside the thief's apartment building, in the street, threats and insults are heard: "Coward. Liar. . . . Big head. You won't get away with accusing [us]." Furious, helpless, Ricci leaves. "Bruno . . . come on."*

There is a sharp contrast between Ricci, with his Roman look and clear Roman accent, and the people in the crowd—immigrants from the south, displaced from their homes by the war—the actual aspect of life in the postwar capital.

Until that point, the search for the bicycle had a pattern of hoping to find it, being almost there, and losing the hope. Although in scene 27, the thief appears, it becomes clearer and clearer that Ricci's bicycle is irretrievable. But Ricci hesitates to accept this.

## Sequence 7

Sequence 7 consists of three scenes, in which the sudden desperate act of stealing someone's bicycle ends any hope (see Figure 6–6).

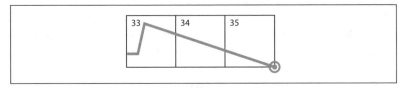

*Figure 6–6. Diagram for Sequence 7*

*33. Ricci and Bruno walk down various streets. Bruno looks at his father with concern. The boy is exhausted and is nearly hit by a passing car without his father even noticing. They go down a long flight of steps . . . Bruno sits down on the curb to get his breath back.*

Here the camera and the plasticity of silent acting take over the narration.

*A medium close-up of Ricci: he is staring determinedly out of the shot. Through his eyes we see "rows and rows of bicycles parked outside the stadium." It is clear that he is struggling with temptation. He walks up and down nervously, looks at the bicycles and turns away sharply.*

*In a long shot of the street we see an old bicycle near the door of a build-*

*ing. No one is around. In a close-up on Ricci, we can recognize his inner strug-*
*gle; but no, he does not want to succumb. He goes and sits on the curb, next*
*to his son.*

The medium shot of the two, in the intensity of their despair, is
one of the most remarkable and famous images in film history.

*Suddenly, Ricci sends the boy home. He gives him a coin: "Run, there's the*
*train." But Bruno misses it. Meanwhile Ricci rushes to the place where the*
*old bicycle is standing against the wall. He approaches the bicycle, jumps on*
*it, and pedals furiously. The bicycle's owner rushes out of the door, shouting*
*the same words that Ricci had shouted a short while ago: "Thief . . . thief!*
*Stop him!"*

*Ricci is pursued by a growing throng. One man grabs his coat. He falls*
*to the ground. The furious, shouting crowd gathers around him. Ricci tries*
*to protect himself against blows and insults.*

After the story with their Fides is over and done with, we see how
the honest man becomes a thief, tries to steal a bicycle, and fails.

*34. From a distance, Bruno sees all this. In a close-up, his horrified face is*
*shown.*

We understand what is going on through Bruno's eyes, and his
viewpoint is what makes the scene so dramatic.

*"Bastard . . . I'll teach you to rob people!" "Prison . . . that'll show him . . .*
*the bugger." They hit Ricci, and now he doesn't even protect himself. Bruno*
*pushes through to his father. "Papa, papa!" Crying, he picks up Ricci's hat*
*and dusts it off. He runs up and grabs his father's legs. They look at each*
*other. The bicycle's owner sees this. He is touched by the look of the boy and*
*lets Ricci go. "That's a nice trick to teach your son!" someone in the crowd*
*shouts.*

This last line of dialogue in the film reveals much more than it says.
Fitting for the situation, it also summarizes the underlying meaning of
the film—a child receives a bitter lesson about the life of adults, and
the paradise of his poor but decent childhood, in which his father has
been idolized, is lost forever.

The final scene is developed entirely without words.

*35. The camera tracks with Ricci and Bruno as they walk slowly across the*
*parking area. The sound of indistinct insults follows them. People walk by, as*
*they do on any Sunday afternoon; Bruno discreetly hands his father the hat.*

*Ricci takes it and straightens his hair . . . his jaw set, eyes empty of emotion, shoulders sagging. . . . Bruno is hugging his father's legs, and still wiping the odd tear from his face. They move through the lolling crowd. . . . Ricci tries to hold back the tears in his eyes. He continues to walk with a faltering step.*

*Bruno, his eyes wet with tears, is walking next to his father. In a close-up we see his hand slipping into Ricci's.*

All the forgiveness and compassion is expressed in this gesture. Ricci squeezes Bruno's hand. He is crying. They both weep at their failure, their loss, and certainly their shame. The story that was so strongly tight to its specific time and place now is elevated to the universal level. Even though the quest for the bicycle has been fruitless, and their efforts to improve their life have resulted in nothing but disappointment, Ricci and his son still have one another.

*In a long shot from behind, we see the father and son move away and disappear in the crowd.*

The open structure of *Bicycle Thieves* doesn't offer a solution to the drama; the ending is inconclusive and the conflict remains unresolved. The job of the director, De Sica insisted, is to reveal situations, not supply solutions.

Once Zavattini spelled out that the ideal neorealist *feature* film should consist of ninety consecutive minutes, showing the routine of a worker's daily life: the filmmaker's camera would faithfully follow the person within a day, because, in Zavattini's words, the everyday life of an ordinary person has innate dramaturgy, and there is no need to invent anything else.

It seems that he, the theoretician and political fighter, completely ignored what he, the writer, always knew and would never question: that film is life transformed by imagination, that it is a form of creation. A skillful professional, he certainly knew about the duality of our perception—we like to think that what is on the screen is real, and at the same time, we don't forget to evaluate how the film was made. When, for example, Bruno sees his father's humiliation by the crowd, we shudder as if it happened in real life, but simultaneously we are ecstatic about the director's work and about the incomparable performance of little Enzo Staiola.

In *Bicycle Thieves* everything is carefully and thoughtfully composed. Look at the pattern:

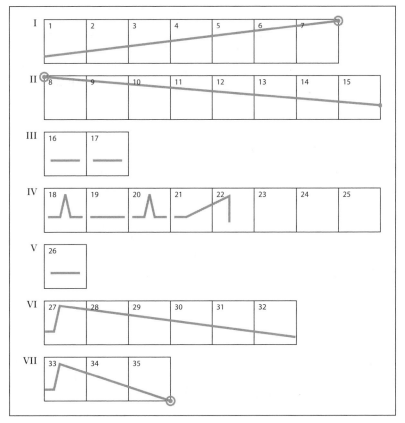

*Figure 6–7. Complete Scene Diagram for* Bicycle Thieves

Bruno saves his father two times (Ricci versus two angry crowds).

There are two stolen bicycles.

The fortune-teller appears two times.

Two boys are in the restaurant.

And finally, there are two thieves in the film and two chases.

This symmetry contributes to the plot's balance and also gives the spectator better understanding of the film: the comparison of the two thieves brings us the hint that perhaps the young man also stole the bicycle out of necessity, for survival, as Ricci did. The comparison of the two boys in the restaurant reminds us about the rich and the poor and accentuates Bruno's genuineness and goodness. The two visits to the fortune-teller demonstrate the changes in Ricci's attitudes and principles. The two chases reveal the bitter irony of Ricci's transformation.

De Sica was happy to free himself from the studio dependence and to take the camera outside, where the people really live. His mise-en-scènes included a pawnshop, an employment office, the church, the Communist Party headquarters, the bordello, the restaurant, the bus stations, people's homes, the markets, and the city itself.

Certainly, Rome's streets and piazzas in *Bicycle Thieves* are authentic, yet they are not just documented but also artistically organized, something that De Sica called *poetic*. The British director David Lean, who attended a shooting of one of the film's outdoor scenes, was overwhelmed by the way De Sica worked with the crowd in the streets.[27]

De Sica was unique in working with nonprofessional actors. His lifelong experience as an actor in theatre and cinema, along with his instinct, intuition, and tireless efforts to find whom he needed, allowed him to get flawless performances from his amateurs. "There are some roles which demand professional actors, while there are others which can come to life only through a certain face, which is only to be found in real life," he wrote.[28]

His greatest success was with Enzo Staiola, who played Bruno. De Sica said that he noticed the boy in a crowd—an odd-looking child with a round face and a weird nose and large expressive eyes. No less fortunate a choice was Lamberto Maggiorani, a steel factory worker, who appeared in the film as Ricci. "The way he moved," De Sica recalled, "the way he sat down, his gestures with his hands hardened from work, the hands of a working man, not of an actor. . . . I made him promise that after the film he would forget the cinema and would go back to his job."[29] For three months, every day, a black limousine would pick him up and bring him to De Sica. But when the shooting was over, he received a very modest sum of money.

In 1973, dying of cancer in a hospital, Lamberto Maggiorani gave his first and only interview. "I never wanted to talk, because all my life [after 1948] had been tied up with Antonio Ricci, there was a complete identification."[30] Admitting his respect for De Sica, he also told how incredibly anxious he was throughout the shooting; how embarrassing it was, with his innate shyness, to act in front of the people and the camera; how sometimes he cried when he wasn't able to do something De Sica wanted. But he also knew very well that the director did not want to allay his frustration, but to use it, transferring it into Ricci's anxiety and tension.

De Sica didn't want, after the success of *Bicycle Thieves*, for Maggiorani to play in other films. "He wanted my face to be exclusively in his masterpiece, nowhere else."[31] Maggiorani believed that the film offered something important to the people, and that he came to the end of his life *not with empty hands.*

But Maggiorani's successful performance, as well as the acting by everyone else in the film, should not lead to the conclusion that nonprofessional actors are just as good as professionals. In this case a highly accomplished actor, as the director was, "played" all the characters in the film. It was a joke that De Sica could teach even a sack of potatoes how to act.

The general reaction to *Bicycle Thieves*, at the time it was made and until our time, has been that it is one of the best films ever made. There were thousands of responses in the press and film literature. The film was compared even to Greek tragedy in its interpretation of the loss of the bicycle as death; it was compared to numerous classics in literature and drama; and Ricci was even compared to Ulysses, while crowds in the film were compared to the modern equivalent of a Greek chorus, representing both the higher and the lower aspects of human character.

There were a lot of surprising reactions, like this one by the director, Michelangelo Antonioni, who said that he would prefer to be told more about the man and less about the bicycle.

One of the most direct and immediate responses was given by the celebrated writer Gabriel Garcia Marquez, then a twenty-two-year-old journalist, when the film was released: "The work by Vittorio De Sica . . . gives one a lot to think about. . . . From the simplicity of the title to the even greater simplicity of the ending, De Sica's work is nothing but an anguished search for a stolen bicycle through the streets of Rome, where is a vast, dizzying bicycle market, on the longest and most pitiless Sunday that a man could live through . . . the bicycle becomes a myth, a divinity. . . . [The film] can be described, without fear of exaggeration, as the most human film that has ever been made."[32]

# Appendix

### De Sica: About Directing[33]

Only by directing can I express what is within me. The Lord and the Lumière brothers have provided me with this wonderful method of writing. I find philosophy very difficult to understand, but nevertheless I have a favorite philosopher—Seneca, the Roman Stoic. I like to think over his moral observations. Besides, I feel particularly well acquainted with him because I once impersonated him in a film. I am basically an unhappy man. Life gives me always the impression of cruelty. I read the newspaper—crimes, murder, divorces, and so on. I do not find evidence of sincerity or solidarity there. I love humanity, I trust humanity, but humanity has a way of disillusioning me. The pictures I direct are nearly always melancholy. This comes from the contrast between my love and my disillusion. I am an optimist. I love life. I seek perfection. If my art seems pessimistic, it is a consequence of my continuing optimism and its disillusion. At least I have an enthusiasm. It is necessary to all professions to have enthusiasm in order to have success.

### De Sica: Bicycle Thieves[34]

Lamberto Maggiorani is the workman in *Bicycle Thieves*. I engaged him to work with me for a while before we started shooting. I talked a great deal with him about Antonio Ricci, the man he was to play, and about Antonio's wife and their son, thus establishing in a roundabout way a hidden but continuous parallelism between that family and his own. In the end, I realized that a kind of *osmosis* had operated between the reality and the fiction, between his life and Antonio's, and that impulses and reactions had been transmitted from one plane to another until he very nearly thought of Enzo Staiola, the boy who played the part of the little Bruno, as his own son. Later, he himself confessed to me that he had experienced this sensation, acutely and poignantly, in the last scene of the film: Antonio, in a moment of revolt against his cruel fate, attempts robbery and is arrested and maltreated in front of his son. When, through his tears, Lamberto Maggiorani felt his hand seized by little Staiola, it seemed to him that it really was his son who took his hand, and his tears became real tears of burning shame. In a few months of patient effort, I had brought this man to the point of being able to forget himself in his role and to enter fully into the sad story. . . .

### From Gideon Bachmann's Interview with Federico Fellini[35]

Fellini: Well, I was one of the first to write scripts for neorealist films. I think all my work is definitely in the neorealist style, even if in Italy today some people don't think so. But this is a long story. For me, neorealism is a way of seeing reality without prejudice, without the interference of reality without any preconceived ideas. . . . For me, neorealism means looking at reality with an honest eye—but any kind of reality: not just social reality, but also spiritual reality, metaphysical reality, anything man has inside him. For me, neorealism is not a question of *what* you show—its real spirit is in *how* you show it. It's just a way of looking around, without convention or prejudice. Certain people still think neorealism is fit to show only certain kinds of reality; and they insist that this is social reality. But in this way, it becomes mere propaganda. People have written that I am a traitor to the cause of neorealism, that I am too much of an individualist, too much of an individual. My own personal conviction, however, is that the films I have done so far are in the same style as the first neorealist films, simply telling the story of people. And always, in telling the story of some people, I try to show the truth.

## Notes

1. Interview with De Sica by Monique Fong, *Sight and Sound,* 1950 (April), p. 62.

2. Mira Liehm, *Passion and Defiance*, Berkeley: University of California Press, 1984, p. 46.

3. Howard Curle and Stephen Snyder, eds., *Vittorio De Sica: Contemporary Perspectives,* Toronto: University of Toronto Press, 2000, p. 23.

4. Vittorio De Sica, "Critics Hurt Me," *Films and Filming,* 1955 (December), p. 5.

5. ibid, p. 5.

6. Andre Bazin (1918–1958), French film critic and theorist, one of the most influential critics in Europe and founded the paramount film magazine *Les Cahiers du Cinema.*

7. Vittorio De Sica, Preface, *Miracle in Milan* (screenplay), New York: Oregon, 1968, p. 5.

8. Curle and Snyder, "De Sica's Interview with Charles Samuels," in *Vittorio De Sica: Contemporary Perspectives,* 2000, p. 33.

9. Already at that time, on a visit to America, De Sica said that the neorealist movement in Italy was finished, though its spirit was still alive. "Whatever people say, neorealism for me is poetry, the poetry of real life. For that reason . . . it will never die." Vittorio De Sica, "On Neorealism," *Film and Filming*, 1956 (March), p. 6.

10. Curle and Snyder, 2000, p. 49.

11. First were the *neorealist trinity*—Roberto Rossellini, Luchino Visconti, and Vittorio De Sica—and then some others, among them Alberto Lattuada and Giuseppe DeSantis.

12. Curle and Snyder, 2000, p. 31.

13. Castor oil was given routinely during Mussolini's police interrogations to induce severe diarrhea as punishment and humiliation.

14. Alan Bullock, *Hitler: A Study in Tyranny*, New York, London: Harper and Row, 1962, p. 710.

15. Liehm, p. 51.

16. For example, Rossellini collaborated with Mussolini's son, Vittorio, on a documentary glorifying Italian aggression in Abyssinia in 1935.

17. Sam Rohdie, "A Note on the Italian Cinema During Fascism," *Screen*, 1981 (22–24), p. 87.

18. There were almost no white telephones in those films. The name of the genre came from white telephones in American movies, the symbol of prosperity in the eyes of the Italian middle class.

19. Nearly all the masters of the postwar Italian cinema were trained at this school.

20. Cinecitta was nicknamed, by Vittorio Mussolini, Hollywood on the Tiber. In the last months of World War II, it was damaged by bombardments and stripped of all the equipment that survived by retreating Germans. Later it was converted to a prisoner-of-war camp and the center for displaced persons. In 1947, it was rebuilt and used exclusively for film productions.

21. In some films expositions are long and detailed (usually combined with credits), in others, very short, or simply absent.

22. Vittorio De Sica, *Bicycle Thieves: Classic Film Scripts,* Lorimar, 1968. (Probably by mistake, Zavattini's name is not mentioned.) All the subsequent quotations from the script are taken from this publication.

23. The *consequential* editing is opposed to *associative* editing, when shots are juxtaposed to each other or even collide for a dramatic or visual contrast, or for certain emphasis, or to give a certain hint to the spectator.

24. Millicent Marcus calls it *adoring mimicry* in his *Italian Film in the Light of Neorealism*, Princeton, NJ: Princeton University Press, 1986, p. 59.

25. Rita Hayworth (1918–1987) starred in *Gilda*, her most celebrated film, in 1946, the time when the action of *Bicycle Thieves* takes place.

26. For the first market scene, De Sica hired forty vendors. They *were* market vendors, but the director carefully chose them and orchestrated their actions and organized *reality* in the most expressive way.

27. Lean said that De Sica was both a commander-in-chief of an army and a conductor of a symphony orchestra.

28. De Sica, "Critics Hurt Me," pp. 5–6.

29. De Sica, "Critics Hurt Me," p. 28.

30. Lamberto Maggiorani, "Sin mi Vittorio De Sica no habria pasado a la historia del cine," *Cine Cubano* 1984 (7), p. 70.

31. Maggiorani, p. 71.

32. This review was published in October 1950, signed with the pseudonym "Septimus," in the Colombian newspaper *Herald of Baranquilla*. The pseudonym comes from Septimus Warren Smith, a character in *Mrs. Dalloway*, by Virginia Woolf.

33. Winthrop Sargeant, "Profiles: Bread, Love, and Neo-realism," *New Yorker,* 29 June 1957, pp. 45–46.

34. De Sica, *Bicycle Thieves*, from Introduction to the script.

35. Gideon Bachmann, "Federico Fellini: An Interview," in *Film: Book One*, ed. Robert Hughes, New York: Grove, 1959.

# RASHOMON

## Akira Kurosawa

| | |
|---|---|
| director: | Akira Kurosawa |
| producer: | Jingo Minoru |
| production company: | Daiei |
| cinematography: | Kazuo Miyagawa |
| screenplay: | Shinobu Hasimoto, |
| | Akira Kurosawa |
| art direction: | So Matuyama |
| lighting: | Kenichi Okamoto |
| music: | Fumio Hayasaka |

### cast

| | |
|---|---|
| tajomaru, the bandit: | Toshiro Mifune |
| takehiro, the samurai: | Masayuki Mori |
| masago, the wife: | Machiko Kyo |
| the woodcutter: | Takashi Shimura |
| the priest: | Minoru Chiaki |
| the commoner: | Kichijiro Ueda |
| the police agent: | Daisuke Kato |
| the medium: | Furniko Honma |

Black and white
*running time:* 88 minutes
*released:* August 1950, Tokyo
*awards:* The Golden Lion from the Venice Film Festival, 1951; Oscar
for the best foreign film, 1952

Akira Kurosawa (1910–1998) was born in Tokyo, the youngest of seven children. His mother was a "very gentle woman," he wrote in his memoir. But his father was "quite severe."[1] A retired military man descended from a samurai lineage unbroken since the eleventh century, he was a judo and sword-fighting teacher as well as one of the first to introduce baseball and swimming pools to Japan. His household was strictly traditional, with an appreciation of Japanese history and the spiritual and cultural rituals. But he was also a devotee of Western culture and of European and American films, regularly taking the whole family to the movies. He was a strong influence in Akira Kurosawa's life, both in his Japaneseness and in his pro-Western infatuation. Akira inherited his father's cultural duality, which became the identity of his artistic persona. A tremendous variety of cultural influences gave Kurosawa's work its uniqueness.

From childhood he was trained in old Japanese arts of both discipline and spontaneity—bamboo sword fencing and calligraphy. Spiritual meditation in a shrine was Kurosawa's daily ritual. But he was passionate about books, especially Western literature ("I was a great reader," he wrote), and about painting. At the age of seventeen, after finishing the School of Western Art, he chose painting as his career. His landscapes and still-lifes won some prizes, but they could not bring any money; he earned a living by doing magazine illustrations and advertisements. His elder brother, Heigo, who was a *katsuben*—a narrator and commentator of silent films—excited Akira's curiosity about cinema. Thanks to Heigo, he acquired a considerable knowledge of Japanese and Western films, their styles, techniques, and history.

In 1928, Kurosawa joined the Proletarian Artists' League, but he left it in a few years. He never was a true Marxist, he recalled, but he had "that tendency."

In 1936, having competed among hundreds of applicants for one of few vacancies at the Motion Picture Company, he became an assistant to Japan's major film director, Kajiro Yamamoto. His apprenticeship lasted for seven years, but Yamamoto considered him a coauthor rather than just an assistant.

During that period, besides his work with the camera, lighting, stage construction, and editing, Kurosawa wrote many scripts. In the future, he would author or coauthor all of the scripts for his films.

His first film ("the first time I said 'Cut!'"), *Sanshiro Sagata* (1943), was about a judo fighter. It was striking visually and his deep interest in characters was, at that time, unusual for Japanese cinema. Kurosawa was noticed and praised by both the public and the press.

In his second film, *The Most Beautiful* (1944), he turned to contemporary life—to an optics plant with women grinding, polishing, and checking lenses. The film's star, Kiyo Kato (her stage name was Yoko Yaguchi), became Kurosawa's wife. Their marriage was happy and lasted forty years, until her death in 1985. They had two children, a son and a daughter.

Of the ten films Kurosawa made in the 1940s, before *Rashomon*, the most remarkable is *Drunken Angel* (1948), about a slum doctor who tries to cure a gangster. "In this picture, I finally discovered myself. It was *my* picture. I was doing it and no one else."[2] The Japanese critics wrote that this picture was to the national Japanese cinema as *Bicycle Thieves* was to the Italian cinema and that it "perfectly epitomizes the period, its hopes, its fears."[3] His next film, *Stray Dog* (1949), was about a policeman who loses his gun. The film's topic and some closeness to documentary style were Kurosawa's tributes to neorealism.

In 1949–1950, Kurosawa completed his work on *Rashomon*.[4] Most of the Japanese critics were puzzled by its complexity, its ambiguity, the idea of the elusive nature of truth, the whole spirit of existentialism. "This is not the Japanese way" was the most common conclusion. The head of the Daiei Studio, which produced the film, walked out of the first screening, telling the press that he had had no idea what the film was about. Kurosawa was reproached as being Western, less Japanese, or not Japanese enough, and at the same time Japanese critics nicknamed him, half ironically, half with servile recognition, Emperor Kurosawa. But he considered himself only a hardworking artist: "I am a kind of person who works violently, throwing myself into it, I also like hot summers, cold winters, heavy rains and snow, and I think my pictures show this. I like extremes."[5]

The Western critics adored him and thought of him as one of their own, but Kurosawa was not happy with them, either: "I have not read one review from abroad," he wrote, "that has not read false meanings into my pictures. . . . I would never make a picture just for foreign audiences. If a work cannot have meaning to Japanese audiences, I, as a Japanese artist, am simply not interested."[6]

Only after *Rashomon*'s immediate success in Europe and the United States, and especially after the film won the Golden Lion at the Venice International Film Festival, did Kurosawa's homeland start taking the film seriously. The Daiei Studio celebrated the success with a glorious reception, which the director did not attend.

"When I received the Venice prize for *Rashomon,* I remarked that I would have been still happier, and the prize would have had more meaning, if I had made and been honored for something showing as much of present-day Japan as *Bicycle Thieves* showed of modern Italy," Kurosawa said.[7]

*Rashomon* was the first masterpiece of Japanese cinema to receive international recognition. With it, the foreign market opened to Japanese films, and in the country, international film festivals became almost state events, comparable to the Olympics. When film delegations returned home without a prize, they would apologize publicly, as if they had personally failed the nation.

In the 1950s, one success followed another: *Ikiru* (1952), a modern-life drama; *Seven Samurai* (1954), a period piece; *The Throne of Blood* (1957), a free adaptation of *Macbeth*; *The Hidden Fortress* (1958), a period piece. The only disappointment to critics, and to a certain extent to Kurosawa himself, was his film *The Idiot* (1951), an adaptation of the famous novel by Fyodor Dostoyevsky, Kurosawa's favorite writer.

Kurosawa usually spent eight months for filming, used three cameras to work on each scene, did not like to repeat takes, and edited everything himself. He worked with rushes the day after shooting "to edit," as he liked to say, "with a fresh feeling."

The 1960s saw Kurosawa's decline from the heights of acceptance and fame, except for *Yojimbo* (1961) and *Red Beard* (1965), which are among his best films. In the second part of the decade, the public's fascination with television almost ruined the Japanese film industry. Even for Kurosawa, there were no Japanese producers who were ready to give him money. He signed a contract with Twentieth Century Fox and moved to America to work on *The Runaway Train,* a film that was not produced.[8] Neither was the second American project, *Tora! Tora! Tora!*—a film about the events leading up to the bombing of Pearl Harbor.

When the American producers invited Kurosawa, they had no idea how independent and uncompromising the director was; that he had never made a film just for money; and that once, when a producer wanted to make his film shorter, Kurosawa said, "If you want to cut my film you can do it only *along* the strip."

His work in the United States was a series of misunderstandings and confrontations. He was accused of failing to fulfill the studio's expectations, of breaking rules, of a short temper.

Upon returning home, Kurosawa and three other filmmakers founded a production company called the Four Musketeers of Cinema, and he made his first color film, *Dodeskaden* (1970), a series of episodes in the life of some slum dwellers. This was a low-budget film, with nonnaturalistic use of color and painted sets. It was a complete financial failure and brought about the end of the production company.

This fiasco, along with the bitterness of his American experience and also a series of aborted projects in the preceding years, all added up to Kurosawa's sense that his creative energy was gone. In December 1971, he attempted suicide—he was found in the bathtub with numerous slashes all over his body. But he survived. In an interview a year later, he called the attempt a foolish and thoughtless act committed in a dark frame of mind.

In a few years, recovered and back at work, he was invited by the Soviet film company Mosfilm to make a film about a Russian explorer of Siberia. The film, *Dersu Usala*, completed in 1975, restored Kurosawa's reputation. Even more successful was his next film, *Kagemusha* (1980), about a man who serves as a double for his lord. This film, made with the financial backing of George Lucas and Francis Ford Coppola, won a Golden Palm in Cannes in 1980. Still, Kurosawa spent several years trying to find producers for his next project, *Ran* (1985), his version of *King Lear*. While waiting for the film's financing, Kurosawa made the film in an extensive series of drawings. "Drawings can be extremely useful in filmmaking, as a way of giving concrete expression to my ideas for the movie," Kurosawa wrote.[9] He mentioned that in his youth, he dreamed about an exhibition of his paintings, but it had never happened. "Life is strange indeed. Now the drawings I made for *Ran* have been made into a collection. Inquiries are coming in from all over the world. It all seems like a dream."[10]

For his next film, *Dreams* (1990),[11] he received financial support entirely from outside his country. Only his subsequent film, *Rhapsode in August* (1991), was financed by a Japanese company, as well as his very last film, *Madadayo* (*Not Yet*) (1997–1998), a cinematic essay depicting the everyday life of the writer Uchida Hyakken, his students, his wife, and his cat, Nora.

Kurosawa's *Dreams* is a grand-scale film, one of his very best works. It is an allegorical autobiography consisting of eight episodes—the various stages of the director's life, from childhood to almost his last days.

Kurosawa died on September 6, 1998, at his home in Tokyo. He himself summed up his life when in *Dreams,* a very old man in a village says, with the merry sounds of waterfalls in the background, "It is good to work hard, live a long life, and pass on at a ripe old age."

Kurosawa left behind some thirty films, numerous scripts, drawings, and a unique book of memoirs, *Something Like an Autobiography*, an account of an honest, uncompromising life, entirely devoted to his work and his family.

In *Rashomon*, a samurai has been killed, his wife has been raped, and several people, including the wife, plead guilty to the murder. Their testimonies cancel out each other, but each of them is entirely convincing. Even at the end of the film we still don't know whom to believe and don't have a clue how to figure this out. We see only how subjective and elusive truth can be, and this is what Kurosawa wanted us to realize.

This existential point of view was totally foreign to the Japanese public; the national motion picture had been based on clarity of cinematic stories and scrupulous attention to the who, what, when, where, how, and why of any film. And this was from the very beginning.

Motion picture production began in Japan a couple of years after the Lumière brothers' invention, and already in 1897, there was the first public film screening in Tokyo.

If in the United States and Europe, especially in England, at that time, the motion pictures were considered a low type of entertainment (Oxford students, for example, to avoid being recognized at the movies, wore false mustaches and beards), in Japan, movies were acknowledged and highly respected. Even the crown prince, later the emperor Taisho, visited one of the first screenings. Earlier than in other countries, in 1903, a special theatre for movies was built in the capital and the admission to the show was as expensive as it was for stage performances.

The first films—the very short documentaries that came from the West—were for the Japanese precious glimpses into the never seen world, from which they were isolated geographically and culturally. But they always were eager to know more about it, about streets, houses, people, manners, clothing, and life. No less fascinating than the movies themselves was the whole technological aspect of filming and projecting.

With the unique ability to absorb foreign cultures (for centuries, it was the Chinese one), and at the same time remain faithful to their own, the Japanese producers and filmmakers assimilated experiences of the West. The strongest influence was Hollywood's structures and methods, its studio system, genres, methods of scene organization, and editing. Even the director's commands were given in English.

American films were maturing *apart* from the theatre, gradually getting rid of the stage modes and developing and cultivating cinematic ones. The expressive power of the close-up, of faces seen very closely, freed cinema from the dependence on theatrical gestures.

The Japanese films, on the contrary, kept close to stage styles, to the theatrical power of gesture, and even the tradition of *oyama*—having male actors play women's roles.

The most outstanding and unique element of Japanese cinema was the *katsuben* (or *benshi*)—the commentator and live narrator of films. He, or sometimes she, would stand at the left of the screen, impersonating voices of film characters, explaining everything, every detail of what was going on on the screen. The narrators' skill was derived from some theatrical traditions, but even more from old narrative performance genres.

Katsuben were no less popular than movie stars, and even when the talkies appeared, some of them continued performing with the sound of the movie shut down in order not to disturb the katsuben.[12]

In the 1920s Tokyo studios developed a system of genres by classifying and separating groups of films with common subject matter, tone, and style—the direct influence of Hollywood, although some of the genres were specifically Japanese. For example, the period pieces called *jidai-geki* (formally, *Rashomon* belongs to this genre), and films set in contemporary times, called *gendai geki,* were devoted to family life and male camaraderie. Not without Hollywood influence, the *comedy genre* was developed. Before there were only foreign comedies, and the most favorite comedian, almost a cult figure, was Charlie Chaplin.[13]

At the end of the 1920s, the Japanese cinema reacted to all of the changes in the country—depression, tensions with China, strikes, the growing influence of the military groups and nationalistic ideologies. A new genre—the *tendency film*—turned attention to everyday life. In the 1930s, another genre appeared—the *war film.*

Political convergence with Nazi Germany influenced cultural policies in Japan. In 1939, the government established motion picture laws, following, in part, Goebbels' film regulations: to create films glorifying patriotism and showing the readiness to serve the country; to create films that did not exaggerate horror in war scenes and destroy fighting spirit, but praised the sacrifice for the nation; to show characters who were patient and were against American individualism.

Comedies were restricted, films with even a touch of sensuality, prohibited, as well as films showing women smoking or drinking. One new genre appeared that very quickly became popular—the *spy film*, generating hate for the enemies. The spies were always American or British, played by Japanese actors.

In 1941, all American films were banned.[14] As we know, Japan lost the war and was occupied by the United States Army. To the country, which never in its history had been defeated, this was not only a catastrophe but also a national shame. Kurosawa recalled how on August 15, 1945, he was summoned to the studio along with his colleagues to listen to the emperor speak on the radio. As he walked there, he saw in the streets people fully prepared for the Honorable Death of the Hundred Million—the mass suicide. He saw some people "who had taken their Japanese swords . . . and sat staring at the bare blades." However, the emperor did not ask his subjects to die. When Kurosawa walked back to his home, on the same route, he saw cheerful faces; people already were preparing for the next day's festivity.

"I don't know if this represents Japanese adaptability or Japanese imbecility. In either case, I have to recognize that both these facets exist in the Japanese personality. Both facets exist within my own personality as well. . . . I would like to look back once more at myself during the war. I offered no resistance to Japan's militarism."[15]

After the war, most of the major Japanese cities were destroyed, and half of all movie theatres disappeared. Now MacArthur's occupation headquarters formulated the policies for motion picture production: to abolish the previous censorship, to allow the foreign pictures. A list of prohibited subjects was announced: no films with themes of militarism, revenge, nationalism, racial or religious discrimination, no direct or indirect approval of suicide, no films with oppression of wives or exploitation of children, no films with cruelty or violence. Filmmakers had to remember that every human being and every class of society had to be highly respected and never forget about the rights of the individual. More than two hundred war propaganda films were destroyed. However, most of the time, the Japanese directors had no problems with the occupation headquarters, and Kurosawa even recalled how an American censor gave a party in honor of one of his films.

Although there was not enough electricity, not enough film stock, the cameras were old and worn out, and awful signs of the disaster of the war were all around, the atmosphere of cultural liberation was evident in rapidly appearing melodramas, films about children, and comedies. Some films had sensual overtones; the recent past taboos were broken. In one film[16] even a kiss was shown, the first ever kiss on the Japanese screen. It was partly covered by an opened umbrella; still, this frivolity was wildly discussed as the beginning of a new trend in cinema.

*Rashomon* was made several years after World War II ended. Although Kurosawa refers to the eleventh century, and there is nothing in the film, directly or allegorically, about wars, the reflection of the recent tragic past can be discerned here. The very first sentence pronounced in the film, "I can't understand it. I just can't understand it at all," could be what Kurosawa and his contemporaries said about the insidious attack on Pearl Harbor, which even the Japanese prime minister at that time called "harmful to [Japanese] national honor and prestige"; the unheard of disasters of Hiroshima and Nagasaki; the threat of the emperor's call for mass suicide; and even the emperor's confession on the radio that *he was not divine.*

Also, *Rashomon's* meditation on the elusive nature of truth, on the unpredictability of human behavior and the dark sides of human nature, on the urge to preserve honor at any cost—all of that undoubtedly also related to more universal and immense events than the one that happened in the grove in Kurosawa's film.

The action in *Rashomon* unfolds in three locations; each of them has a distinct visual image, mood, and texture:

The gate—huge, gloomy, enveloped in a downpour

The courtyard—with a bare ground and a plain white wall, with an endless horizontal line at its edge

The forest and grove[17]—with a density of trees, light, shadow, and emotional tension

Before anything else, let us talk about the *story* of *Rashomon.*

*The story [18] of a fiction film is the totality of events, everything that we see and hear, taken in chronological order from the earliest moment in time to the very end.*

So the *story* in *Rashomon* could be defined as follows:

The samurai and his wife pass the priest on the road.

The bandit sees them.

The rape occurs.

The samurai is killed.

The police agent arrests the bandit.

The witnesses and participants in the drama testify in the courtyard.

The priest and the woodcutter seek shelter under the gate.

The two tell the commoner what happened in the forest and grove, and in the courtyard that morning, some hours earlier.

All of them hear the abandoned baby's cry.

The commoner steals the baby's clothes and leaves.

The woodcutter takes the foundling to his family and is praised by the priest.

Thus, the *story* reveals in chronological order, first, what happened in the forest and grove three days ago; second, the police agent arresting the bandit two days ago; third, the action in the courtyard today, in the morning; and, finally, what is going on under the Rasho gate later that day, in the afternoon.

Of the twenty-nine scenes of *Rashomon*, five are located at the gate, ten at the grove, twelve at the courtyard, one at the riverbank, and one at the lake. Arranged according to the chronological order, the diagram looks like that shown in Figure 7–1.

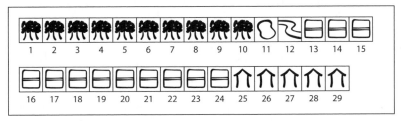

*Figure 7–1.* Rashomon's *Story in Chronological Order*

The *story duration* is three days—from the earliest point, when the priest meets the couple on the road, to the latest point, at the end of the film, when the woodcutter leaves the Rasho gate with the abandoned baby in his arms.

The film's *plot* arranges and presents the events of the *story* in the most expressive way. Notice in the diagram in Figure 7–2 (see next page) the constant location changes: from the intense passions in the grove

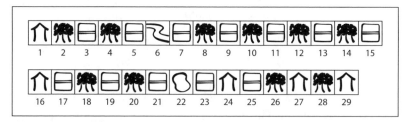

*Figure 7–2. Diagram of* Rashomon's *Plot*

, to the sober emptiness of the courtyard , to the gloomy entrapped Rasho gate . stands for the riverbank; for the lake.

But the plot disrupts the continuity of the *story*. Notice how completely restructured, dynamic, and active the organization of the *plot* is. The scenes there derive not only from different points in time but from different viewpoints—recollections of the woodcutter, the bandit, the woman, and the samurai (also, very briefly, from the priest and the police agent). There are three different narrative times here: the *present,* at the gate; the *past* of the grove; and the more *immediate past* of the courtyard.

There are 408 shots in the film, plus 12 for the titles. All of them are masterfully structured. The variety of visual compositions reveals Kurosawa's past as a painter and calligrapher.

So the point of departure, as Kurosawa called the film's exposition, in this film happens under the Rashomon, the half-ruined gate of eleventh-century Kyoto.

*1. A Buddhist priest and a woodcutter take shelter from a rainstorm. They are shocked by an event that has recently occurred. The priest says that there has never been anything "as terrible as this."*[19] *The woodcutter recounts the story to a commoner who also seeks refuge from the pouring rain. "It was three days ago," begins the woodcutter. "I'd gone into the mountains for wood." [A flashback follows.]*

Flashbacks usually re-create the way the events took place in the past. In *Rashomon,* we see flashbacks instead made up by the characters' imagination. In the scholarly world, this type of flashback is called *mindscreen.*

With a sharp rhythmic beat of music, the next scene starts.[20]

2. *The woodcutter walks through the woods. His ax glints in the sunlight. He stops in surprise when he notices a woman's reed hat and veil hanging from a branch and several other small items scattered nearby. Suddenly, the woodcutter notices a corpse, and in a panic, runs away, dropping his ax.*

Although the woodcutter's walk contains twenty-nine short shots (average length, eight seconds), the editing of this scene as well as in the rest of the scenes is almost invisible. Notice how, after seeing the samurai's corpse, the woodcutter runs back by the same route. One cannot escape thinking about some similarity to an old scroll that has unrolled from right to left and now is rolling back.

3. *The woodcutter, kneeling in a prison courtyard, testifies to the unseen judge: yes, he was the first person to find the dead body. He lists the articles he discovered and swears that he left nothing out.*

*The priest testifies to the same unseen judge. He says that three days prior he had seen the murdered man while he was still alive.*

We don't see the judge and don't hear his questions, and it seems that the testimonies are given to us, the spectators. Notice the severe simplicity of the prison courtyard's mise-en-scène: only the bare wall, which leaves some space to the sky, and people who testify sitting on the ground. All attention is on what they are saying.

4. *The priest walks through the woods. From the opposite direction comes a samurai leading a horse by the bridle. On the horse rides a woman; her face is veiled.*

5. *Back in the courtyard, the priest claims that he could see the woman's face through her veil and that the man had a sword, a bow, and arrows. "What a pity he should die like that," the priest says.*

The transition to the next scene is done by a *wipe*, the punctuation device when a shot is wiped from the screen by the movement of a new image. The technique was widely used in silent films but had been almost forgotten in the sound era. Kurosawa wanted to return to pictorial values of the silent films and to bring back the lost beauty of them. The wipe also gives a pause between actions and suggests a passage of time.

*A police agent testifies. Beside him sits Tajomaru, the bandit, tied up. The police agent says that when he caught Tajomaru, the bandit was carrying a Korean sword, a bow and arrows and that he had been thrown by a horse.*

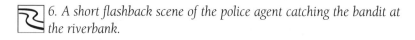 *6. A short flashback scene of the police agent catching the bandit at the riverbank.*

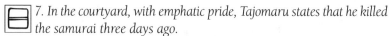 *7. In the courtyard, with emphatic pride, Tajomaru states that he killed the samurai three days ago.*

Notice that the courtyard and, to a point, the gate are the scenes of talking, describing, and confessing, in contrast to the grove, which consists of the scenes of action.

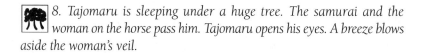 *8. Tajomaru is sleeping under a huge tree. The samurai and the woman on the horse pass him. Tajomaru opens his eyes. A breeze blows aside the woman's veil.*

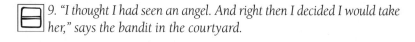 *9. "I thought I had seen an angel. And right then I decided I would take her," says the bandit in the courtyard.*

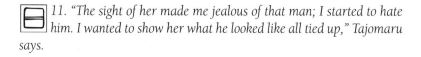 *10. Tajomaru tells the samurai that in the grove he keeps antique swords and daggers, which he is willing to sell cheaply. The men leave together and the woman remains alone on the road.*

*As the samurai nears the grove, Tajomaru suddenly attacks him. They fight; the samurai loses. Tajomaru ties him to a tree and triumphantly tears through the woods to the woman and tells her that her husband has been bitten by a snake.*

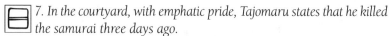 *11. "The sight of her made me jealous of that man; I started to hate him. I wanted to show her what he looked like all tied up," Tajomaru says.*

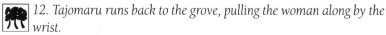 *12. Tajomaru runs back to the grove, pulling the woman along by the wrist.*

This swift movement seems as one uninterrupted pan of the camera, but there are seven invisible cuts in this fleeting episode.

*When the woman sees her husband, she attacks the bandit with her dagger, misses, and attacks him again. "She fought like a cat," Tajomaru says. But eventually, she succumbs and gives herself to the bandit. Her fingers loosen, and the dagger drops to the ground.*

The whole scene is shot in the dazzle of the sunlight. At a certain moment the sun itself is filmed.

The scene is replaced by the gate scene with the heavy rain "pouring as though it is *trying to wash away the greatest of sins.*"

13. *Tajomaru is laughing and kicking his feet excitedly. "And I had her." He testifies that he did not intend to kill the samurai. "But then . . ."*

14. *When the bandit is ready to leave the grove, the woman runs after him. She says that either the bandit or her husband must die; she wants to belong to the one who kills the other. The bandit cuts the rope that binds the samurai and gives him back his sword. They cross swords again and again. The bandit kills the samurai.*

15. *The bandit says that the woman ran away. She turned out to be like any other woman, he says. His biggest mistake was that he forgot about her dagger.*

16. *At the gate, the rain continues to pour. The priest tells the commoner that he saw the woman in the prison courtyard and that she was not at all as willful as Tajomaru has described her. On the contrary, she was rather miserable and meek. "Tajomaru's confession, the woman's story—they're lies," says the woodcutter.*

Notice the shocking contrast of the fast-moving, dancing camera in the forest and the unmoving camera in the courtyard; the unchangeable, static mise-en-scène of the courtyard and the noisy, disturbing, continual rain of the gate scene; the accentuated horizontal composition of the courtyard and the repetition of verticals in the gate structure and the transparent streams of rain.

17. *The woman testifies. She says tearfully that, after having taken advantage of her, the bandit sneered at her husband, took the samurai's sword, and left.*

18. *The woman rushes to her husband. She lies crying at his feet. The samurai looks at her coldly and cynically, despising her. Cutting the rope with her dagger, she asks him to kill her, but not to look upon her with hatred. She cries and begs; it does not help. In total despair, she raises the dagger above the samurai.*

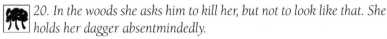 19. The woman is saying that in the eyes of her husband was not sorrow or anger, but a cold hatred of her.

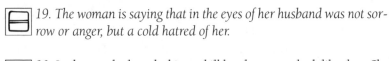 20. In the woods she asks him to kill her, but not to look like that. She holds her dagger absentmindedly.

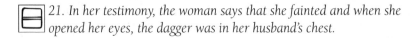 21. In her testimony, the woman says that she fainted and when she opened her eyes, the dagger was in her husband's chest.

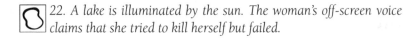 22. A lake is illuminated by the sun. The woman's off-screen voice claims that she tried to kill herself but failed.

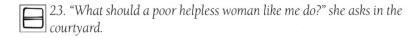 23. "What should a poor helpless woman like me do?" she asks in the courtyard.

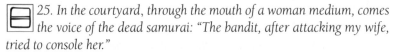 24. The rain keeps on as the three men huddle together under the Rashomon. The story confuses the commoner. The priest informs him that there is also the husband's account of the murder, which was related through a medium.

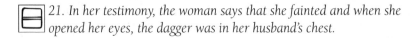 25. In the courtyard, through the mouth of a woman medium, comes the voice of the dead samurai: "The bandit, after attacking my wife, tried to console her."

Now the samurai tells what happened.

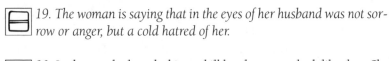 26. Tajomaru asks the woman to go with him. But she wants him to kill the samurai first. Her words shock the bandit. He throws her to the ground and holds her down with his foot. He asks the husband what to do with her. Kill her? Spare her? "For these words I almost forgave the bandit," says the samurai. The woman manages to free herself and flees into the woods. Tajomaru tries but cannot catch her. He returns to the samurai, cuts the ropes that bind him, and leaves.

The samurai is weeping. He notices the woman's dagger on the ground, takes it, raises it high above his head, and thrusts it into his chest. "I lay quietly in this stillness . . . then someone's hand grasped the dagger and drew it out."

The dagger is a detail that matters, in various ways, to all of Rashomon's characters, except the priest: the bandit is sorry for forgetting to take it; the woman fights with it, drops it when she succumbs to the bandit, and maybe kills with it; the woodcutter steals it; and the commoner figures out who has stolen it.

*27. Under the gate, the woodcutter protests: there was no dagger when he found the corpse. The samurai was killed by a sword, he insists. The commoner accuses the woodcutter of having viewed the entire scene and not having testified about it. The woodcutter explains that he simply did not want to get involved with the police, but now he will tell the truth:*

*28. The woman cuts the rope that binds her husband. She wants him and the bandit to fight. But the samurai refuses to risk his life for the "shameless whore." She accuses both men of being weak and cowardly. They fight lazily, almost grotesquely, and the bandit kills the samurai. Meanwhile, the woman flees into the woods.*

Notice how the following episode turns the scene of talking into a scene of action.

*29. The three hear a cry of an abandoned infant. The commoner steals its clothes. The woodcutter accuses him of being evil. The commoner accuses the woodcutter of stealing the woman's valuable dagger—he figured it out. The woodcutter admits his guilt. The commoner comes out in the rain and disappears.*

*The woodcutter and the priest, holding the baby, stand motionless under the gate. We see them in a long shot. It dissolves to a medium shot, with them in the same positions, and then the camera comes even closer to them. The rain stops, and now the cry of the baby is heard.*

*The woodcutter takes the baby. He has six children of his own. "One more wouldn't make it any more difficult," he says. The priest claims that the wood-cutter has restored his faith in mankind. They bow to each other.*

This theatrical gesture emphasizes that the story and the presentation of it are over.

*The rain stops. The sun comes out and shines directly into the lenses. The men bow to each other again. With the baby in his arms, the woodcutter leaves the gate.*

Looking at the first and final scenes in the diagram in Figure 7–2 on page 186, it is clear that the plot duration is only the few hours spent under the gate. The grove and the court scenes are inserted into the present as flashbacks. Note that the plot condenses the three-day duration of the story into several hours; in turn, the *screening time* condenses the plot duration into eighty-eight minutes. (The screening time of *Rashomon* was finalized by Kurosawa in the editing room, where every shot's length was determined.) *Screening time, plot duration,* and *story duration* are the three categories of time in the film.

One more look at the diagram (Figure 7–2): it clearly reveals the temporal mosaic of the scenes when the story's chronological continuity is broken up into pieces and then put together in a completely different succession: the first scene starts in the present; the second moves to the past, three days prior; the third scene takes place in the morning of the present day; the fourth, again, three days ago; and so on.

The jumps in time give *Rashomon* its dramatic intensity. Because the samurai's corpse is seen (scene 2) before the samurai and his wife are seen traveling through the woods (scene 4), the audience is more alert than they would have been if the events had appeared in chronological order. The audience should be more focused on the characters' reactions than on the events themselves. Otherwise, the same action would not be repeated several times.

There are many other instances in which the film alienates the audience from the action and draws attention to the unpredictability of human nature in general by presenting, in succession, episodes taken out of their original continuity. For example, the bandit's account of the rape and murder is interrupted several times by the courtyard scenes (scenes 9, 11, 13, and 15), which removes us emotionally from the drama. We are forced to evaluate the action rationally and to contemplate it from a distance.

If the gate scenes are singled out, as in the diagram in Figure 7–3, the role of their position becomes clearer. They frame the rape-murder

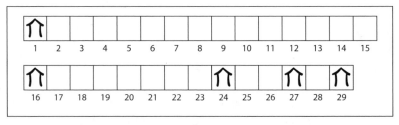

*Figure 7–3. The Gate Scenes in* Rashomon

drama (scenes 1 and 29) and constitute the beginning and the end of the film, and one of the gate scenes (scene 16) marks the middle of the plot.

The first half of the film focuses on the interplay between the events in the grove and the investigation in the courtyard. In the second part, the gate scenes appear more frequently. From being just supportive to the grove drama, the gate scenes become a drama in themselves. A parallel is subtly drawn: in both dramas, there are three participants, among them one villain (in the grove—the bandit; at the gate—the commoner). There are also similarities between the gate and the courtyard scenes: in both a trial is under way, but the trial at the gate is more successful. It is here, not at the court, that the truth is revealed—the commoner, himself a villain, figures out that the woodcutter stole the dagger, and the woodcutter is truly repentant; "I am the one who ought to be ashamed," he admits.

The diagram in Figure 7–4 illustrates how balanced the organization of the courtyard scenes is. The placement of the courtyard scenes has a clear rhythm: one-two, one-two, one-two.

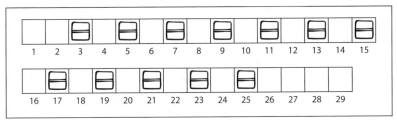

*Figure 7–4. The Courtyard Scenes in* Rashomon

As we have seen, the plot of *Rashomon* destroyed the temporal order of the events as they originally happened. But another unity between the scenes was established.

The last scene, in which the woodcutter adopts the baby, brings a positive finale to the entire film. Now faith in human compassion is restored. The ego as a source of misdeeds is balanced by this act. The priest summarizes this change by saying to the woodcutter that, thanks to him, *"I think I will be able to keep my faith in men."* The priest and the woodcutter *"bow to each other. . . . The woodcutter, holding the infant, leaves the gate; the sky is clear . . . sunny."* The sunny sky here symbolizes hope and goodness.

Kurosawa was one of the first in the cinema who entered the modernist artistic world where the *how*—the technique, the method of expression—became the essential part of the content. Painting and literature had taken that step years before. We know, for instance, that our fascination with Cézanne comes, to a large extent, with *how*—the structure and the technique of his works. The same is true with Joyce. "While *Rashomon* is historical and classical in subject matter and setting, the methods of narration are insistently modernist."[21]

Breaking the chronological flow of time; having the multiple perspectives on the same characters and events; unexpectedly switching back and forth among the three locations; creating a certain distance between the screen action and the spectator to give the latter some space to reflect and judge—all of these are signs of the new modernist sensibility coming to cinema. We see it even in Kurosawa's acute attention to geometric forms and numbers. In *Rashomon*, the number three is the basic element in the film structure. There are three locations, three characters in the forest scene, and three characters under the gate. There are six testimonies (three plus three). The triangle very often visually organizes the composition of a shot. There is even a sort of triangle unfolded in time when, at a certain point, the camera goes to the woman, then to the husband, then to the bandit—every time from the same distance, the medium shot, and with the same duration, four seconds.

Why does the woman plead guilty if she did not stab her husband? Why, if the bandit did not kill the samurai, does he request punishment for himself? Out of honor? And what disturbs the eternal rest of the dead samurai? If he did not commit suicide, what drives him to invent his story now? Unlike the other characters, the woodcutter wants to hide his crime; still, he too would like to consider himself nobler than he is.

Piecing together different moments of the drama, making comparisons, observing, alternating from one version to another, believing them all, and doubting them all, one arrives at the same conclusion that Kurosawa formulated in his memoirs that human beings are unable to be honest about themselves even with themselves.

## Appendix

### *Akira Kurosawa: Some Random Notes on Filmmaking*[22]

*What is cinema?* The answer to this question is no easy matter. Long ago the Japanese novelist Shiga Naoya presented an essay written by his grandchild as one of the most memorable prose pieces of his time.

He had it published in a literary magazine. It was entitled *My Dog*, and ran as follows: "My dog resembles a bear; he also resembles a badger; he also resembles a fox . . ." It proceeded to enumerate the dog's special characteristics, comparing each one to yet another animal, developing into a full list of the animal kingdom. However, the essay closed with, "But since he's a dog, he most resembles a dog."

I remember bursting out laughing when I read this essay, but it makes a serious point. Cinema resembles so many other arts. If cinema has very literary characteristics, it also has theatrical qualities, a philosophical side, attributes of painting and sculpture and musical elements. But cinema is, in the final analysis, cinema.

## Notes

1. Most of Kurosawa's quotes are from his book, *Something Like an Autobiography*, New York: Vintage, 1983.

2. Interview with H. Sams, *Sight and Sound,* 1964 (3–4, Summer and Autumn).

3. Donald Richie, *The Films of Akira Kurosawa*, Berkeley: University of California Press, 1984, p. 47.

4. The script was based on two short stories by Rynosuke Akutagawa (1892–1927), a well-known Japanese writer who committed suicide, leaving a statement that he couldn't cope with a world that lacked moral standing.

5. Andrew Sarris, *Interviews with Film Directors*, New York: Discus, 1967, p. 293.

6. Donald Richie, *Japanese Movies*, Tokyo: Japan Travel Bureau, 1961, pp. 149–150.

7. Joseph Anderson and Donald Richie, *The Japanese Film: Art and Industry,* Princeton, NJ: Princeton University Press, 1982.

8. Some ten years later, Soviet director Andrei Konchalovsky made the film, using Kurosawa's story.

9. Akira Kurosawa, *Ran* (screenplay), Boston, London: Shambala, 1986, p. 5.

10. Ibid, p. 5.

11. Sometimes the film is called *Kurosawa's Dreams*.

12. Katsuben performances were abolished in the mid-1930s. Katsuben had a double identity on the stage—the narrator himself and the film's

characters. One of the most famous impersonations in foreign films was in *The Blue Angel* (1931). Marlene Dietrich's songs were sung live in the Japanese language by some katsuben.

13. When Chaplin visited Japan in the early 1930s, he was treated like a national hero.

14. More about the political and cultural atmosphere of those years was published in *The Japanese Film: Art and Industry*, by Joseph Anderson and Donald Richie.

15. Kurosawa, *Something Like an Autobiography*, p. 145.

16. *A Certain Night's Kiss* was a film by Yasuki Chiba.

17. *Forest* and *grove* are used interchangeably in this text.

18. *Story* as opposed to *plot*.

19. All of the script's quotes are taken from Akira Kurosawa, *Rashomon* screenplay, New Brunswick, London: Rutgers University Press, 1986.

20. Composer Fumio Hayasaka worked very closely with Kurosawa until the last days of his life in 1955. For *Rashomon* he wrote a score with Japanese music, but Kurosawa insisted on something in the mode of Maurice Ravel's *Bolero*.

21. See James Goodwin, *Akira Kurosawa and Intertextual Cinema*, Baltimore, London: Johns Hopkins University Press, 1994, p. 144.

22. Kurosawa, *Something Like an Autobiography*, p. 191.

DAVID GLENN HUNT
MEMORIAL LIBRARY
GALVESTON COLLEGE